A SHORT ECONOMIC HISTORY
OF MODERN JAPAN

A SHORT ECONOMIC
HISTORY OF
MODERN JAPAN

1867-1937

*With a Supplementary Chapter on
Economic Recovery and Expansion
1945-1960*

by

G. C. ALLEN

FREDERICK A. PRAEGER, PUBLISHER

NEW YORK

BOOKS THAT MATTER

Published in the United States of America in 1963
by Frederick A. Praeger, Inc., Publisher
64 University Place, New York 3, N.Y.

PRINTED IN GREAT BRITAIN
in 10 point Times Roman
BY T. AND A. CONSTABLE LTD
EDINBURGH

PREFACE

This book is a result of a study of Japan's economic affairs that has extended over a considerable period. The study began during my residence in the country between 1922 and 1925, and much of the material that forms the basis of the later chapters was collected during a second visit paid to Japan in 1936 for the purpose of investigating economic conditions at first hand. I began to write the book early in 1939, but the outbreak of the war compelled me to lay it aside for five years, and at the same time deprived me of access to some of the primary sources on which I should have liked to draw. The book was completed on the eve of Japan's surrender.

I have tried to describe the process of economic development in Japan between the time when she first entered upon her career of Westernization and the beginning of the war with China in 1937. I have written in the belief that an appreciation of this process of development is necessary both to an understanding of recent events in the Far East and also to the formulation of a wise economic policy towards Japan now that she has been defeated. But the book is intended to provide a background of knowledge rather than suggestions for policy or speculation about what is to come. The main emphasis throughout has been on industrial and financial development and on economic policy, although the study has not been confined to those fields. It is hoped that economists and others who concern themselves with economic affairs and policy will find some general interest in tracing the evolution of a modern industrial system within a society so differently constituted from that of Western nations.

So far as possible, I have supported general statements by statistical evidence; but in order to avoid cumbering the text with tables and to provide the means of convenient reference, I have relegated most of the figures to a statistical appendix. I have included a bibliography which, though by no means complete, indicates some of the main printed sources that I have found useful and also offers suggestions for further study.

I am greatly indebted to my wife for help in preparing the book for publication.

G. C. ALLEN

August 1945

PREFACE TO REVISED EDITION

In preparing the present edition for publication I have benefited by the extensive research into Japan's modern economic history that has been carried out since the book first appeared (in 1946). I have thought it necessary to make a considerable number of detailed amendments and additions to the original text, but I have tried to introduce these changes without disturbing the former structure of the book or its scale. The chief new feature is a long supplementary chapter on Japan's economic recovery after the Second World War and her subsequent progress. I have also revised the statistical appendix and the bibliography.

UNIVERSITY COLLEGE, LONDON

September 1961

G.C.A.

CONTENTS

CHAPTER I

THE DISINTEGRATION OF
THE OLD RÉGIME

The rise of Japan to the position of a Great Power ranks along with the reconstruction of Germany as the most significant of the political changes of the fifty years before 1914. To many Westerners the Japanese achievement, in the economic as well as in the political sphere, seemed so astounding as to defy rational explanation. Some of them were at times inclined to acquiesce in the views of those Japanese who sought the clue to their new-found glory in the realms of mysticism, while others attributed Japan's advance to a series of lucky accidents and prophesied that time would presently reveal an essential mediocrity. In the economic sphere especially, forecasts of imminent disaster and decay have been numerous and impressive at every stage of her modern history, and it was not until she plunged into war with the United States and the British Empire that a shrewder estimate of her strength became common in the West.

Some acquaintance with Japanese history during the Tokugawa era is necessary for an understanding of the circumstances that made possible the country's transformation after 1867 and her more recent progress. The popular conception of a people living for centuries under a system of picturesque feudalism and suddenly awakened to practical ambitions by the guns of foreign warships is far from the truth. The Japanese did not suddenly acquire that energy and restless ambition which have so disturbed the Western nations. Throughout their history they have shown a gift for rapidly assimilating new ideas and practices, a boldness in executing large projects and, above all, a trained and frequently exercised capacity for organization.[1] Furthermore, modern Japan inherited from her past certain political and economic institutions that could be easily adapted to serving the nation in its new rôle. Her social organization, rooted in a special kind of family system, and the long centuries of feudal discipline, helped to produce a capacity for extreme self-abnegation on the part of individuals and an aptitude for corporate effort which served the country well in a time of rapid social and economic change; and the institution of an Imperial House which mythology invested with divine attributes provided a focus for patriotic fervour. Japan

[1] Cf. J. Murdoch, *A History of Japan*, Vol. I, pp. 1-30.

entered upon her course as a Great Power with an inheritance of political ideals and emotional dispositions well-fitted to supply driving force and unifying power in the task of nation-building.

These factors, though they cannot be neglected in an account of Japan's economic progress, belong rather to the sphere of political history, and it is upon others that we must dwell here. It has been customary for some foreign writers to refer to the primitive nature of Japan's economy before 1867, and to treat the Tokugawa period as though it were an era of almost complete stagnation. Recent work by Japanese and Western scholars, however, goes to show that in the seventeenth, eighteenth and early nineteenth centuries important industrial and commercial developments took place, and that the break between the old and the new Japan was much less sharp than has hitherto been supposed in the West. We shall begin with a brief description of the outstanding characteristics of the political, economic and social condition of the Tokugawa era and then examine the process of disintegration which ultimately led to the changes of the Restoration.

The outcome of the prolonged civil wars of the sixteenth century had been the establishment of the House of Tokugawa as Shogun, or secular rulers of Japan. The Shogun in theory owed allegiance to the Emperor, whose family from time immemorial had been the *de jure* head of the State. During the Tokugawa era, however, the practice of acknowledging this allegiance lapsed; and the Emperor lived in seclusion at Kyoto, surrounded by his Court and playing no part in the government of the country. Indeed, foreigners who came to Japan in the seventeenth and eighteenth centuries commonly regarded the Shogun as the real head of the State. The form of government instituted by the Tokugawas was a military dictatorship, known as *Bakufu*. The Shogun, together with the various branches of the Tokugawa family and its immediate vassals, owned between a quarter and a fifth of the agricultural land of the country, and derived the major part of his revenues from that source. The rest of the country was held by lords, or *daimyo*, who enjoyed a considerable degree of autonomy in the administration of their territories (*han*), and over whom central control was exercised chiefly through the requirement of the *sankin kotai*. This meant that each important *daimyo* was obliged to spend several months every year at Yedo (Tokyo), the seat of the Shogunate, and to leave hostages there when he returned to his fief.[1] The retainers of the lords and Shogun formed an 'estate' known as *samurai*. This class appears originally to have consisted of farmers who had the right of carrying arms, and who, in time of war, were called upon to serve their lord. With the alteration in the methods of warfare during the sixteenth century they had

---

[1] *Sankin kotai* may be translated 'alternate attendance'.

for the most part broken their links with the land and had come to live as military retainers in the castle-towns (*joka-machi*) of their lords, who granted annual allowances of rice for the maintenance of the *samurai* families and their hereditary servants.

The *samurai*, though all members of the privileged class, differed widely from one another in power and wealth. Some of them had large allowances and exercised the chief administrative functions of the *han*; but the majority received meagre grants of rice and acted as ordinary men-at-arms. During the long period of peace, both internal and external, which prevailed during the Tokugawa era, the *samurai* had little opportunity of practising their traditional function as warriors, and since industry and commerce were supposed to be unworthy of them, they became, with the exception of men who had administrative duties, a functionless and parasitic class. This indeed was the inevitable consequence of the Tokugawas' success in establishing peace after a long period of civil strife during which the warrior had risen in prestige and importance. As the *samurai* and their families, together with their hereditary servants, numbered about two million persons, or one-sixteenth of the population, on the eve of the Restoration, the maintenance of this large idle class must have constituted a heavy burden on the rest of the nation.

Among the non-privileged classes the peasants formed a large majority, and at the end of the Tokugawa period they possibly represented three-quarters of the whole population. They were subjected to many of the restrictions on their liberty with which the European serf was familiar. They were forbidden to leave their land and to migrate to the towns. Their freedom of cropping was restricted by the lords in the interests of a local self-sufficiency in foodstuffs, and sumptuary regulations governed the style of their clothing and dwelling places. Individual liberty was limited not merely by rules imposed from above, but also by the spontaneous growth of associations for mutual assistance from among the peasants themselves. Each village formed a unit which assumed a joint responsibility for the payment of taxes and for the proper cultivation of the land.

The peasants were the source of the major part of the revenue received by the Shogun and the *daimyo*. The annual land tax formed the most important payment. This varied widely from province to province and was altered frequently at the will of the lord. It was paid in rice, and it usually amounted to between 40 and 50 per cent of the total yield of the paddy-fields. In addition, other payments in kind and service were exacted from the peasants. Japanese writers are at one in declaring that this tribute reduced the peasants to a condition of extreme indigence—'their lot was so hard that they appeared to exist solely for the purpose of paying taxes'[1]; but whether they were worse off than the European peasant of the eighteenth century is a question that has not yet been answered, and is probably unanswerable.

The chief crop consisted, as today, of rice grown in irrigated fields. On the upland fields, the farmers raised millet, barley, wheat, soya beans, vegetables and tea. They produced also industrial crops, such as mulberry leaves for the silkworms, lacquer, indigo, hemp and cotton. In the early days of Tokugawa, when a 'natural' economy prevailed to a considerable extent in the rural areas, the peasants bought from outside their villages only such goods as salt, metals, medicines and, in the case of inland communities, fish. But they at no time confined themselves to purely agricultural pursuits. Those who lived near the sea-coasts combined fishing with farming, and nearly all the peasant families carried on subsidiary industrial pursuits. A large part of the manufactured articles in ordinary use was produced by them, either for their own consumption, or to the orders of merchants according to a 'putting out' system. During the winter months there was a seasonal migration of workers from rural to urban districts. This description of the activities of the Tokugawa peasants applies with surprisingly slight modification to those of the Japanese farmer in modern times.

In the course of the Tokugawa period the feudal system of tenure was affected by the intrusion of commercial influences, despite the opposition of the lords. In the first place, the scope and methods of farming changed. The range of crops was extended, some of the peasant's subsidiary activities, such as sericulture, grew substantially, and improvements in agricultural methods, including the increased use of fertilizers, led to a rise in productivity. These changes were accompanied, and made possible, by a modification in the organization of agriculture. In the seventeenth century farming operations had been conducted by co-operative family groups composed of units of various sizes, and hereditary servants and cultivators of subservient status then made up a large proportion of the working force. The innovations in farming technique required more highly intensive cultivation and gave the individual farmer with a small-holding a decided advantage over the large co-operative group, which gradually disappeared. While the majority of the peasants remained subject to feudal obligations, relationships within the rural communities became increasingly commercialized. City merchants invested in land and they, and the more prosperous peasants, rented farms to a new class of tenant. Most of the hereditary servants were either transformed into wage labourers on the farms or impelled to seek opportunities for employment in the expanding towns. At the same time,

[1] E. Honjo, *A Social and Economic History of Japan*, p. 231.

production for a market in some degree replaced purely subsistence agriculture.[1] Such changes as these hardly accord with a progressive impoverishment of the peasants that was the subject of popular declamation, although their economic condition certainly varied widely.[2]

All this implies the emergence long before the end of the Tokugawa era of social and economic relationships familiar to a modern economy. 'Commercial farming and the experience of working for wages had taught the peasant to respond with alacrity to monetary incentives',[3] and the gradual penetration of a money economy into the country districts was exerting the same kind of influence as in Europe in breaking down the old political and social system.

The specialized manufacturing industries of the towns depended largely on the demands of the privileged classes. In the *joka-machi*, or castle-towns of the *daimyo*, groups of handicraftsmen produced clothing, furniture, metal articles, swords and other military equipment for the *samurai*; and while in general the market for these products was local, some of the craftsmen catered for a wider demand. Numerous highly skilled crafts were also carried on at Kyoto, the artistic centre of Japan; and at Yedo many trades had appeared after its establishment as the Shogun's capital and after the institution of the *sankin kotai*. In the later days of Tokugawa the population of Yedo was about one million persons, and it was the chief consuming centre in the country. Osaka, 'the city of merchants' and the main breach in the feudal citadel, had a population of three or four hundred thousand and was another important manufacturing centre.

The crafts were controlled by guilds which bore a fairly close resemblance to the European craft guilds. The guilds regulated prices and conditions of production, sale and apprenticeship. Membership was limited and hereditary, and it could be acquired by a newcomer only through the purchase of the *kabu* (membership-privilege) from a retiring member. The guilds which had been recognized by the central government in the Trade Association Decree of 1721, paid taxes to the Shogunate or the *daimyo*, and the names of members were registered with the authorities. Unlike their European counterparts, they seem to have taken little part in the political or administrative life of the localities in which they were formed. Important as they may have been in the sphere of trade regulations, they seldom ventured beyond these narrow boundaries, and they remained essentially subordinate to the feudal society around them.

Industrial activity was by no means limited to the guilds. As already

---

[1] *See*, T. C. Smith, *The Agrarian Origins of Modern Japan*, *passim*, especially Part II.

[2] *See* the discussion of this question in G. B. Sansom, *Japan: A Short Cultural History*, pp. 454 *et seq.*   [3] T. C. Smith, *op. cit.*, p. 212.

shown, a form of domestic system was widespread in Tokugawa times. Articles manufactured by peasant families and urban workers were bought by merchants and distributed in the chief consuming centres. Sometimes the merchants made advances of raw materials and equipment to the producers, and in trades in which the operations were numerous and complex they assumed the responsibility for dividing the work in its various stages among the producers. Much of the raw silk, cotton and silk textiles, paper, mats, lanterns and many other articles were produced according to this system, and some of these industries became localized in particular districts or provinces. This system persists to a remarkable extent, even to the present day, and the manufacture of many of the older types of product is still localized in the same districts in which the trades were conducted a century ago. Nor were factories unknown during this time, although they were all small and relatively unimportant features of economic life. Workplaces employing up to one hundred persons were to be found in several of the textile trades; small factories existed in the *sake*-brewing industry and in wax manufacture; and there were some comparatively large enterprises in the gold, silver and copper-mining trades. These were for the most part operated by the Shogun or by *daimyo*, and the importance of copper among Japanese exports during this era testifies to the magnitude of this industry. From the later years of the seventeenth century coal also was produced, and from early in the eighteenth century the famous Miike mine was worked by the local *daimyo* as a fairly large-scale undertaking. Iron, produced from iron sand, was another industry into which large-scale capitalistic methods were intruding. That the iron and mining industries should provide the chief exceptions to the prevailing methods of production under the domestic system need cause no surprise. For obvious reasons this has been the case in most countries in a similar stage of development, just as in Japan, as elsewhere in early times, the conduct of these industries rested mainly in the hands of the Government or large landed magnates. Towards the close of the Tokugawa era these authorities began to take the initiative in setting up other large-scale trades—a development to be examined later.

In spite of the largely self-sufficient character of many of the peasant communities, the volume of trade between different parts of the country was far from negligible. It was indeed stimulated by the political system of the time. Just as the establishment of castle-towns led to the growth of handicrafts to cater for the needs of privileged groups of consumers who lived in them, so the institution of the *sankin kotai* necessitated a system of communications, a large movement of goods from the provinces to Yedo, and highly developed forms of financial and commercial organization. Rice and other products of the lords' territories were consigned to Osaka and Yedo for sale, so that the *daimyo* might be provided with funds to cover the expenses of their periodical journeys to the capital and their residence there. As a result there grew up an important merchant class to handle the various financial and commercial transactions to which this business gave rise. Great warehouses were built in the two chief cities to store the commodities brought from the provinces, and organized markets appeared there in which transactions in futures took place. The *daimyo* frequently raised money on the security of their revenues, and a class of financiers developed to provide these loans and to arrange for the transmission of funds from one part of the country to another. Various types of credit instruments, such as bills of exchange and promissory notes, were in common use, and the chief financial houses had a network of branches in different parts of Japan. The merchants were highly specialized as to goods and function, and they formed themselves into guilds for the regulation of trading conditions and for restricting their numbers. With the growth of the cities during the Tokugawa period retail shops became very numerous, and even in the early eighteenth century Kaempfer had commented on the number of these shops in Kyoto and the variety of goods sold in them. Some of these retail enterprises were on a very big scale; the House of Mitsui, for example is said to have employed over a thousand people in its Tokyo shops at the end of the eighteenth century,[1] and there were other forerunners of the great stores so characteristic of the cities of modern Japan.

The *sankin kotai* had led to a marked improvement in the roads. There was fairly rapid communication between Eastern and Western Japan along the famous Tokaido, although traffic was impeded by the barrier gates erected along the highways by the Shogun for the purpose of controlling the movements of his subjects, and also by the policy of limiting the building of bridges over the rivers which intersected the main roads. The coastal trade reached a considerable volume. Although the Government forbade the building of large ships because of its policy of isolating Japan from the rest of the world, yet there was a large and high organized traffic between the chief ports, especially between Yedo and Osaka.

The regulations of the Shogunate had a crippling effect on foreign commerce. As is generally known, from the early days of the Toku-

---

[1] *The House of Mitsui*, p. 6. These shops appear in some of Hiroshige's prints; they were also depicted in a painting by Buncho. The Mitsuis had little to learn of the arts of salesmanship and publicity. They provided free umbrellas to customers caught unprepared by unexpected showers; each umbrella bore the sign, or trademark, of the House. They paid popular actors to introduce subtle references to the firm in their lines. They had a Code in the best traditions of Rotary.

gawa era the policy of seclusion was followed, and for many years Japan's economic development was only slightly affected by the influences that result from international trade. After 1641 commerce between Japan and the outside world was restricted to that conducted by the Chinese at Nagasaki and by the Dutch merchants whose factory was established at Deshima in the same neighbourhood. The volume and composition of this trade were strictly controlled. The chief imports consisted of raw silk and silk piece-goods, and as these were paid for by exports of gold, silver and copper, the trade was regarded with some disfavour by the Government, since it seemed to endanger the country's supply of precious metals. The main purpose of the seclusion policy was to assist in the preservation of the rigid political system which the Shogunate had established, and the policy naturally extended to foreign cultural influences. In the early part of the era even translations from European languages were proscribed. Japanese were forbidden to leave Japan and foreigners to settle there. Although with the connivance of the southern *daimyo*, who were hostile to Tokugawa, some of these regulations were evaded, especially towards the end of the era, the policy of seclusion was on the whole effectively carried out. This served to intensify the shock to the economic system of contact with the outside world when the country was at last thrown open to foreigners.

We must now consider the reasons for the collapse of the Tokugawa régime and of the economic system associated with it. To European observers in the third quarter of the nineteenth century this change appeared to be both sudden and catastrophic, and the impression that it represented a complete transformation still remains among many Westerners. Yet, in reality, it came as the culmination of a series of developments that had been steadily weakening the Shogunate; and profound though the subsequent changes undoubtedly were, Japan carried into her modern era many vestiges, economic as well as political, of the older forms. The contention that the main cause of the Shogunate's collapse was the forced opening of the ports to foreigners cannot, of course, be sustained, although pressure from abroad was undoubtedly a contributory cause. From the later years of the eighteenth century the difficulty of preserving seclusion, the keystone of Tokugawa policy, was increasing. English and other European traders were insistent on the need for opening up relations with Japan, and they tried repeatedly to obtain from the Shogunate the right of calling at the ports and trading with the people. The Russians descended on Saghalien and made several attempts to establish diplomatic relations with the Japanese Government. The settlement of the west coast of the United States brought American ships to the Western Pacific, and American whalers were frequently observed in Japanese waters.[1] For a time the Shogun was able to evade the demands for permission to trade or to shelter; but when Perry steamed for a second time into Suraga Bay in 1854 and refused to leave without an agreement which meant in effect the end of Japan's seclusion, the Government had to acquiesce.

The breach once made was very soon enlarged. In 1858 the Government was compelled to sign treaties which conferred rights of trade on British, French and other nationals; five ports were opened to foreign shipping; and extra-territorial rights were granted to foreigners.[2] The irresistible might of Westerners' naval equipment was demonstrated to the clans most hostile to this enforced change of policy by the bombardments of Kagoshima and Shimonoseki in 1863 and 1864. Foreign aggression thus brought to light the weakness of the old régime, emphasized the need for change and, to some extent, determined the nature of the transformation in Japan's economic and political life that subsequently occurred. But the view, once widely held in the West, that 'the bombardment of Kagoshima was the paramount cause that impelled Japan to adopt the foreign civilization' was rightly criticized by Griffis as early as 1875.[3] As he says, 'the foreigners and their ideas were the occasion, not the cause, of the destruction of the dual system of government. . . . Their presence served merely to hasten what was already inevitable. The true cause of the recent marvellous changes in Japan . . . operated mainly from within, not from without; from impulse, not from impact.'[4]

The internal influences chiefly responsible for the changes are to be sought in the political, religious, intellectual and economic life of the country. Our concern is with the economic causes of change; but lest these should be given a disproportionate weight, a brief reference must be made to others. Tokugawa Iyeyasu (1603-16) and his immediate successors had made Buddhism the national religion, had discouraged inquiry into the past history and traditions of Japan and had fostered Chinese scholarship, particularly that of the Sung school. For many years under rigid governmental censorship these influences were paramount. But gradually they were undermined. The fall of the Ming dynasty brought many Chinese scholars to

---

[1] J. Murdoch, *op. cit.*, Vol. III, p. 527. Cf. also J. F. Kuiper, 'Some Notes on the Foreign Relations of Japan, 1798-1805', in *Trans. of Asiatic Society of Japan*, December 1924.

[2] These treaties, much resented by the Japanese in subsequent years, were known as the 'unequal treaties'.

[3] W. E. Griffis, *The Mikado's Empire*, Vol. I, pp. 292-3.

[4] *Ibid.*, p. 291. Cf. also G. B. Sansom, *op. cit.*, p. 460, where he states: 'What opened the doors was not a summons from without but an explosion from within.'

Japan and provided a new intellectual stimulus. There was a revival early in the eighteenth century of interest in ancient Japanese history and literature. The publication of the Prince of Mito's *History of Great Japan* informed the literary classes of a time when the Emperor, not the Shogun, held sway over the country, and towards the end of the eighteenth century scholars and propagandists, among whom was the celebrated Nobunaga Motoori, proclaimed the necessity for casting off Chinese and Buddhist influence and for returning to the ancient beliefs associated with Shinto. Among these were the doctrines of the divinity of the Emperor, of the descent of the Japanese from the gods and of their possession of peculiar virtues by right of this distinguished descent.[1] These movements in the world of thought had important political repercussions, for they were all antagonistic to the Shogunate as well as to the forms of scholarship which those rulers had fostered. The slogan *Sonno Jo-i*[2] which roused the clans to action after the incursion of Perry is said to have been 'a compendious and practical summing up of the logical results of Motoori's teaching'. The propaganda was gratefully received by the Western clans which, though subdued by Tokugawa in the sixteenth century, still smarted under the government of a house of which they had once been the peers. Their dissatisfaction was constantly stimulated by the arrogant attitude of the Shogun's own retainers. Being most distant from the capital these clans were difficult to control, and they formed the natural seat of political movements hostile to Tokugawa. When the Shogun was forced to come to an agreement with foreigners and in doing so appeared to sacrifice Japan and the Emperor to the barbarians, they were able to demand in the name of patriotism the change of government which their interests and ambitions had long required.

Hostile as these clans were to the encroachment of Western nations on the independence of Japan, they themselves in the eighteenth and early nineteenth centuries had provided a channel for influences that helped to shatter the old Japan. The lord of Satsuma in Kyushu connived at illicit trading on the part of Chinese and European merchants. He encouraged the study of English and Dutch, and Kagoshima, his capital, became an important centre of intellectual activity and a source from which the knowledge of Western ideas and practices spread over the rest of Japan. In the second quarter of the nineteenth century several young Japanese *samurai* secretly left the country against the explicit orders of the

[1] 'Little credence was reposed either in the ancient myths in general or in the theory of the divine descent of the Mikado in particular in eighteenth-century Japan before Motoori began his thirty years polemic in their support.' J. Murdoch, *op. cit.*, Vol. III, p. 482.

[2] 'Reverence the Emperor and exclude the foreigners.'

central Government for the purpose of studying Western civilization, and these included many Satsuma men who played a prominent part in the creation of new Japan. Long before this, moreover, Western intellectual influences had been gradually permeating the country. In the eighteenth century the Japanese intellectual classes began to acquire what was known as the 'Dutch learning' (*Rangaku*), that is to say, a knowledge of Western sciences (particularly astronomy, anatomy, medicine and military science) through the medium of the Dutch language. In the early part of the nineteenth century this tendency grew in strength and some three thousand students are said to have passed through the Dutch School at Osaka during the twenty-four years after its establishment in 1838. The Japanese intellectual classes were thus not ignorant of the material progress of the West, nor were they unacquainted with its pre-eminence in applied science. This knowledge made them critical of the existing forms of government and apprehensive of the dangers to Japan that the growing power of the Western States might bring.

The economic causes of the change were of profound, perhaps of pre-eminent importance. Prince Matsukata, the great financial administrator of the Meiji era, was one of the most notable of the public men in new Japan to emphasize these causes,[1] and recent investigations bring out clearly the economic disintegration that had been taking place for many years before 1867. It is evident that from the early years of the nineteenth century, and indeed before this, the Tokugawa régime was being shaken by serious financial difficulties and by changes in the social and economic structure of the country which were the source of widespread discontent.

Let us first examine the financial position of the central Government. The first of the Tokugawa Shoguns, Iyeyasu (1603-16), had accumulated a large reserve of treasure, chiefly through seizing the property of *daimyo* who had been hostile to him; but this was dissipated during the second half of the seventeenth century, partly through rising administrative expenses and partly through numerous earthquakes and fires which devastated Yedo. In the next century efforts to maintain financial stability were successful only for short intervals. Apart from his rice-revenues, the Shogun derived an income from taxes imposed on traders resident in the ports and large towns, which were mainly under his control, and from mining properties operated by the central Government. The restrictions on foreign trade meant that only a meagre income was available from import or export duties. So the Shogun had not at his command a source of revenue which rulers in Europe had found increasingly important as the income from their domains became insufficient to meet the growing expenses of government during the same period.

[1] Cf. S. Okuma, *Fifty Years of New Japan*, Vol. I, p. 359.

Financial administration was lax, and owing to the corruption of officials, a considerable part of the proceeds of the taxes failed to find its way into the Treasury. Attempts to wrest higher taxes from the peasantry led to frequent jacqueries and to a tendency for the farmers to desert the land for the towns, a movement which struck at the whole basis of the revenue and which official prohibition seems to have done little to check. From the latter part of the eighteenth century, moreover, the country was visited by a series of natural disasters, including earthquakes and famines. Historians have concluded that the population, which had steadily increased in the early part of the Tokugawa era, declined in the subsequent period.[1]

To meet his growing difficulties, the Shogun did not hesitate to resort to the traditional expedient of governments in financial distress. The currency suffered successive debasements so that the purchasing power of the standard coin by the middle of the nineteenth century was only one-eighth of its purchasing power in 1661.[2] The rise in prices which debasement caused provoked great discontent among the classes injured by it, and the trouble was accentuated as a result of the issue by the *daimyo*, for the purpose of meeting their own financial difficulties, not merely of illegal coinage, but also of large quantities of notes secured against stocks of rice and other consumable goods, including even umbrellas. A second expedient of which the Shogunate made increasing use was the exaction of benevolences (*goyokin*) from the *chonin*, the rising merchant and financial class. After the collapse of the seclusion policy the Shogunate's finances rapidly degenerated. The danger from abroad obliged the Government to incur heavy expenditure for improving the national defences and for maintaining diplomatic representatives. Moreover, it had to pay heavy indemnities to foreign States for outrages on their nationals committed during periods of anti-foreign feeling.[3]

Meanwhile, feudal society in the provinces was breaking up. The maintenance of hordes of idle retainers absorbed a large share of the

---

[1] R. Ishii, *Population Pressure and Economic Life in Japan*, pp. 13-15.

[2] A. Andreades, *Les Finances de l'Empire Japonais et leur Evolution*, p. 26.

[3] The disorganization of the currency was completed by the impact of foreign trade on the supplies of metallic money in existence at the time. The Tokugawa Government maintained a monopoly of silver and found it profitable to overvalue, in terms of gold, the silver coins which it issued. The gold-silver ratio was accordingly fixed at 1 : 5 compared with a ratio in the outside world of 1 : 16. When the Treaties were signed with foreign Powers in 1858, in was agreed that the Japanese Government would exchange Japanese silver coin for foreign silver weight for weight. The Government evidently did not realize the inevitable result of this provision. Foreigners imported large quantities of Mexican dollars, the chief medium of exchange in the Far East, exchanged them weight for weight with the Japanese token silver coin (the *ichi-bu*), turned the *ichi-bu* into gold *ko-ban* at the ratio of 5 : 1, and shipped the gold to Shanghai where it could be exchanged for silver at a ratio of 16 : 1.

daimyo's revenue, while the *sankin kotai* proved to be an increasingly heavy burden as the lords vied with each other in conspicuous expenditure at Yedo. Attempts were made to reduce expenses by cutting down the *samurai's* allowances with the result that the lower strata in this class became impoverished. In their search for additional revenue, the *daimyo* increased their issues of paper money, which tended further to disorganize the economic life of their *han*, and they also established various industrial and trading enterprises of a monopolistic kind, a policy which helped to modify the character of the feudal society. After the middle of the eighteenth century the *daimyo* resorted increasingly to loans. These were secured on their rice revenues, and they were raised from the merchants who acted as the *daimyo's* agents for selling their rice. The result was that the merchant classes increased in wealth and influence. 'Sometimes the finances of the *daimyo* were controlled by a certain money-lender who loaned money to a *daimyo* with rice as a security'.[1] Great merchants like Konoike who acted as agents and bankers for the lords were able to live like princes. A contemporary chronicler wrote 'Although in form the *samurai* govern and the commoners obey, in reality it seems to be an age when the *chonin* rule'[2]; and another declared 'The anger of the wealthy merchants of Osaka has the power of striking terror into the hearts of the *daimyo*.'[3]

The merchants' influence on the development of Japan in the Tokugawa period was unquestionably profound. They created a new urban culture and contributed lavishly to the superb artistic flowering of the Genroku era (1688-1703). Their commercial and financial activities helped to undermine the economy of a régime based on peasant agriculture and payments in kind and service.[4] But they never made any serious attempt to wrest political power from the feudal classes to whose authority they were in the main content to defer. And the central and local authorities for their part regarded them as instruments of the existing feudal order, never as possible agents of economic growth.[5]

If the position of the lords was shaken by these changes, that of their retainers, especially those in the lower ranks, became deplor-

---

[1] E. Honjo, *op. cit.*, p. 197.   [2] *Ibid.*, p. 199.   [3] *Ibid.*, p. 201.

[4] Saikaku, a writer of the Genroku period, gave vigorous expression to the spirit of the rising merchant class, praising its audacious enterprise and its urgent pursuit of economic advantage. His concept of an ideal economic man seemed as strange and repellent to the typical *samurai* as was the idea of competition for which, when Western economic writings were first translated, it was necessary to make a new word. (See T. Ueda, 'Saikaku's Economic Man', in *Annals of the Hitotsubashi Academy*, October 1956, and G. B. Sansom, *The Western World and Japan*, p. 248.)

[5] C. D. Sheldon, *The Rise of the Merchant Class in Tokugawa Japan, 1600-1868*, *passim*, esp. Chap. IX.

able. Their impoverished lords often held back part of their rice grants. Since the *samurai* were paid their incomes in a commodity liable to violent fluctuations in price, their economic position became increasingly unstable as a result of the spread of a money economy in the towns where they lived for much of their time. Many of them were even obliged to sell or pawn their swords and armour, the insignia of their privileged rank, and to engage in occupations traditionally despised. They often entered the service of merchants or set up in trade on their own. By the nineteenth century the majority of them had given up the practice of maintaining hereditary servants, and the strong personal ties which previously existed between the family of the *samurai* and that of his servant were thus destroyed. The sharp divisions of status and function that were characteristic of early Tokugawa society became blurred in consequence of these changes. The formerly despised merchants, as we have seen, acquired wealth and influence. The *daimyo* were engaging in trade and industry, and their *samurai* were beginning to follow commercial occupations. It became the practice for the *samurai* to adopt the sons of rich commoners into their families; while others even sold their *samurai* status to commoners.[1] Thus the whole system of personal relationships upon which the old scheme of society rested was falling to pieces. It is ironical to reflect that the very success of Tokugawa in imposing rigid control over the feudal classes contributed ultimately to the destruction of the social and political system. For the bulk of the *samurai* became functionless, and the *sankin kotai*, besides impoverishing the lords, stimulated the development of trade, a money economy, and so a financial and commercial class which could not be easily accommodated within the old feudal structure. Feudalism was losing its grip even on the peasants who were exposed increasingly to the corrupting influences of a market economy.

During the last few decades of the Shogunate, and especially after the opening of the ports to foreigners, the central Government seems to have accepted the proposition that fundamental changes were required in administration and economic policy. At all events, it began to introduce a series of reforms which the Meiji Government later carried through. Envoys were sent abroad to study foreign conditions; restrictions on the building of ocean-going ships were abolished; and warships and merchant vessels were purchased from abroad. During the last ten or fifteen years of his rule the Shogun was busily engaged in constructing dockyards, ironworks and other industrial plants modelled on Western lines. He borrowed from France and the United States to finance these new enterprises. He

---

[1] Prince Ito, the great statesman of the Meiji era, was the son of a farmer who had purchased *samurai* status from a retainer of the Mori family in Western Japan.

introduced administrative reforms and threw open important offices, previously the perquisite of men of high rank, to men of talent, He was even contemplating the abolition of the *han* and the establishment of a modern system of centralized government.

The Shogun also attempted to deal with the rise in prices, which was causing unrest in the early decades of the nineteenth century. This rise in prices was commonly attributed at the time to the activities of the guilds. These organizations were pursuing an increasingly exclusive policy. In consequence, there was a considerable growth in the number of journeymen (*shokunin*) who, though qualified by apprenticeship for the status of master craftsmen, were not admitted to full membership of the guilds. Disputes between the *shokunin* and the guilds were frequent, and the latter found increasing difficulty in maintaining their monopolistic rights over trade. Meanwhile the *samurai*, who saw the *chonin* class usurping their traditional place in society, had conceived a deep detestation of the merchants and the guilds in which they were associated. This sentiment was felt especially for the merchants engaged in foreign trade which in the fifties and sixties began to disturb the old economic structure. The monopolistic practices of the guilds had already been challenged in the provinces by the tendency of the local governments to set up their own manufacturing and trading organizations in order to improve their financial position. The Shogun hoped to follow this example in his own domains, and by generalizing this practice, to prop up the decaying structure of feudalism. A blow was given to the merchants' privileges by the decrees of 1831 and 1843 which abolished all forms of guild. The immediate result of this step, however, was to disorganize economic life still further; for the abolition of the guilds involved the destruction of the credit system that rested on the *kabu*, or membership privilege. The disorganization was so serious as to compel the Government in 1851 to make some attempt to revive the guilds in a modified form. But since the number of *shokunin* had by then greatly increased, it was not possible to restore the monopolistic privileges which the guilds had enjoyed, and they were finally swept away during the next few years. Thus, institutions which the Shogun had recognized for the purpose of enabling him to control the economic life of the country, and which provided him with a useful adjunct to his revenue in the form of licence fees, had crumbled even before the political revolt had begun. When foreign trade began to increase after 1858, the social distress that had attended these economic troubles was intensified. The distribution of economic resources that had been stereotyped by a policy of seclusion and rigid trade regulation could not be preserved once Japan was exposed to the conditions of the world market. Old trades decayed as cheaper substitutes for their products began to be imported, and contact with the West was accompanied by alterations in the tastes of the people which diverted demand into new channels. Adaptation to these new circumstances was not easy and was often attended with hardship for the older types of producer.

The effect of the impact of the outside world was especially obvious in the relative prices of the period 1859-67. There was an enormous rise in the price of raw silk, egg cards, rice, tea and, in general, articles for which a foreign demand became keen. On the other hand, imports of cheap cotton textiles, yarn and other products of machine industry brought about a steep fall in the price of such goods.[1] Naturally these changes caused economic dislocation. The silk-weaving trade suffered through the rise in price of its raw material, and the producers of cotton textiles were damaged by the influx of foreign goods. Many of the farmers, however, benefited as a result of the expansion of the foreign demand for raw silk and tea. Capital began to flow into Japan from abroad not merely through the loans raised by the Shogun and *daimyo* but also through the financial activities of foreign merchants who now settled in Japan. This affected the whole organization of industry. Factories for turning out textiles and metals were set up both by central and local governments, and the domestic system, characterized by the commercial predominance of the merchant over his dependent groups of craftsmen or peasants, was widely extended.

The process of adjustment to these new conditions gave rise to social and economic strain, and, among the groups damaged by the changes, to serious unrest. Thus, just as the opening of the country and the conclusion of agreements with foreigners—a policy which force of circumstances compelled the Shogun to follow—brought him in the eyes of his enemies to the position not merely of a usurper of Imperial rights but also of a betrayer of his country, so both the financial difficulties of the régime which the Shogun had striven to preserve and the economic chaos that attended the transition to a new order could be placed to his account. The Shogun suffered discredit both for the economic and political evils attendant on the old régime and also for his actions calculated to change it. He had alienated the most powerful classes in the country, and any step he took, however necessary or inevitable it might prove in the light of subsequent judgment, was mistrusted because of his equivocal position in relation to the Emperor, and so provided another argument for his overthrow. At a time when the nation needed bold and vigorous leadership, the Shogun was precluded by his loss of prestige from supplying it. Other men and other institutions had to be used.

It was not, however, among the *chonin* that the leadership needed

[1] Cf. S. Okuma, 'The Industrial Revolution in Japan', in the *North American Review*, Vol. I, p. 72; and E. Honjo, *op. cit.*, Chap. XI.

to usher in the new world was mainly found. Some of them, notably Mitsui, helped to finance the revolt against Tokugawa. But, as a class, the *chonin* owed their wealth to their position as financial and commercial agents of the *daimyo* and Shogun; the interests of most of them were bound up with the old régime, even though they might sometimes suffer from its exactions. Insulated by the Seclusion Edict from the vitalizing impact of foreign trade, they had become as a class conservative in temper and restrictionist in commercial policy. With a few notable exceptions, the great merchants failed to seize, either before or after the Restoration, the new opportunities offered to them by the opening of the country to the commerce of the world and by the development of new industries. It was the *samurai* of lower rank from the 'outside' clans who initiated the revolt and played the major rôle in weaving both the political and the economic fabric of New Japan. This class, during the Tokugawa period, had become increasingly impoverished, and their social privileges had been curtailed as a result of their economic distress. Far from having any stake in the old régime, their interests lay entirely in the direction of change.

At the time of Perry's first arrival (1853) the Shogunate still seemed impregnable. But the foundations of its rule had been undermined by political, economic and intellectual changes, and it needed but the shock of foreign aggression to bring down the whole edifice. When the Western clans, led by an extremely able group of *samurai*, moved against the Shogunate in the name of the Emperor, the resistance was trivial. In 1868 the House of Tokugawa was overthrown, and the Emperor was restored to a constitutional position which he had not occupied for some 800 years. This Restoration almost coincided with the death of the Emperor Kei-o and the enthronement of his successor, then only sixteen years old. The Meiji era had begun and, with it, the career of Modern Japan.

CHAPTER II

RECONSTRUCTION, 1868–81

The Restoration Government, though composed of many men who had bitterly opposed the Shogun's policy of coming to terms with the foreigners, advanced further in the same direction once the new régime had been established. It recognized that Japan's military weakness and her economic backwardness might make her the easy spoil of Western Powers, and it judged that the rapid adoption of Western methods in war and industry could alone enable her to retain her independence and ultimately to secure the abrogation of the 'unequal treaties'. In a sense Japan was fortunate in that the breaking down of her seclusion was not delayed. In the fifties and sixties the liberal international outlook of the most powerful European countries was not conducive to colonizing adventures by ambitious statesmen, while the United States was distracted by internal feuds. Had the opening up of the country been deferred until the new era of imperialist expansion, Japan might well have succumbed to attack from abroad. Even as it was, Japan formed a field in which French and British rivalries displayed themselves, for France in the years preceding the Restoration lent her support to the Shogunate, and England to the revolting clans. What had been an especially potent influence in awakening Japan to her danger was the 'Opium War' of 1839-42, which demonstrated both the superiority of Western armaments to those of the East, and also the possible fatal consequences of that superiority to the territorial integrity of Oriental nations.[1] Defence, therefore, became the main task of the new Government, while those numerous Japanese whose fear of the Western nations was mingled with admiration of their prowess overseas considered that the adoption of Western material equipment might enable Japan to find a place among the aggressors instead of among the victims of aggression.[2]

After the Restoration the control of the central Government rested, under the Emperor, in the hands of those vigorous leaders of the

[1] Cf. G. F. Hudson, *The Far East in World Politics*, pp. 24-6.

[2] Some interesting reflections on this point are to be found in T. Kada, *Social and Political Factors in Japan's External Economic Policy*, pp. 3-6 (Japanese Society of International Studies, Tokyo). Cf. also I. F. Ayusawa's statement: 'The slogan of the Meiji era which permeated all thinking minds and inspired the New Japan was "Fu-koku Kyo-hei", or "Rich Nation, Strong Army" ' (in H. A. Marquand's *Organized Labour in Four Continents*, p. 483).

Satsuma, Choshu, Tosa and Hizen clans who had led the revolt against Tokugawa. There was naturally discontent among the *samurai* who were shut out from power, especially among the clans which had supported the Shogun, and it was not until 1870 that opposition to the new Government was finally put down. Even within the clans now in control of the State there was no unanimity about policy, and in 1874 there took place a rebellion in the Saga clan and in 1877 the more serious Satsuma rebellion, the last fight of expiring feudalism. Not until this rebellion had been suppressed could it be said that the political revolution had been completed and the country unified.

1. *General Economic Changes*

These political struggles naturally imposed a severe strain on the administrative capacity and the financial resources of the central Government. At the same time the country was still in process of adjusting itself to the new economic conditions created by the opening of the country and by the decay of the political institutions on which economic life had depended. Nevertheless, the achievements of the new Government were remarkable. A mere enumeration of the reforms and innovations for which it was responsible during the first fourteen years of its existence is sufficient to indicate the energy and determination which it brought to its policy of Westernizing the country's institutions. In 1869 feudalism was abolished and the clans surrendered their fiefs to the Government. In 1871 prefectures were established in place of the *han* and the old financial and administrative system associated with feudalism disappeared, while shortly afterwards far-reaching reforms in taxation were introduced; these will be further discussed when we come to consider the fiscal and financial history of the period.

The changes effected by the Government in social, industrial and commercial organization were as important as those in finance and politics. Most of the remaining restrictions on freedom of movement and enterprise that had been a legacy of the old régime were abolished. In 1869 the equality of the various social classes before the law was declared; local barriers to communications and restrictions on internal trade were swept away; freedom of cropping was allowed; entry into professions and trades was thrown open; and individuals were allowed to acquire property rights in land. The Government's attempts to introduce a new régime were not confined to permissive measures; for it was realized that in the absence of an industrial and commercial class familiar with Western trading methods and technique the State was obliged to take positive action to bring about the modernization of the country's economic life. The business class which had been left as a legacy of the Shogunate consisted for the most part of mere financial agents of the old régime, and few of its members were fitted to act as entrepreneurs in the new era. Even under Tokugawa foreign experts had been engaged to instruct the Japanese in Western methods of mining and manufacture. This policy was pushed much further in the early years of Meiji. In 1875 when, according to official statistics, the number of foreigners in the service of the central and prefectural governments reached the maximum, 527 were employed, of whom 205 were technical advisers, 144 teachers, 69 managers and administrators and 36 skilled workmen.[1] Japanese were encouraged to go abroad to acquire Western knowledge, and means were devised to provide technical training. For instance, samples of foreign foods and foreign machinery were imported by the Government and lent to the prefectural authorities who used them as models for the producers in their locality. Itinerant teachers were sent round the country. Schools and colleges were soon established by the State, including engineering, mining and agricultural colleges. Agricultural experimental stations were set up to assist in the adaptation of foreign crops to Japanese conditions and to work out improved methods of farming. In 1869 the Government founded a Commercial Bureau to supervise and encourage foreign trade, and it provided for the establishment of organizations for developing the exports of artistic products. In 1877 it organized an Industrial Exhibition at Ueno Park, Tokyo.

The Government had a particularly keen interest in foreign trade at this time. Large payments had to be made in foreign currencies in return for imports of equipment, such as merchant vessels, warships, munitions and machinery, needed to carry out its programme of Westernization. Imports of consumer goods, especially textiles and kerosene increased, and interest payments had to be made on foreign loans. Yet, in the undeveloped state of Japan's commerce and finance, the necessary foreign exchange was scarce, and there was pressure on the balance of payments. On many occasions during the seventies the State itself engaged in export transactions in order to obtain foreign currency. For instance, it purchased domestic stocks of rice, tea and silk, sold them abroad and used the proceeds of the sale to finance the imports it urgently required.[2] The Government's preoccupation with the balance of payments lay behind some of its industrial ventures also. In establishing factories for producing

---

[1] *The Fifth Annual Statistical Report of the Japanese Empire* (1886), pp. 935-7. The number declined sharply in the later seventies, but in 1880 237 were still employed. In addition, there were foreigners in the employment of business firms; their number is unknown.

[2] *The Currency of Japan* (A Reprint of Articles and Reports: published by the *Japan Gazette*, 1882), pp. 185, 198, 219.

cement, glass and building materials it hoped to replace imports by home-produced supplies.

The State soon realized the necessity of introducing the new methods of communication that had played so important a part in the industrialization of the West. In 1871 a postal and telegraph system was introduced, and six years later Japan joined the Postal Union. In 1869 a steamship line between Osaka and Tokyo was formed, and shortly afterwards the first railway was built—it connected Tokyo and Yokohama—on the proceeds of a Government loan raised in England. What is more, the State took the initiative in establishing a large number of manufacturing establishments equipped with Western machinery for producing new products or goods hitherto manufactured by primitive methods. In this it was but carrying further a policy begun before the Restoration. We have already seen that several of the more enterprising *daimyo* had set up Western-style factories during the first half of the century. The lord of Satsuma, for example, had founded works for the manufacture of pottery, cannon and cotton yarn. Indeed, the first cotton-spinning mill in Japan was started in 1861 by this *daimyo* who imported Lancashire textile machinery for the purpose. The Shogun himself had founded Western-style enterprises, including two shipbuilding yards, during the later fifties. The new Government pursued systematically a policy which the feudal chiefs and Tokugawa had only tentatively begun.

A brief reference to some of the Government's activities in the industrial field will demonstrate their wide range. To begin with, the State took over many of the undertakings of the Shogunate and the *daimyo*, re-equipped and re-organized them. During the seventies it built and operated cotton-spinning mills of a Western type in the Aichi and Hiroshima prefectures; and in order to encourage private enterprise, it imported and then sold foreign spinning machinery to entrepreneurs on the instalment plan. From 1858 onwards exports of raw silk had grown rapidly, but even so the development of this trade was handicapped by the lack of suitable equipment. For instance, the Japanese type of reeling machine, driven by manual or water power, was incapable of producing the standardized qualities of silk demanded abroad. So, in 1870 the Government established at Maebashi and Tomioka factories on French and Italian models. Other model factories built during the seventies with the object of encouraging the importation of Western technique, were the Shirakawa White Tile Works, the Fukugawa Cement Works, the Senji Woollen Web Factory, and a sodium sulphate and bleaching powder works.[1] Certain factories were established for the specific purpose of

[1] Y. Honyden, 'Der Durchbruch des Kapitalismus in Japan', in *Weltwirtschaftliches Archiv*, July 1937, pp. 31-2.

C

stimulating the development of particular localities; for instance, the Development Commission of Hokkaido set up at Sapporo a brewery and a sugar factory.

The creation of a munitions industry was, of course, the most urgent requirement of the period, and here the Government had two foundations on which to build. These were, first, the workshops in which arms had been made for the *daimyo*, and secondly, the powder and munitions factories of the Shogunate. The new Government took them all over and re-equipped them. Thus, the Nagasaki Iron Foundries which had belonged to the Shogun were the parent of the new Government's artillery works, and the Kagoshima shipbuilding yard, originally owned by the lord of Satsuma, was adapted to the manufacture of warships. A woollen mill to supply the army with uniform cloth was built in 1876 and an engineering factory in 1879.[1] All mineral properties were declared to belong to the Government which leased mining rights to persons desirous of working them. In the late sixties and early seventies nine large mines (gold, silver, copper, iron ore and coal) were actually operated by the State as model enterprises. The Government also gave attention to the development of a mercantile marine. In 1874 it bought ocean-going ships from abroad, and later transferred these to the Mitsubishi firm which, with Government assistance, operated both coastal services and lines to Formosa and China. Foreign captains were engaged to command its ships and to train its seamen, just as the services of foreign technicians and workmen were made use of in the organization of the new manufacturing enterprises. It can be said with truth that there was scarcely any important Japanese industry of the Western type during the later decades of the nineteenth century which did not owe its establishment to State initiative.[2] In 1880 Count Okuma, in a summary statement of Government-owned industrial undertakings and properties, enumerated 3 shipbuilding yards, 51 merchant ships, 5 munition works, 52 other factories, 10 mines, 75 miles of railways, and a telegraph system which linked all the chief towns.[3] At that time the Government was giving help to several shipbuilding yards, besides those which it owned, and it was subsidizing mail steamship services. It had taken steps to develop Hokkaido and to encourage emigration to that thinly populated island. All this was achieved during a period when the Government was faced with great financial difficulties and with two major rebellions.

[1] *Ibid.*, pp. 31-2.
[2] 'We find that every company or manufactory deserving of notice in any way has been furnished with capital by the Government or has been endowed with special privileges by the same power' (*The Currency of Japan*, p. 260).
[3] *The Currency of Japan*, pp. 76-80.

It is not to be thought that strategy and difficulties with the balance of payments provided the only motives for the Governments' policy of sponsoring industry. Another reason was to find employment for the *samurai*. These had not only lost their privileged status but also, as a result of the commutation of their pensions, had suffered grievous financial loss. They were not a submissive class like the peasants and, if their smouldering discontent were to be blown into flames, the Restoration Government might well be consumed. To find them remunerative occupations was, therefore, a condition of the Government's survival. As we shall see presently, the new banking laws were framed to some extent with this object in mind. Similar motives lay behind decisions to establish certain manufactures and to provide for the training of *samurai* both as managers and skilled artisans. But in this context the Government was not concerned solely with turning the edge of political revolt. *Samurai* themselves, the new rulers were moved by a conviction that men of their own class possessed unique qualities of character which could contribute much to the development of their country.[1] As events were to prove, they judged well.

If the establishment and growth of the more highly capitalized industries and the basic services can be attributed mainly to Government initiative, the inception of other new industries and expansion of several old ones came largely as the response of private enterprise to the opportunities presented by the opening of the country to foreign trade. Here an essential part was played by European and American merchants settled in the ports. Japan's experience of world markets and sources of supply as well as of the technique of foreign commerce was at this time narrowly limited. So, until the end of the century, foreign merchants conducted the major part of the overseas trade. They and the branches and agencies of such foreign banks as the Oriental Banking Corporation and the Hong Kong and Shanghai Banking Corporation financed much of this trade and, incidentally, the dealers from whom the foreign merchants obtained their supplies. European and American merchants and bankers can, therefore, be regarded as one of the chief instruments of economic change during these early years.[2]

Under the stimulus of Governmental example and of the new opportunities caused by the freeing of trade and the opening of the country, industry and commerce began to advance. The railway mileage, including State lines, increased to 122 by 1881. The tonnage

[1] Cf. T. C. Smith, *Political Change and Industrial Development in Japan: Government Enterprise, 1868-1880*, p. 33.

[2] For a more detailed account of the activities of foreign merchants in Japan, see G. C. Allen and A. G. Donnithorne, *Western Enterprise in Far Eastern Economic Development: China and Japan*, especially Chap. XII.

of the mercantile marine grew from some 26,000 in 1873 to about 50,000 in the early eighties. There was a gradual increase in the number of ships built in Japanese yards, although in 1880 the tonnage constructed amounted to only 3,200 tons of steam and 1,100 tons of sail. Various public utilities spread slowly to the chief cities, including gas supply and tramway services.

The new communications, especially railways and steamships, played an indispensable part in promoting economic growth. Markets were enlarged and local specialization encouraged. Prince Matsukata was certainly right in suggesting, with an eye on his own country's needs, that there was a high correlation between railway development and general economic progress in the various parts of the world.[1] Yet, it is probable that mechanized transport, at any rate in the early years of Meiji, was less significant for Japan than innovations that were technically quite primitive, It has been well-said that the construction of 'dirt' roads and the replacement of pack-horses and human porters by rickshaws and carts pulled by horses, oxen, dogs and men, probably exerted a more powerful influence on the development of the new economy than the railways.[2] In the same way, the new highly capitalized and newly equipped factories, though important both from the standpoint of their own production and from that of their rôle as models, may well have made a smaller contribution to Japan's progress in the early years than the work-shops that were now provided with simple, if novel, types of machinery. Apart from the new enterprises in the hands of the Government, the number of large establishments engaged in the manufacture of Western-style products remained small; but the foundations of many undertakings which later became important were laid. For example, in the early seventies, plants for the production of beer and cigarettes were initiated by private individuals; and the Ashio copper mines were acquired and re-organized by the Furukawa family in 1877. A number of new small-scale manufacturing industries appeared, such as the manufacture of matches; while many of the old-established trades succeeded in adjusting themselves to the new conditions. In particular, the steady increase in the demand for raw silk for export continued to bring advantages to the peasantry.

This progress, however, was not evenly spread; for certain groups of producers who had already been injured by the opening of the country to foreign trade, suffered further injury through the abolition of feudal institutions. 'A vast number of occupations which had hitherto been thriving had suddenly to be abandoned, and skilled labourers and artisans were thrown out of employment in thousands.

[1] T. C. Smith, *Political Change and Industrial Development*, p. 43.
[2] W. W. Lockwood, *The Economic Development of Japan*, p. 107.

Moreover, all kinds of monopolies and business privileges which the *daimyo* granted to their favourite merchants and to themselves ceased to exist with the fall of feudalism.'[1] When the Shogun gave up his residence at Yedo (Tokyo), this meant the withdrawal of an enormous number of retainers, both his own and those of the *daimyo*. The economic life of the town was for a time paralysed by this loss of a large consuming class. Similarly, when feudalism was abolished, the Osaka merchants whose business had been to sell the rice crops sent to that city by the *daimyo* lost their chief function. In the provinces industrial life had formerly centred round the castle towns. 'Many tradesmen of all occupations whose labour once found a market at the castle or among the hosts of retainers quartered near it, now found but scanty occupation and poor recompense. The productions of many of them (were) superseded by foreign goods.'[2]

Foreign trade, though still small by the standards of later times, increased considerably in the decade following the Restoration. In 1868 the total value of foreign trade, calculated in silver yen, amounted to about 26 million; by 1873 it had risen to about 50 million yen, and by 1881 to 62 million yen. In interpreting these figures we should remember that during the seventies silver was depreciating both in terms of gold and of commodities in general, and that, therefore, the growth was less than at first sight appears. This is borne out by the fact that between 1873 and 1880 the tonnage of merchant ships entered at Japanese ports from abroad rose only from 566,000 to 691,000.[3] Except for the years 1868 and 1876 the value of imports far exceeded that of exports, and the total adverse balance on the visible trade between 1868 and 1881 amounted to nearly 79 million yen. The adverse balance of payments was far greater than this because Japan had to remit large sums abroad for financial services rendered by foreign merchants and banks who handled nearly all the foreign trade, and for shipping services, as well as for various Government payments. This debit balance was met partly by foreign capital movements, namely the proceeds of the two loans raised in London and the short-term capital imported by foreign merchants and financial houses, but chiefly by the export of specie which the inflationary policy of the time encouraged. The net export of specie from 1872 to 1881 amounted to over 70 million yen.[4]

The composition of the foreign trade was typical of a country in Japan's stage of development. The bulk of the imports consisted of

[1] S. Okuma, 'The Industrial Revolution of Japan', in *North American Review*, Vol. 171.

[2] *The Currency of Japan*, p. 37.

[3] Even in 1880 only about one-fifth of the total tonnage entering the ports was Japanese-owned.

[4] *The Currency of Japan*, pp. 287, 326.

manufactured goods, of which textiles, particularly cotton, formed by far the most important group of commodities. The import of cheap Manchester goods rose very rapidly in the early seventies and displaced many of the domestic fabrics formerly produced in the homes of the people. Other fairly important items consisted of capital goods, such as machinery, ships, railway equipment, munitions, and other manufactured metal products. Great Britain occupied a pre-eminent position in Japan's import trade at this time and was responsible for about half of it. This was due not merely to the superiority of England's manufacturing industry but also to her highly developed organization for conducting foreign trade, her experienced merchant houses and her financial machinery.

Exports consisted mainly of raw products of which raw silk and tea were the chief. Raw silk had long been produced in Japan, but the development of the industry had been handicapped by sumptuary laws which forbade the wearing of silk clothes by commoners. By one of the many fortunate accidents that have attended Japan's modern development it happened that the opening of Japan to foreign intercourse coincided with the outbreak of silkworm disease in Europe. A strong demand for Japanese silkworm eggs and raw silk developed, and silk became at once, what it long remained, by far the most important item among the exports. Although the competitive position of Japanese raw silk in European markets was assisted by the opening of the Suez Canal in 1869, yet the trade did not expand very rapidly in the seventies, because the French had by then been able to rebuild their industry by importing supplies of healthy eggs from Japan. Nevertheless, the relative importance of this trade to Japan is shown by the fact that the only occasions on which she had an export surplus during this period (namely in 1868 and 1876) were years in which demand for her silk rose sharply owing to the failure of the French and Italian crops. Japan would necessarily have encountered far greater difficulties in carrying out quickly her programme of Westernization if this accident of nature had not created a large foreign demand for one of the few products which she was capable of producing for export in the early days of the modern era.[1] The second most important export commodity was also a product of Japanese agriculture, namely tea, which was sent for the most part to the United States. In addition, an export trade grew up in rice, from which the former export prohibition was removed in 1873, and in marine products. Copper, the chief export in Tokugawa days, remained fairly important. Manufactured goods came low on the list and they consisted almost entirely of the traditional products of the Japanese craftsman—pottery, fans, Japanese-style paper, lacquer and bronze wares. With the exception of copper, all the

[1] In 1876 nearly half of Japan's exports consisted of raw silk.

Japanese exports came from the small-scale industries many of which were conducted in peasant households. In the raw silk trade, for example, the peasants at that time produced not only the cocoons, but also reeled the silk in their farm-houses. The few manufactured articles among the exports were produced either by localized groups of skilled craftsmen or, as with matches, by women and children working in small workshops or in their own homes.

2. *Financial Problems*

In 1868 the new Government found itself faced by grave budgetary difficulties. Because of the cost incurred in crushing the clans hostile to the Imperial régime, public expenditure was heavy, while revenue was difficult to obtain. The whole of the revenue which the Shogun drew from his own domain and on which that ruler had mainly relied for meeting his administrative expenses was not yet available for the Meiji Government, and the local governments still preserved financial autonomy. The chaotic state of the country made it difficult for the Government to impose new taxes, and agreements with foreign Powers strictly limited the amount that could be secured from customs duties. The expenditure in 1868 was 25 million yen; while Government revenue from ordinary sources amounted to no more than 3·7 million yen.[1] The Government obtained *goyokin* from Mitsui and other merchants who were among its chief supporters, and it borrowed on short term from several Japanese and foreign merchant houses. Total receipts from these sources were only 5·4 million yen and consequently there was a deficit of nearly 16 million yen in that year. In 1869 expenditure amounted to 20·8 million yen, while revenue from taxes, short loans, fines and *goyokin* came to only 10·5 million yen.[2] In these circumstances the Government was obliged to resort to the printing press, and in those two years notes to the value of 48 million yen were issued. Some of them were issued through the medium of the old Exchange Companies (*Kawase-gumi*) which made large profits on the business. Prominent among these companies was the house of Mitsui. The issue was resented by the *daimyo* who feared the effect of the Government notes on their own paper money, and the general distrust of the Government's position led to a heavy depreciation in their value. At one time during 1868 the notes exchanged for specie at a discount of 55 per cent. The currency situation was, indeed, alarming; for the monetary circulation comprised not merely these new issues of inconvertible notes, but also gold and silver coins in varying degrees of debasement—an inherit-

[1] M. Takaki, *The History of Japanese Paper Currency*, p. 11.
[2] This account of Japanese finances is based largely on S. Okuma, *A General Review of Financial Policy during Thirteen Years* (1868-80), and on other articles and reports in *The Currency of Japan* (Japan Gazette).

ance from the Shogunate—and about 1,500 varieties of clan notes.

The forces hostile to Meiji had been finally crushed by the end of 1869. In consequence the Government's expenses diminished, and in 1870 there was no considerable rise in the note issue. The cessation of inflation, together with the increasing confidence in the new régime, was responsible for an appreciation in the value of the notes which, the Government had announced, were to be redeemed in 1873. In 1871 the abolition of the *han* widened the sources of State revenue, and in the same year an attempt was made to reform the coinage. A law was passed defining the content of the gold yen and making it the standard coin, although at the Treaty Ports the silver yen, equivalent in bullion content to the Mexican dollar, was declared to be legal tender. At the same time the Government set up a mint at Osaka equipped with modern machinery and staffed by foreign experts.

But there were still serious difficulties to be overcome. With the abolition of the *han* the Government assumed responsibility for local administration. Although the revenues which the *daimyo* had previously received from their subjects were henceforth due to the central exchequer, it was not easy at first to ensure the collection of these sums. The Government, moreover, had to compensate the lords for surrendering their rights, and at the same time to take over their former liabilities. The most onerous of these was the provision of annual pensions for the *samurai*, whose functions as feudal retainers had now ceased. Further, the Government made itself responsible for the debts of the *daimyo*, and it had to provide indemnities for the Buddhist church on its disestablishment. These measures increased the budgetary difficulties. In 1872 while total expenditure was 58 million yen, revenue reached only 33 million yen. New issues of paper money were accordingly made, and the amount of Government notes in circulation rose to over 73 million yen in that year.

The State next assumed responsibility for the local notes formerly issued by the *han* governments. For redemption purposes these notes were valued at the market rate then ruling in terms of Government notes, and the amount was placed at 26 million yen. Thus, at the end of 1872 the total volume of paper currency in circulation amounted to just under 100 million yen. In the next year the Government, in fulfilment of its promise to redeem its notes, offered bonds bearing interest at 6 per cent in exchange for the paper currency. Fewer of these bonds were taken up than had been anticipated, partly because the current rate of interest was far above that carried by the bonds, and partly because of the rise in the value of the notes. Nevertheless, by June 1876 the note issue had fallen to 94 million yen, and by that time the notes were practically at par with specie. Indeed, because of the sudden increase in the foreign demand for Japanese silk at that time through the failure of the European crops, they actually stood at a premium in terms of Mexican dollars and silver yen in the latter part of 1876. Thus, by that year the Government seemed to have solved its chief currency difficulties, and this success had been achieved in spite of the expenses in connection with the annual payment of pensions to the privileged classes, the expedition to Formosa and the Saga Rebellion in 1874. At first sight it may seem surprising that the great expansion in the note issue during the first eight years of the new régime had failed to bring about a larger depreciation. But Japan at the time was passing quickly from a natural to a money economy. Industry and population were increasing; local barriers to trade had been destroyed; and money payments had been substituted for rice payments in the case of the land tax. Thus, along with the rise in the quantity of money, there had occurred simultaneously a considerable expansion in the demand for it, and so its value had been largely maintained.

During this period, while the greater part of its budgetary deficits had been met by note issues, the Government had also raised loans for the same purpose. The money borrowed on short term during the first two years of the régime had all been repaid by 1871. Apart from these short-term loans, others were also contracted during the period before 1876. Two were raised abroad—in London. The first, in 1867, was a loan of 3¾ million yen, mainly for the purpose of constructing the Tokyo-Yokohama railway, and the second, 10·7 million yen, was raised in 1872 to provide funds for meeting the obligations incurred through the abolition of feudalism. In addition to these, domestic bond issues were made. One, as already mentioned, was used for the redemption of paper money. Two others were issued in 1873 to cover the liabilities of the Government incurred through taking over the debts of the *han*, and a further issue consisted of Pension Bonds. The Government offered these to members of the privileged classes who wished to capitalize their annual pensions. By June 1876 the total unredeemed liabilities of the Government in the form of bonds amounted to 55 million yen.

In the meantime an attempt had been made to reform and systematize taxation. In the days of the Shogunate the chief revenues of the local and central governments, as we have seen, had come from the land tax, arbitrary in amount and payable in rice. In the years immediately following 1872 a new assessment was made with the object of producing a revenue which, though broadly the same as before, was less liable to fluctuate in money terms. The net average produce of the various holdings during a five-yearly period was valued at the prices then ruling and was capitalized at rates varying from 6 to 7 per cent. On this a land tax of 3 per cent was at first imposed, but in 1876 it was reduced to 2½ per cent. Under the old régime the people had also been subjected to a large number of miscellaneous taxes which scarcely repaid the cost of collection. In 1875 the whole system was drastically reformed, and in the course of the next five years the number of taxes was reduced from nearly 1,600 to 74. The land tax, however, remained for many years the only important source of revenue, and in 1879-80 it accounted for four-fifths of the whole tax revenue.

Although by 1876 these reforms in taxation had not yet yielded their fruits, the fiscal position at that time was by no means unsatisfactory, especially in view of the difficulties with which the Government had been confronted. A large part of its liabilities was an inheritance from the Shogunate, and its period of office had been one in which it had been engaged in suppressing rebellion and in transforming the administrative and economic life of the country. Some of its debts were covered by valuable assets, such as a railway and several industrial and commercial undertakings.

Its financial troubles, however, were not yet over. In 1877 the Satsuma Rebellion broke out and heavy expenditure was incurred before it was finally subdued. This expenditure was covered, in part, by another issue of Government notes to the amount of 27 million yen, and, in part, by a bank loan of 15 million yen. About the same time, the State decreed that the pensions of the privileged classes should be commuted, and to this end it issued to them interest-bearing pension bonds to the amount of 174 million yen. The national debt was thus raised in the course of 1877 from 55 million yen to over 240 million yen, although of course most of this increase represented merely the capitalization of an existing annual liability. The commutation of the pensions is of great importance because of its indirect effect upon the currency situation. To understand how this might be, we must consider the circumstances in which the first banks of a modern type were instituted in Japan.

The collapse of the old régime had meant the destruction of the financial machinery dependent on it. The last vestiges of the guild system had been swept away 'as being opposed to the principles of political economy',[1] and the old merchants and financiers whose credit was bound up with that system suffered severely. 'For a time all dealings on credit came to an end',[2] and there was in consequence a great tightness of money. The abolition of the *han* also struck a blow at the structure of commerce and finance. The merchant-bankers of Osaka and Tokyo had acted as the *daimyo's* agents for the disposal of their rice revenues. They were accustomed to make loans on the security of this produce, and they possessed an organization for remitting money from one centre to another. The disappearance of the *han* brought this business to an end and swept away many of the old merchant houses in a common ruin. Two of the

[1] *See* S. Okuma's Report.   [2] *Ibid.*

wealthiest merchants, Ono and Shimada, went bankrupt in 1873, and a large number of smaller firms ceased business. At the same time the establishment of a centralized Government meant that taxes formerly paid to the local governments were now sent to a central exchequer, and this produced a pronounced tightness of money in the distant provinces at tax-collecting time. Thus, with the old financial mechanism in chaos and with new financial problems arising as a result of the political changes, fresh banking institutions were obviously required. In the early years of Meiji several new *Kawase-gumi* (exchange companies) had been formed by wealthy merchants. These carried on ordinary banking business and were authorised to issue notes against their reserves. But they scarcely met the needs of the new era, and in 1872 the establishment of Western-style banks with the right of note issue was authorized.

On the advice of Prince Ito the American system of national banking was taken as a model, in spite of opposition from those who favoured a central banking system. According to the Regulations issued in 1872, a national bank was to deposit Government paper money equal to three-fifths of its capital with the Treasury, and to hold gold equivalent to two-fifths of its capital as a reserve. The Treasury handed to the banks Paper Money Exchange Bonds bearing 6 per cent interest in return for the notes deposited with it, and the banks were then permitted to issue their own notes redeemable in gold up to the amount of the security which they possessed. In this way it was expected that part of the Government's inconvertible note issue would be replaced by notes convertible into gold, and that effective banking machinery to serve the needs of the new economic system would be brought into being. The operations of these banks, it was also hoped, would lead to a fall in the rate of interest which, since 1868, had apparently ranged between 13 and 14 per cent per annum.[1]

These expectations were not realized. Only four national banks were established under these regulations, the first and fifth in 1873 and the second (which was a converted Yokohama Exchange Company controlled by Mitsui) and the fourth in 1874. Their actual note issue never exceeded 2,300,000 yen. The reasons for the failure of this experiment are not difficult to discover. The relatively low rate of interest paid on the Government bonds, which the banks received in exchange for the Governmant paper money deposited with the Treasury, made an investment of this kind unprofitable. Further, the banks found difficulty in keeping their notes in circulation. Since these notes were convertible into specie, whereas the Government paper money of the same face value was at a discount, merchants who had to pay for imports naturally found it profitable to present

[1] Rates charged by Mitsui on commercial loans of 10,000 yen and over (S. Okuma's Report).

the bank notes at the issuing bank and so to obtain gold for their foreign payments. In this way the national banks were drained of their reserves.

In 1877 the hereditary pensions of the privileged classes were commuted for public bonds. 'Now this class, beyond the functions which had appertained to it under the régime which had passed away, was ignorant of the ordinary means of gaining a livelihood, and now being suddenly released from these functions, was greatly in danger of falling into a state of indigence and perhaps into pauperism, unless some calling could be found for its members. The Government consequently, with the object of finding a means by which the military class could turn their public debt bonds to account in obtaining a livelihood, and moved also by the want of circulating capital in the country and the general tightness of money, adopted a plan calculated to confer a double benefit, the principle of which was the establishment of national banks by the military class on the security of the public bonds held by them.'[1] It should be added that the very existence of the new Government might have been endangered if the military class had been antagonized by the financial settlement which the Government had enforced on them. Because of the relatively low rate of interest on the bonds (7 per cent) and of the large volume that had been issued, there was every likelihood that they would depreciate in value. Indeed, even the bonds issued in 1874, when the commutation was on a voluntary basis, changed hands at a discount of from 40 to 50 per cent a year or two later.[2]

So the National Bank Regulations were revised, and from 1876 onwards bank notes, within a limit of 34 million yen, could be issued by national banks against the deposit with the Treasury of Government bonds equal to 80 per cent of their capital. Instead of a specie reserve only a currency reserve was now required. Since the currency was Government paper money, the bank notes thus lost their characteristic of convertibility. Banking now seemed, however, to offer good prospects to the holders of the pension bonds. Between 1876 and 1880 148 new national banks were founded, and at the end of this period the limit set by the Government on the total issue had been reached. The largest of these banks was the Fifteenth Bank, established in 1877 with a capital of 18 million yen by a group of nobles. As its main function at this time was to lend the State 15 million yen towards the expenses of suppressing the Satsuma Rebellion, it cannot have played an important part in financing trade and industry. This seems to have been true of the majority of the banks. Formed by men without business experience, they were in general badly managed, and most of the real banking business of the country was conducted either by foreign banks or by those native institutions

[1] S. Okuma's Report.   [2] *The Currency of Japan*, p. 141.

which had been established by the mercantile class before the amended regulations of 1876. The large note issues made by the banks, however, contributed substantially to the inflationary movement which began with the Government's own issue of 27 million yen of paper money in 1877. In June of the previous year the total issue of Government and bank notes amounted to just over 95 million yen; by the end of 1878 the volume had risen to over 150 million yen. State indebtedness had also grown—from 55 million yen in June 1876 to 254 million yen in June 1878. The greater part of this increase had, of course, been occasioned by the pension bond issue and by the loan from the Fifteenth Bank already mentioned. But in addition an Industrial Works Loan of 12½ million yen was raised in 1878 to provide for railway construction and the improvement of harbours, roads and bridges.

All the symptoms of a violent inflation now showed themselves. General prices rose rapidly, and the price of rice, by far the most important commodity, was doubled between 1877 and 1880. Specie left the country. The rate of interest rose and Government bonds fell in price. The silver yen, which became legal tender throughout the country in 1878 when a bi-metallic standard was officially adopted, rose in terms of paper money, and by 1881 1 yen of silver was equivalent to 1 yen 80 sen of paper. The depreciation of the notes was accompanied by frequent and violent fluctuations in their value in terms of silver, and it was not uncommon for a rise or fall of 10 per cent to take place in the course of a single day. The profit inflation which accompanied these financial disturbances gave a temporary stimulus to certain branches of industry, as we have already shown. Enterprises in many sections of manufacture and mining were newly established or were re-organized and expanded. The farmers are said to have benefited greatly.[1] While the burden of their debts and taxes payable in paper money remained constant, their money receipts from sales of rice and silk were augmented. 'New farm houses sprang up in every province; new clothes and ornaments were freely purchased; landed property came into great demand . . . and in general everybody rejoiced in hope and a sense of prosperity.'[2] The landlords, in particular, received a windfall, for their rents were paid in rice while their tax obligations were expressed in the depreciating currency. They applied their capital gains partly to the purchase of more land and partly to investment in trade and industry in which many of them already participated. It was from the landlords that many of the new industrial entrepreneurs were recruited at this time.

The Government was not ignorant of the dangers of this inflationary boom. The cost of living was steadily rising, and the exchange

---

[1] *The Currency of Japan*, p. 271.
[2] *U.S. Consular Reports*, Vol. XIX, No. 68, p. 655.

fluctuations made foreign trading exceptionally hazardous. The foreign merchant class was loud in its complaints, declaring that the Japanese dealers repudiated their contracts when price changes made the terms unfavourable to them. In 1879 and 1880 the State tried to check the depreciation of notes by disposing of part of its reserve of silver through Mitsui and certain of the national banks, and by cancelling the notes so acquired. Its own issue of paper money fell in consequence of this step by some 12 million yen between 1879 and 1880, although the circulation of bank notes rose by about 5 million yen in the same period. Furthermore, the Government tried to improve its budgetary position by increasing taxation; but it was not until October 1881 when Count (later Prince) Matsukata was appointed Minister of Finance that the financial situation was finally brought under control. The story of the establishment of a sound budgetary and financial system, however, belongs to the next chapter in Japanese history. On the whole, in view of the enormous difficulties that faced the new Government—both those inherited from Toku-gawa and those inseparable from the consolidation of the new régime—the Government's record can scarcely be condemned. Most of the financial troubles of the period were the consequence of events beyond the Government's control rather than of mistakes of policy. Even the unsuccessful experiment in national banking was deter-mined by the peculiar conditions of the time, and chaotic as the situation appeared in 1881, only a few years of resolute administra-tion were required before stability was established.

Japan, shaken by the repeated political and financial crises, gave at this time little promise of her future development, save in the deter-mined way in which her leaders faced their difficulties. Even some of the more prominent Japanese were pessimistic. The foreigners in Japan contemplated with complacency the mediocrity of achievement which the future promised. 'Wealthy we do not think it (Japan) will ever become: the advantages conferred by Nature, with the exception of the climate, and the love of indolence and pleasure of the people themselves forbid it. The Japanese are a happy race, and being content with little are not likely to achieve much.'[1] Clearly Japan could not expect to rival the West in the realms of high finance. When he considered the unsuccessful banking experiments of the seventies, a contemporary foreign resident found an unflattering explanation of their failure. 'The national banking system of Japan is but another example of the futility of trying to transfer Western growth to an Oriental habitat. In this part of the world principles, established and recognized in the West, appear to lose whatever virtue and vitality they originally possessed and to tend fatally towards weediness and corruption.'[2]

[1] *The Currency of Japan*, p. 121.   [2] *Ibid.*, p. 112.

CHAPTER III

FINANCIAL FOUNDATIONS, 1881–1914

The last two decades of the nineteenth century were noteworthy for the creation of a stable monetary system which, in spite of many difficulties, was adequate to withstand both the strains of rapid economic expansion and the crisis produced by the Russo-Japanese War. During the seventies Japanese finances had been disturbed by the political troubles incidental to the Restoration, and the banking experiments of that period yielded results that were hardly satisfactory. With the appointment of Count (later Prince) Matsukata as Minister of Finance in 1881 a determined and successful attempt was made to introduce order into the chaotic financial situation. It was decided to abandon the experiment in national banking, to establish a central banking system on the European model, to balance the budget and to restore parity between the silver yen and the notes.

In the first place reforms were effected in the system of land taxation, and increased taxes were levied on *sakē* and tobacco.[1] Economies in administration were achieved; grants for public works and private enterprises ceased; and many Government factories and other properties were sold. A sinking fund was instituted to provide for the redemption of the public debt, and in consequence of this and of successful efforts to balance revenue and expenditure, the public debt which had stood at 245 million yen in 1880 was only 5 million more ten years later when the national income and the taxable capacity of the country had considerably risen. A marked reduction was effected in the service charge on the debt. In 1880 the Government had paid rates of interest ranging from 7 to 10 per cent even on short loans. In 1885 it was possible to raise a foreign loan for building the Nakasendo Railway at 6 per cent, and in 1886 all public bonds carrying interest over 6 per cent were redeemed by a 5 per cent conversion issue. In the same year the Government began the practice of drawing up regular annual budgets. Thus, in a very short time the disorderly state of the public finances had been remedied.

Japan's newly found financial strength was tested in the Sino-

---

[1] In 1875-76 the total tax revenue was 57,800,000 yen, of which 50,000,000 yen came from the land tax; by 1883-84 the tax revenue was 69,200,000 yen, of which 39,000,000 came from the land tax. *See* A. Andreades, *Les Finances de l'Empire Japonais et leur Evolution*, p. 50 and *passim*.

Japanese War of 1894-95. On the eve of that war annual public expenditure was about 80 million yen and was completely covered by revenue from taxes and other non-loan receipts. The war expenditure amounted to about 200 million yen, and this was met almost entirely from internal bond issues (117 million yen), appropriations from surplus accounts, revenues from occupied territories and part of the indemnity received from China. There was no increase in taxation and the net addition to the national debt was relatively small.[1] As a result of the war Japan was able to annex Formosa and the Pescadores, to secure an indemnity of 366 million yen, to bring the régime of capitulations to an end and with it the restrictions on her right to direct her own tariff policy. This last result was signalized in a number of treaties with foreign Powers signed in 1899. But her victory brought her into direct rivalry with Russia in Northern Asia, and she was obliged to undertake a burdensome policy of armament. The development of Formosa, moreover, involved the granting of substantial annual subsidies. Annual State expenditure rose from about 80 million yen in the early nineties to between 250 and 293 million yen in the fiscal years 1900-04. The greater part of this increase was absorbed by the Army and Navy. To meet these new expenses the Government instituted national monopolies of tobacco and camphor from which a large revenue was subsequently derived, and it greatly increased existing taxes, especially the *sakē*, income, business and land taxes.

To cover the rising expenditure it was also necessary to raise loans both at home and abroad, and the national debt rose from 207 million yen in December 1894 to 435 million yen in December 1903. These figures do not cover loans raised to provide capital for the State railways. If these are included, the total national debt in 1903 amounted to 539 million yen, of which 98 million yen had been raised abroad. Although some of this money had been used for public works of a revenue-earning character, the greater part of the loans had been raised for financing war-preparation.

The war with Russia cost the State about 1,500 million yen, which was covered mainly by foreign borrowing, although there was an increase in taxation and domestic bond issues. By December 1907 the aggregate national debt reached 2,244 million yen (including the railway and ironworks debts) and of this more than half was foreign debt. Thus between 1894 and 1907 the national debt had increased tenfold. The territorial acquisitions that resulted from the war imposed additional financial burdens. Japan now had to spend money on the development of Korea, the Kwantung Peninsula and South Manchuria; while fear of Russia still obliged her to add to her

[1] A. Andreades, *op. cit.*, pp. 51-60; and Foreign Affairs Association of Japan, *A History of Japanese Finance*, pp. 8-10.

expenditure on armaments. The annual public expenditure, therefore, continued to increase, and in the years just before the First World War it amounted to nearly 600 million yen, more than twice that of the early years of the century. But the national income of the country was growing, and Japan was able to meet this expenditure out of taxation. The increased taxes imposed at the time of the Russian War, however, had to be maintained during the subsequent period. For instance, the land tax which in 1899 had been raised from 2½ per cent to 5 per cent for urban sites and 3·3 per cent for rural sites rose again in 1905 and later reached 11½ per cent on the most highly taxed sites.

ORDINARY REVENUE[1]

(in thousand million yen)

	1893-94	1903-04	1906-07
Land Tax	38·8	46·9	85·6
Income Tax	1·2	8·2	21·8
Patent Fees	—	7·0	19·4
Drink Excise	16·7	53·1	59·2
Shoyu Excise	1·3	3·5	5·3
Sugar Excise	—	6·9	16·8
Customs Duties	5·1	17·4	31·8
Stamp Duties	0·8	14·2	27·4
Receipts from Public Undertakings and State Property	11·6	55·7	104·7
Miscellaneous Receipts	10·3	11·5	20·5
Total	85·8	224·4	392·5

If the amount of the national debt did not increase after 1907,[2] its composition altered very considerably. Military success had raised Japan's credit-standing, and she was able in the years before 1914 to float a number of foreign loans for conversion purposes. Part of the proceeds of these loans was used to repay domestic debt raised at a higher rate of interest. So in 1914, out of a total national debt of 1,832 million yen (excluding the railway debt), 1,524 was foreign debt, whereas in 1907 when the total debt was 2,064 million yen, the shares were much more evenly balanced. The State Railway Debt, which falls into a special category, has been excluded from these figures.

[1] A. Andreades, *op. cit.*, p. 79; also *The Financial and Economic Annual of Japan* (various issues), which is the source used for most of the statistical data on public finance.

[2] That is if the State Railway Debt is excluded.

D

In 1906 the Government, which had previously owned only a few lines, began to execute its plan of nationalizing the railway system, and it borrowed money for this purpose. In 1914 the amount of railway debt outstanding was 729 million yen, compared with 117 million yen in 1906.

The three main features in the history of Japanese public finances during the twenty years before the First World War were, first, the large increase in annual expenditure, secondly the growth of the national debt, and thirdly, the large import of foreign capital. These were the necessary consequence of Japan's policy of developing her resources in the interests of national power; for the increased expenditure and borrowing were incurred mainly in connection with war, armaments, colonial exploitation and the establishment of industries of 'national importance'. The growth in her productivity had greatly increased her tax revenue, and her success in raising loans abroad at relatively low rates showed that by this time foreign investors were confident of her future. The rapid pursuit of ambitious political objectives, however, had strained her financial strength, and as by 1914 she had nearly reached the limit of her foreign credit, it seemed that her expansionist programme would have to be executed more cautiously.

We must now turn to the history of banking and currency during this period. In 1881 the chief financial objectives were the redemption of the inconvertible paper money, the legacy of the seventies, and the accumulation of a specie reserve which could serve as a backing for a new issue of convertible notes. With these ends in view Count Matsukata, in a memorandum of March 1882, advised the immediate establishment of a central bank modelled on those of European countries.[1] He argued in this document that the evils from which the country was suffering were the excess issue and unequal distribution of the currency, the shortage of liquid capital and the depletion of the specie reserves. He criticized the national banks for their lack of co-operation with one another, and he declared that a central bank was needed to co-ordinate the financial activities of the State. Its formation, he said, would help to equalize rates of interest in different parts of the country; hoarding would cease; and, as the operations of the Treasury would be entrusted to the Bank, the tightness of money at tax-collecting time would be mitigated. The immediate task of the Bank, however, was to redeem the inconvertible notes and to provide a unified note issue backed by adequate specie reserves.

The regulations of the Bank of Japan, as later drawn up, provided that it was to issue its notes only against a specie reserve, except for a

[1] See M. Matsukata, *Report on the Adoption of the Gold Standard in Japan*, passim.

fiduciary issue on which a tax of 1½ per cent was to be paid.[1] In times of crisis the Bank, with the permission of the Minister of Finance, was empowered to increase its fiduciary issue on the payment of a tax of not less than 5 per cent on the amount of the increased issue. At the same time, provision was made for the withdrawal of the

NOTE ISSUES

(in million yen)

End of Year	Government Paper Money	National Bank Notes	Bank of Japan Notes
1881	118·9	34·0	—
1885	93·4	30·2	4·0
1890	40·1	26·4	102·9
1895	15·7	22·3	110·5
1900	5·1	1·6	179·8

inconvertible Government notes and the national bank notes, and the regulations governing the Bank's own note issue were suspended until parity between the notes and silver had been reached. Funds obtained from the sale of Government factories were used for the purchase of specie, and part of the budget surplus after 1881 was used for acquiring foreign bills of exchange or for the redemption of Government notes. The national banks were required to transfer their reserves to the Bank of Japan and to make annual payments into a fund which was to be employed for the redemption of their notes. The retirement of the inconvertible paper money was rapidly brought about, and by 1886 specie payments were begun. Thus, after only four or five years the paper money, which at the beginning of the period was from 70 to 80 per cent depreciated in terms of silver, had been brought to par. The Government paper money was finally redeemed in 1899 and the last national bank note in 1904. A law of 1896 provided that national banks on the expiry of their charters were to be dissolved, and by the end of the century 132 of them had been transformed into private banks, while the rest (21 in number) had been wound up.

The deliberate contraction of the currency during the early eighties was naturally accompanied by a fall in prices, including the price of rice. While this raised the real revenue from the land tax, it imposed

[1] The following account of Japan's banking history is based largely on: *United States' National Monetary Commission* (1910), Vol. XVIII; M. Takaki, *The History of Japanese Paper Currency*; M. Matsukata, *Report on Post-Bellum Financial Administration in Japan*; Japanese Department of Finance, *A Brief Outline of the Financial System of Japan* (1905); US Department of Commerce, *Japanese Banking*.

additional burdens on the agricultural community, for more rice had to be sold to meet the tax demands. In consequence, many of the small peasant proprietors at this time were forced to sell their land and there was an increase in the proportion of arable land held in tenancies. In other words, the result was to bring about some concentration of land ownership. The industrial sector was similarly affected. Many small enterprises collapsed under the deflationary pressure or passed into the hands of those with larger resources. The Government's policy of selling its industrial properties—mainly for the purpose of providing additional revenue—contributed to the same result. There were very few business houses at that time ready or willing to invest in or to operate large industrial establishments. Those who had the resources and the enterprise were able to acquire the plants at low prices and later to employ them very profitably.[1] This transference of State factories to a few private firms marks an important stage in the evolution of the *zaibatsu* who in later years dominated the modern sector of the economy.

The deflationary policy was robbed of some of its less agreeable consequences by the contemporaneous depreciation of silver both in terms of gold and of commodities. Undoubtedly this depreciation assisted the Japanese Government in restoring and maintaining its specie payments. From the later years of the decade prices turned sharply upwards, and the *Oriental Economist's* index of wholesale prices (base=1873) which stood at 97 in 1886 had risen to 156 by 1897. Meanwhile rates of exchange on gold standard countries with which Japan was conducting two-thirds of her trade were highly unstable. When the Indian currency reform plan was put into operation in 1893, Japan decided to adopt the gold standard at the earliest favourable opportunity. The transition from silver to gold was facilitated by the receipt of the indemnity from China after the war of 1894-95. Arrangements were made to have this indemnity (230 million taels or 38 million pounds sterling) paid in sterling instead of in taels. Part of the sum was brought home in gold, and part was kept on deposit in London or invested in British securities and maintained as a foreign exchange reserve. The adoption of the gold standard formally took place in 1897.

Meanwhile, Count Matsukata was steadily putting into operation a banking principle which he had enunciated in his memorandum of 1882. This principle was that a healthy financial system required the existence of banks with specialized functions, which he defined as the provision of long-term investment in industry and agriculture, the

---

[1] The prices were low in relation to the Government's initial investment in these properties. Of course, the current market price depended on the earning power of the industrial assets which itself was low; indeed, many of the factories were making losses at the time of the sale.

mobilization of the savings of the poorer classes, the handling of foreign exchange transactions and the conduct of domestic commercial business. The most important of these specialized banks, the Yokohama Specie Bank, had been founded in 1880. It was not until 1887, however, when its regulations were revised, that it entered upon its career as the chief foreign exchange bank in the country. Like the Bank of Japan, the Specie Bank from the beginning was closely supervised by the Government. The State provided one-third of its initial capital and the appointment of its President and Vice-President required the authorization of the Minister of Finance. The Specie Bank was entrusted with funds from the Treasury Reserve Fund to enable it to deal in foreign bills of exchange, and when this support was withdrawn in 1890 the Bank of Japan was authorized to advance to it a permanent loan (later fixed at 20 million yen) at the rate of 2 per cent. Furthermore, large quantities of the Specie Bank's foreign bills were discounted by the central bank at a specially low rate, and these bills from the first constituted the bulk of the central bank's holdings. Indeed, the Bank of Japan was during this period the only large outlet for the Specie Bank's paper, and for many years constituted the only outlet for it.

After the stabilization of the currency, and the establishment of a central bank and a foreign exchange bank, the next step, in accordance with the principle that Count Matsukata had laid down, was to create financial organs for providing long-term loans. There was an urgent need for such institutions, for a well-to-do middle class, prepared to invest in industrial securities, scarcely existed. What were required were institutions formed for the purpose of mobilizing the savings of the community through the medium of bank debentures guaranteed by the Government. In this way resources could be collected and directed towards enterprise. It was not possible to proceed with this plan during the eighties, for Government bonds then stood at a considerable discount. But by the end of the Sino-Japanese War in 1895 Government credit had improved sufficiently to make the scheme practicable. So, by a law passed in 1896, the Hypothec Bank of Japan was set up, modelled on the Crédit Foncier of France, with a capital of 10 million yen. This bank was empowered to make loans, redeemable by annual instalments within fifty years, on the security of immoveable property, such as paddy fields, upland fields, salt fields, forests and fishing waters and rights. It was also permitted to make advances without security to public authorities, co-operative societies and fishery guilds. In order to obtain funds, it was authorized to issue debentures to an amount not exceeding ten times (later fifteen times) its paid-up capital. It could also accept deposits which it had to employ in the purchase of national bonds and bills of exchange. For the first ten years of its life the Government guaranteed its dividends at the rate of 5 per cent. At the same time forty-six Agricultural and Industrial Banks were established, one in each prefecture. Their business was similar to that of the Hypothec Bank, to which they acted as local advisory bodies. They were permitted to raise funds to the extent of five times their paid-up capital, and they were accustomed to resort to the Hypothec Bank for other advances. The latter acted as a kind of central bank for these local institutions. It supplied them with funds by taking up their debentures and it employed them as agents in making advances to its clients. The Government exercised close supervision over the business of these banks and granted them financial help. Apart from the guarantee of dividends already mentioned, it advanced a loan of 10 million yen to the prefectural authorities to enable them to subscribe to shares in the Agricultural and Industrial Banks, and in 1898 it used $3\frac{3}{4}$ million yen of the Chinese Indemnity for the purchase of the Hypothec Bank's debentures.

The next stage in the realization of Matsukata's systematic programme was the creation of a bank for the purpose of providing long-term loans to industry on the security of moveable property, including bonds and shares. So, by a law passed in 1900, the Industrial Bank of Japan (*Nippon Kogyo Ginko*) was set up, modelled on the Crédit Mobilier. It was empowered to raise funds by issuing debentures up to ten times its paid-up capital, and its shareholders received a Government guarantee of dividends similar to that given to the Hypothec Bank. In the early days of its operation the Bank's loans were made for the most part to firms in the newly established large-scale industries, such as the public utilities and the shipbuilding, iron and steel, chemical and machine-making trades. In this way it served to assist the Government's policy of developing the new forms of industrial activity that were believed to be necessary for political as well as for economic reasons. The term of these loans was usually five years, although in the case of advances on ships repayment could be effected in annual instalments over a period of fifteen years. One very important function assumed by this bank was that of providing a channel for foreign investment in Japan. A substantial part of its capital was held by foreigners, and during the first eleven years of its existence some 350 million yen were raised abroad by the sale in foreign capital markets either of its own debentures or of those of municipalities or of public undertakings with which it was associated. Among the latter the South Manchuria Railway Company had an important place, and the bank guaranteed and sold several issues of SMR sterling debentures in London between 1907 and 1911. Its financial relations with this company were a precursor of its later activities in the financing of Japanese penetration on the Continent of Asia.

Japan's colonial expansion after the war with China meant that the original pattern of Government-controlled special banks had to be extended. The acquisition of Formosa (Taiwan) by the Treaty of Shimonoseki led to the establishment of the Bank of Taiwan in 1899. Its functions in that colony were in many respects similar to those of the central bank in Japan Proper, since it had the right of note issue and was entrusted with the colonial revenues. It also undertook foreign exchange business, and later became responsible for financing a substantial proportion of Japan's trade with Formosa and the South Seas. The Bank of Japan maintained close connections with this bank, and provided it with advances at low rates of interest. After the Russo-Japanese War the First Bank (Dai Ichi Ginko) acted as a note-issuing central bank in Korea (Chosen). In 1909 it was replaced in this capacity by the Bank of Korea, which took over the note issue and most of the branches of the First Bank. After the annexation of Korea a year later the new institution came to be known as the Bank of Chosen. It was given a monopoly of the note issue in Chosen; it handled the Government account; and it also acted as an ordinary commercial and foreign exchange bank in that colony and in the Kwantung Peninsula.

These two note-issuing banks should be distinguished from another group of colonial banks founded for the provision of long-period loans. The Hokkaido Development Bank was created in 1899 to provide finance for the colonization and development of the northern island. In Korea a number of local hypothec banks were set up in 1906 to make long-period loans to industrial and agricultural enterprises, and it was these banks which in 1918 were merged to form the Chosen Industrial Bank. Another industrial bank in which the Government was interested was the Oriental Development Company established in 1908. Its functions were to finance industrial enterprise both in Korea and in Manchuria.

All these special banks were capitalized in part by the Government and the Imperial Household, and were subjected to strict official control. They were closely linked with one another through the granting of mutual financial help and through co-operative investment in enterprises of national importance both at home and on the Continent of Asia. Some of these activities will be discussed later on. Here it is sufficient to emphasize that they were all instruments of a national purpose which changed little during the period of their existence. From the beginning they had close financial connections not merely with the Government but also with the great financial institutions of the *zaibatsu*, themselves in part the agents of national policy.[1]

Before concluding this account of Government-supervised banking

[1] *See* Chap. VIII.

institutions, we must refer to another most important component of Japan's financial machinery, namely the Deposits Bureau of the Ministry of Finance. To this Bureau, which was founded in 1877, were entrusted postal savings besides postal transfer savings and certain other funds belonging to the Government. As in other countries the savings were provided by numerous small depositors, especially farmers. In 1885 there were about 300,000 depositors and about 9 million yen of deposits; in 1896 $1\frac{1}{4}$ million depositors and 28 million yen of deposits; and in 1914 12 million depositors and 189 million yen of deposits. The significance of the Bureau lies in the fact that it provided a channel for directing the savings of the people towards enterprises sponsored by the State. The Bureau invested its funds mainly in the bonds and debentures issued by the Government and the municipal and prefectural authorities, and in the debentures of the special banks. It also made extensive loans to semi-official concerns, such as the public utilities, the Oriental Development Company and other colonial enterprises. Thus the savings of the poor were canalized to furnish capital for modern large-scale enterprise and for the exploitation of Japanese territories overseas.

Japan's financial development in the period now under review was by no means limited to these official or semi-official institutions. Indeed the deliberately specialized functions which had been given to these banks left opportunities for the growth of banks of another kind. Some of the old money-lending and exchange houses had been reorganized shortly after the Restoration and before the end of the century a few of them developed into flourishing commercial banks of the modern type. After the revision of the National Bank Regulations which provided for the gradual withdrawal of the note issue, many national banks were re-formed as private commercial banks. During the nineties the number of these private banks grew rapidly, along with the industrial and commercial development of the period. By 1901 there were 2,359 separate banking concerns in the country with aggregate deposits of 516 million yen. Many of them were very small; for instance 940 had a capital of less than 100,000 yen, and only 78 had a capital of over 1 million yen. It was recognized in official quarters that a system composed of a multitude of very small banks unrelated to one another was likely to be unstable. So in 1901 it was decreed that joint stock banks should have a capital of at least 500,000 yen and private banks a capital of 250,000 yen. This encouraged the consolidation of the banks, and by the end of 1913 their number had fallen to 2,158, inclusive of 648 savings banks. But, in spite of the increase in the size of the banks during this period, 550 of them still had a capital of under 100,000 yen, and four-fifths of them a capital of 500,000 yen or under. Most of the banks worked without branches; in 1913 the average number of branches to each head office was only 1·5.

For an explanation of the rather peculiar system of banking which had been built up in the years before the First World War we have to bear in mind both the nature of Japan's economy and also the State's economic policy. The special banks were essentially instruments of the Government and to them particular tasks were entrusted. In the first place the Bank of Japan and the central colonial banks had the function of reforming and controlling the currency. Secondly, as Japan was engaged in building up powerful armaments for which she needed large imports of war materials and also equipment for the industries that were necessary for national power, the financing of foreign trade was of great political importance. Hence the creation of the Yokohama Specie Bank. Thirdly, the absence of a large class of investors in industrial securities justified the formation of a group of special investment banks charged with the duty of financing large-scale enterprises of national importance both in Japan and on the Continent. The character of the ordinary commercial banks was determined by the structure of Japanese industry as well as by the undeveloped state of the securities market. On the one hand, there were numerous small industrial and commercial enterprises which were growing rapidly at this time, and were in need both of short- and long-term capital. Small local independent banks rose to cater for these needs. On the other hand, large city banks, affiliated to the great business houses with a wide range of commercial and industrial activities and with close relations with the State, grew up to mobilize part of the country's capital and to direct it into the enterprises controlled by those houses. Finally, the Treasury Deposits Bureau and the private savings banks were organized to collect the savings of the poor and to provide a demand for the bonds issued by the Government or by concerns in which it was especially interested at a time when the State's financial position was weak. The operations of the financial system have been extremely susceptible to political influence. In the case of the official banks and the Treasury Deposits Bureau this need not be insisted upon. It is true, however, even of the larger banks owned by the *zaibatsu* because of the association of those houses with the Government and the close relationship which they have had with the political leaders.

It is only by observing how institutions work that their true significance can be realized, and we shall therefore briefly analyse the actual operations of the banking system before the First World War. It is clear that the central bank's functions were more narrowly restricted than those of the central banks in most European countries. It failed, for example, to act as a bankers' bank in the sense commonly understood abroad. Many of the larger ordinary banks held deposits at the Bank of Japan, but only such as were needed for clearing purposes, and it could not be said that the banking reserves of the country were centralized through the medium of that institution. Nor did the Bank of Japan furnish the money market with funds in ordinary times. In periods of financial emergency it was compelled by the Government to make heavy advances to the ordinary banks; but its slender connections with them in normal times meant that it was unable to exercise control over their policy, even though it might be obliged to come to their aid when that policy threatened their solvency. In times of stringency the ordinary banks resorted to the central institution for the re-discount of their bills; but the bank rate was in no sense a controlling rate. Indeed it commonly followed the market rate and was in any case of slight significance because of the Bank's slender connections with the market. Apart from its functions in connection with the note issue, the Bank's main activities were of two kinds. The first of these related to foreign exchange. In the years before 1914 from 40 to 50 per cent of its total loans were made on foreign bills of exchange, and of this amount about four-fifths went to the Yokohama Specie Bank.[1] The central bank was obliged to give this support to the exchange bank because, in the absence of an organized discount market, the funds of the commercial banks were not available for this purpose; while at the same time the problem of international payments was of extreme urgency for Japan. The other main activity of the Bank was the provision of financial aid to the Treasury and official institutions. In addition to the heavy loans which it made, often at a low rate of interest, to the special banks, in times of emergency it invested a large part of its resources in Government bonds. Indeed, its discount rate and its Open Market Policy were much more closely related to the requirements of the Treasury than to the control of the money market. The lack of close contact between the Bank and the ordinary commercial banks can also be explained by reference to the nature of the leading banks themselves. Many of them were part of great business enterprises (Mitsui, Mitsubishi, Sumitomo and Yasuda) with wide ramifications, and the financial resources of these groups enabled the affiliated banks to remain independent of the central institution and to pursue an autonomous policy.

The principle of specialization, as formulated by Matsukata and embodied in the structure which he created, broke down in practice. For instance, the division of function between commercial banking and industrial banking was never fully realized. The commercial banks obtained the bulk of their resources from fixed deposits, and a large part of their assets consisted of industrial securities, long-period

[1] S. Furuya, *Japan's Foreign Exchange and Her Balance of International Payments*, p. 160.

loans to industrial concerns and advances on real estate and personal property. Many a small country bank was in effect a partner in a very few industrial or agricultural businesses, and even the great city banks tied up their resources in investments in the industrial groups of which they formed part. The call funds of these banks, in the absence of an organized bill market, were lent almost entirely to the special banks, particularly to the Yokohama Specie Bank. Thus, not merely was there no clear division of function in practice between the commercial banks on the one hand and the Industrial Bank of Japan and the Hypothec Bank on the other, but the absence of a short-loan market made the commercial banks exceptionally dependent on a very few special banks in acquiring liquid assets.

This situation was inevitable in the circumstances of the time. The ordinary banks could not develop deposit banking of the English type in a country which was unsuited to a cheque currency and where no large supplies of first-class commercial bills were available. The concentration of the majority of large-scale enterprises in the hands of the Government or a few great family businesses, which scarcely ever made public issues of shares, produced a lack of easily market-able industrial securities. The Japanese public, faced with this posi-tion in the capital market and having no tradition of industrial investment, preferred to use their savings by putting them on fixed deposit at the ordinary banks, and these resources were for the most part invested by the banks in industrial concerns. This increased the financial power of the great business groups, since each of them through the bank under its control could easily obtain funds for its enterprises. The Government realized the dangers inherent in a commercial banking system working with illiquid assets and with loans narrowly spread; but rapid industrial development along lines considered necessary for national power could scarcely have been fostered without some such method of mobilizing and canalizing the country's scanty supply of savings. Furthermore, the Government was dependent upon the big financial groups as well as on the special banks for assistance in times of national emergency. The absorption of its bonds issued at the time of the wars of 1894-95 and 1904-05 was only made possible by the creation of syndicates for this purpose by the Mitsui, Mitsubishi and Yasuda Banks and by the Yokohama Specie Bank.

We have seen that the connections between the Bank of Japan and the Yokohama Specie Bank were necessarily intimate in the period before 1914 because of the difficulty in preserving equilibrium in the balance of payments. The increase in loan-financed expenditure during the war against Russia caused Japanese prices to move out of line with those in the outside world; while the armament policy necessitated heavy foreign payments for imported munitions. Further

Japan's territorial gains on the Continent obliged her to make considerable investments in the development of those regions. The money market, in its undeveloped condition, was not able to attract short funds from abroad quickly in times of stringency, and the gold reserve was exiguous. Thus every effort had to be made to increase the supply of export bills and to guard against movements which might force the country off the gold standard and render her unattractive to the foreign investor. But the inability of the central bank to control the credit policies of the ordinary banks left the authorities without an effective weapon for protecting the gold reserve. That part of the Chinese indemnity which had been kept in London as an exchange fund was replenished from time to time from the proceeds of foreign loans. These sterling balances were counted as part of the specie reserve against the note issue, and Japan, actually if not ostensibly, came to possess a variety of the gold exchange standard, in common with many of the weaker financial countries. The maintenance of these foreign balances at an adequate level was a source of considerable anxiety in the decade preceding 1914. Between December 1905 and December 1914 the gold reserve at home and abroad fell from 479 million yen to 342 million yen, and a Japanese Minister of Finance has testified to the growing anxiety felt by the responsible authorities in consequence of this decline.[1] The financial troubles were a measure of the strain which the rapid growth of a modern industrial system accompanied by territorial expansion was imposing on a poor country. The expansionist policy was, in other words, endangering financial stability; but to that policy Japan was irrevocably committed. In these circumstances, it is natural that the Bank of Japan and the Government should have strained every effort to encourage the export trade and to support the Yokohama Specie Bank which occupied a key position in Japan's struggle for power.

[1] J. Inouye, *Problems of the Japanese Exchange*, 1914-1926, Chap. I. These figures include the specie holdings of the Government as well as of the Bank of Japan.

CHAPTER IV

AGRICULTURE, RAW SILK AND THE TEXTILE INDUSTRIES, 1881–1914

The forces of change which had been released by the Restoration and strengthened by the deliberate policy of the Meiji Government affected in some measure every branch of agricultural, industrial and commercial life. But it would be wrong to imagine that all parts of the Japanese economy were brought quickly under the direct influence of the West. For many years after 1868, and even up to the end of our period (1937), the changes in many branches of economic life were slow and often imperceptible. Some of the older industries, as we have seen, were damaged by the impact of foreign trade, and most of them had to adapt themselves in some degree to the new circumstances. Yet this did not prevent a substantial section of Japanese industry from preserving in essence its former character, nor indeed from developing upon lines not vastly different from those of the Tokugawa period. The preservation of the familiar, however, seldom attracts the attention excited by the appearance of the novel and the strange. It is natural therefore that what observers in the latter decades of the nineteenth century were inclined to stress was the rise of new industries and new forms of organization rather than the persistence of the old. These innovations were, in part, the result of the appearance of new wants among the Japanese public in consequence of Western influences. But they can also be attributed to the governmental policy of creating foreign-style industries and institutions such as were considered necessary for national power. The Japanese economy thus came to possess a curious dual character. Its foundations were formed by a peasant agriculture and a variety of small-scale manufacturing industries, many of which were peculiar to Japan. On these foundations was erected a superstructure of large-scale enterprise, an important part of which owed its existence to official initiative or encouragement. Much of the interest which attaches to modern Japanese history is associated with the comparative developments of these two divisions in her economy. Though distinct, they impinge upon one another at many points, and where the interests bound up with them come into conflict there results a social and political strain which has been the chief source of instability in modern Japan.[1]

[1] Cf. G. E. Hubbard, *Eastern Industrialization and Its Effect on the West* (2nd edition), pp. 35-6.

1. *Agriculture*

In the nineteenth century, the distinction between the traditional foundations and the novel superstructure was hardly apparent because the latter was still small and insecure. We have seen that in Tokugawa times some three-fourths of the population consisted of peasants, and in 1872 out of an occupied population of about 19·5 million, not far short of four-fifths were estimated to be engaged in agriculture, forestry and fishing.[1] From that time onwards the proportion steadily declined and in 1913 it was just over three-fifths. The relative decline, however, was consistent with a considerable absolute increase. From 14·5 million in 1872, it is estimated that the agricultural population grew until it reached nearly 17·5 million in the last decade of the century. Subsequently there was a fall, but on the eve of the Second World War over 14 million were still engaged in agriculture, forestry and fisheries.

These changes in the occupied population naturally correspond to changes in the distribution of the total population between urban and rural centres. As late as 1893 about 84 per cent of the population was still found in places with under 10,000 inhabitants, and while these were not all members of agricultural families, the vast majority of them was engaged in traditional economic activities. Only 6 per cent of the population then lived in towns with 100,000 inhabitants or over.[2] Even during the middle nineties, when modern industrialism first made a notable advance, the bulk of the increase in population was still confined to the rural communities. Thus, in the period from 1893 to 1898, out of a total increase in population of 3·33 million, over 2 million were absorbed by the rural centres. During the next five years, however, the tendency towards urbanization became stronger. Although after the turn of the century the rural population continued to grow slowly, the bulk of the increase in population from then on was concentrated in the towns. Consequently, the proportion of the population found in rural communities (places with under 10,000 persons) had fallen to 72 per cent by 1913, compared with 84 per cent twenty years previously. These figures show that the tendency to urbanization did not become strong until the turn of the century, and that even in 1913 it had not gone far enough to threaten seriously the overwhelming predominance of the rural communities which were still absorbing population.[3] This distribution of the people corresponds, as we shall see, with the progress of industrialization.

[1] R. Ishii, *op. cit.*, p. 78. Other authorities suggest an even larger proportion; see K. Ohkawa, *The Growth Rate of the Japanese Economy since 1878*, pp. 147-9. The female workers in agricultural households are included.

[2] R. Ishii, *op. cit.*, pp. 68 *et seq.*

[3] Between 1903 and 1913 the population increased by 6,588,000; towns with 10,000 inhabitants and over absorbed 5,175,000.

In the first half of the Meiji era the Government, having freed the peasants from feudal restrictions, concerned itself with encouraging the introduction of new crops and better methods of cultivation. It sent experts abroad to study foreign agricultural systems; it established agricultural schools and colleges; and it provided instructors who travelled round the country giving guidance and information to the farmers.[1] Some of the innovations which were tried at this time failed to establish themselves. For instance, the attempt to create a sheep-rearing industry in the seventies and early eighties had to be abandoned. Yet, on the whole, progress was considerable. Despite the mountainous nature of the country, it was found possible to extend the land under cultivation. In the thirty years after 1878 the area under rice increased from 2,579,000 cho to 2,922,000 cho, and that under the other chief cereals also grew substantially. Several important new crops were introduced. But the great increase in production during this period can be attributed mainly to improved methods of farming, including more efficient irrigation, better crop strains, pest control and, above all, a lavish application of fertilizers.[2] Agriculture succeeded in supplying all but a small part of the enlarged demand for rice that accompanied the growth in population and the rise in consumption a head. The expansion in the production of the chief cereals is shown in the following table[3]

ANNUAL AVERAGE PRODUCTION OF CEREALS

(in thousand koku)

	Rice	Barley	Naked Barley	Wheat
1879-83	30,874	5,516	3,786	2,219
1889-93	38,549	6,945	5,287	3,102
1899-03	42,268	8,330	6,386	3,700
1909-13	50,242	9,677	7,813	4,901

Despite the improvements in farming methods and the advance in production, agricultural life, in essence, was slow to change. Before the Restoration a holding of half a cho (1·225 acres) was reckoned a good average-sized farm, and the holding of a farmer was commonly formed of strips scattered about the lands of the village. The small size of the agricultural unit is usually attributed to the concentration

---

[1] S. Nasu, 'Ziele und Ausrichtung der Japanischen Agrarpolitik in der Gegenwart', in *Weltwirtschaftliches Archiv*, July, 1937.

[2] The yield of rice per cho rose from 11·6 koku in the early eighties to about 17·0 koku in the years just before the First World War.

[3] *The Statistical Year Book of the Empire of Japan.*

of Japanese agriculture on rice, which is grown in irrigated fields and requires a vast amount of tedious manual labour, especially in the transplanting of seedlings. A contributory cause is undoubtedly to be found in topographical conditions. Because of the hilly nature of the country much of the rice has to be grown in small terraced fields. The abundance of labour and the scarcity of arable land—under 15 per cent of the total area in 1910—also predisposed the Japanese to follow an intensive system of cultivation. These conditions did not change appreciably during the Meiji era. There was a slight tendency for very small farms to decline in numbers; but even in 1910 well over one-third of the farms had an area of under half a cho, and over two-thirds of one cho or under. The larger farms were found mainly in Northern Japan, especially in Hokkaido which was colonized during the Meiji period and where climatic conditions are very different from those in the main islands. If Hokkaido were excluded from these calculations, the proportion of small farms would be still higher. Thus the typical small holding of cultivated land persisted unchanged.

This could not be said of the system of tenure. In the early years of Meiji the proportion of arable land farmed by tenants, as distinct from peasant proprietors, is supposed to have been about one-fifth. It increased after the ban on the sales of land had been removed along with other feudal restrictions, and during the deflationary period of the early and middle eighties the process was rapid, so that in 1887 the proportion had reached nearly 40 per cent. In 1910 it was 45 per cent. At that time about one-third of the farmers were tenants, two-fifths were peasant proprietors, and the remainder owned part of their land and rented the rest. The rents of the paddy-fields continued to be paid in rice, as previously, and these rents ranged between 25 and 80 per cent of the total crop, the average and median being about 50 per cent. The rents of the upland fields also were frequently paid in produce, although here there was a tendency for money rents to be substituted.[1]

As in earlier times, the peasants by no means confined their activities to the production of cereals. Those who lived near the sea-coast combined in-shore fishing with agriculture, and this occupation increased with the rise in the demands of the growing population. Further, the peasants continued to produce industrial crops, although here there were some striking changes. The raw cotton used in the manufacture of Japanese clothing had long been produced domestic-ally, and with the growth in the demand for cotton textiles in the seventies and eighties, and under the shelter of a small import duty, the production of this crop expanded. In 1887 it reached a maximum of nearly half a million piculs, and the country was then self-sufficient in cotton except for a small import from China. After this date,

[1] R. Ishii, *op. cit.*, pp. 153-8.

however, Indian cotton began to replace the home product. In 1896 the Government removed the duty on imported cotton, and by the end of the century the home production had become insignificant. Various other subsidiary industries formerly practised by the peasants were also destroyed by the impact of international trade and new technical methods. For instance, the home production of lacquer was affected by imports from China; while several manufacturing trades were taken from the peasant household through the rise of specialized producing units which employed more efficient technical methods. Most important of these were the cotton-spinning, and to a less extent the cotton-weaving trades. Formerly the women had carded, spun and woven domestically produced cotton for the requirements of their household and for sale to merchants. Spinning was taken from them first by the import of foreign yarns and later by the appearance of Japanese spinning mills. This process had been completed by the nineties, and from then on the weaving activities of the peasant households began to diminish through the rise of specialized weaving sheds. Other traditional peasant trades, however, revived and even expanded. For instance, in certain areas the cultivation of reeds and the manufacture of *tatami*-covers remained a substantial peasant industry; in other districts, the production of paper lanterns, fans and pottery. The greatest development of all occurred in the silk trade. This deserves a fairly detailed treatment, for it provides an illuminating illustration of how an economy adapts itself to changes in demand and technique.

2. Silk

Originally, all the processes in the production of raw silk had been conducted in the peasant household. The farmers and their families grew the mulberry trees, reared the silkworms in sheds attached to their houses, and reeled the silk on simple instruments. The product was then woven on hand-looms either by weavers situated in towns such as Kyoto or in peasant households in specialized weaving areas. On the opening of the country the industry was at once set the task of meeting a large foreign demand both for silkworm eggs and silk in consequence of the outbreak of silkworm disease in Europe. It was taken up by increased numbers of peasants during the sixties and seventies, and it replaced some of the activities which they had lost. The expansion of the industry was accompanied by incipient changes in organization. One of the main difficulties that confronted a peasant reeling industry was the provision of silk of the uniform quality required for export. The spread of the industry to households without previous experience naturally accentuated this difficulty, and as a means of overcoming it and at the same time of enlarging the output, small specialized reeling mills equipped with improved types

E

of hand and treadle machines were set up during the seventies and were staffed by the daughters of the farmers. A few mills in which the machinery was driven by water or steam power were also established. Thus, the silk industry was subject to a technical revolution very early in the new era. Reeling began to appear as a separate industry, although its differentiation from other sections of the trade was not completed for many years.

The initiative came from several quarters. The first machine-weaving mill was founded in 1870 by a former *daimyo* whose territory lay in one of the chief centres of the ancient industry. Filatures were also set up in the early seventies by Ono, one of the great merchant families of the Tokugawa period, and others followed his example. The Government likewise played its part. In 1872 it built a filature at Tomioka which was soon employing some 400 operatives. A second Government mill was founded in 1873. For many of these ventures equipment was imported from Europe, and foreign technicians were brought in to build the mills, train the workers and organize production.[1]

Between 1868 and 1883 the output of raw silk grew from 278,000 kwan to 457,000 kwan, and exports from 175,000 kwan to 365,000 kwan.[2] The export of eggs, which in the first three years of Meiji amounted in value to half that of the raw silk export, declined absolutely as well as relatively in the later seventies; but there was still a fair export in 1880. After that year it fell rapidly and became insignificant by the end of the decade. Those peasants who had hitherto been concerned mainly with egg raising for export now turned to cocoon production. They were able to effect this transference because the foreign demand for Japanese silk continued to grow. Competition with French and Italian silk was assisted not merely by the improvements in methods of production which lowered Japanese costs, but also by the depreciation of silver which conferred a bounty on Japanese exporters to gold standard countries. From this time onwards the reeling process passed rapidly into the specialized reeling establishments, and machine reeling made a great advance. In 1893 there were 3,203 reeling factories employing more than ten persons each, and of these 2,602 practised machine reeling.[3] But a great part of the industry was still conducted either in very small specialized establishments or in the household, and in the period 1889-93 well under half of the silk output was filature silk.

[1] T. C. Smith, *Political Change and Industrial Development*, pp. 57-60.
[2] Figures of exports and imports throughout this book have been, in general, taken from *Foreign Trade of Japan, A Statistical Survey*, compiled by the *Oriental Economist*.
[3] Information about the organization, output, number and size of mills, and employment has, in general, been based on the *Japan Silk Year Book* (various editions).

The filatures themselves were very small; in 1893 only 473 had more than fifty basins, 2,129 from ten to fifty basins, and there was a much larger number with under ten basins.

The next twenty years saw a great expansion both in production and exports, improvements in productive methods in all branches of the trade, a rise in scale in certain branches, and a persistence of the tendency towards vertical disintegration. The growth in output and exports is shown in the following table:—

(in thousand kwan)

Year	Production	Export
1883	457	365
1889-93 (annual average)	1,110	662
1899-03 (annual average)	1,924	1,110
1909-13 (annual average)	3,375	2,563

The costs of cocoon raising were reduced by the introduction of new methods of feeding; cocoons of better quality with a higher yield of silk were produced through the greater attention devoted to rearing the silkworms; and in the filatures improved machinery raised the output per basin. There were also a number of minor technical changes, such as the introduction of a quicker method of killing the pupa on the completion of the cocoon. A major innovation of the period was the rise in the importance of the summer-autumn crop of cocoons. In early Meiji times production had been confined to the spring; but gradually the farmers began to produce a summer-autumn crop, which by 1900 amounted to one-third of the total annual output. This lowered costs by enabling the farmers to be more continuously employed in cocoon raising, and it also substantially reduced the capital requirements per unit of output in the filatures. In the sphere of organization the period between 1893 and the First World War was noteworthy for the triumph of the filature over the hand reel. In 1899-1903 the amount of filature silk was just over half the total (including dupion silk). Up to that time the hand-reel output had continued to grow, though at a much slower rate than filature silk. After 1903 the former ceased to expand, and by 1909-13 the filatures were producing 72 per cent of the total output.

The size of the filatures also increased. During the boom of the middle nineties several large establishments were founded, and in the depression that followed many small firms went out of business. This tendency persisted in the new century and was strengthened during the severe depression that accompanied the American crisis of 1908. By 1913 there were 546 filatures with over a hundred basins, compared with 124 in 1893; while the number of filatures with from ten to fifty basins had been greatly reduced. In spite of this growing concentration of production in larger establishments, the small hand-reeling shop, and even household production, had by no means disappeared. Although in 1913 the hand-reels now accounted for only 22 per cent of the output (apart from the dupion production which amounted to 6 per cent of the total), there were still 284,000 hand-reeling establishments with under 10 basins each, and there were many filatures of similar size also. As often happens during a process of mechanization, the industry had developed two distinct branches. The filatures, especially the larger ones, had arisen to cater for the increased foreign demand for standardized qualities; while the old hand-reeling branch of the industry was left with the task of supplying the needs of domestic weavers.

Another change, which was associated with and was made possible by the rise in the production of uniform silk for abroad, took place in the egg-raising industry. Numerous small producers had flourished in the days when there was a large foreign demand for eggs. But the production of standardized cocoons which the filatures now required was impossible as long as egg production remained in a multitude of independent enterprises. During the nineties, along with the rise of larger filatures, egg production came to be concentrated in fewer hands, and this tendency was encouraged by Government regulation. The number of egg-producers fell from 45,000 in 1895 to 12,000 in 1914. By that time the larger reelers were beginning to exercise a greater degree of control over egg production and cocoon raising. For instance, they imported eggs from Europe and China and developed hybrids which they distributed among the silk raisers who supplied them with cocoons. This practice, however, was in its infancy in the days before the First World War.

The raw silk trade, as we have shown, was an outgrowth of peasant agriculture. In 1914 not merely silk raising but also an important section of the reeling industry was still conducted by peasants or very small-scale producers. Even the filatures were comparatively small establishments, and there were only a few firms owning several plants that could be regarded as large undertakings. These had all risen from small beginnings. The greatest of them, Katakura and Company, started as a small family concern with thirty-two reeling basins in 1878, and it only gradually developed into an important business owning a number of filatures.[1] The capital for such undertakings was for the most part drawn from the country districts in which the mills were located, and thus it might seem that the raw silk industry owed a little of its astounding growth to the great city financial houses which played a predominant part in large-scale

[1] Pamphlet issued by Katakura and Company (Tokyo, 1934).

manufacturing industry. This generalization, however, must be qualified. One of the reelers' major problems was connected with the provision of working capital for the purchase of the cocoons at harvest time from the peasants. A large part of this capital was in fact provided by, or through the medium of, the *tonya*, or commission houses, who acted as intermediaries between the reelers and the exporters of Yokohama and Kobe. Many of these exporters were foreign merchants and much of the export was financed by foreign banks, although after 1890 Japanese export houses and the Yokohama Specie Bank began to participate. These financial relationships, therefore, meant that a considerable part of the working capital was provided indirectly either by foreign financiers or by the larger Japanese merchant and banking houses. Substantial loans to the reelers were of course made by the local bankers; but these obtained a high proportion of their funds by discounting promissory notes with the city banks. Thus, although the great silk industry might seem to be rooted in the old economy of the countryside, it was nourished by streams flowing from the terrain where the great Japanese merchant houses and foreign financiers had their homes.

The Government, by its system of regulation, also made an essential contribution. This point must be emphasized, for it furnishes a clue to Japan's economic progress as a whole. There can be no doubt that the success of the Japanese silk industry and export trade during this and later periods depended closely on the fruitful co-operation among the State, the modern and the ancient sectors of the economy, just as the failure of the Chinese silk industry, in the face of Japanese competition, is largely attributable to its inability to provide for any such co-operation. The silk industry, wherever conducted, needed a wide dispersion of productive units; for the production of cocoons was essentially a small-scale peasant process. But if filament of a uniform quality suitable for use on power looms and knitting frames was to be provided, centralized control at a few points had to be imposed. Apart from the important financial links already described, in Japan this centralized control or supervision was realized through the official licensing of the egg-raisers and by the growth of large filature firms whose plants were scattered over the silk-raising districts and who were consequently able to remain in close touch with the cocoon producers. The contrast with China is striking. In that country no authority capable of, or interested in, imposing control existed. The Government was indifferent. Foreign firms in whose hands much of the trade reposed lacked the power to institute control. The filatures were concentrated in the ports and the Concessions—for reasons of security—and no intimate contact between them and the silk raisers was possible. Central control was again required at the ports through which the silk passed for sale abroad, for at that point reliable testing and conditioning arrangements were essential. To this end silk-conditioning houses were established at Yokohama and Kobe in 1896.[1] In China, on the other hand, conditioning arrangements were not introduced until very late and then only on foreign initiative.

Certain enterprises on the periphery of the industry could be conducted economically only if the scale of operation was large. This sector of the silk trade, therefore, soon engaged the attention of the great capital interests. A mill had been established in 1877 by the Government to spin waste silk according to Western methods, and ten years later this mill passed under the control of Mitsui. The spun silk industry subsequently grew up entirely under the direction of the great cotton-spinning concerns (Kanegafuchi and Fuji), and it was conducted in mills of a modern type. By 1914, however, its development had not gone very far. There were then only about 120,000 spindles in the spun silk trade, and the bulk of the waste silk was still exported.[2]

The silk-weaving industry was only slightly affected by change during this period. Formerly the production of the highest grade silk goods had been in the hands of groups of famous specialist weavers, such as the famous Nishijin producers of Kyoto, whose trade had an elaborate organization; and this branch continued without much modification. Most of the weaving, however, had been conducted in peasant households. Each district specialized in a particular class of silk fabric, and some of them enjoyed a national reputation. The goods were sold to local merchants who often provided the weavers with their raw silk, and these local merchants in turn supplied the wholesalers (*toiya*) of Kyoto, which was the commercial centre of the industry.[3] The *toiya* sent out the fabrics for dyeing and finishing processes and then supplied distributors throughout the country. This organization has persisted to the present time, and a considerable proportion of the better grade goods for home consumption are still made on hand-looms by weavers working in their own homes or in small workshops. The main alteration that took place between 1880 and 1913 was the replacement, in some measure, of domestic weaving by work in small specialist workplaces where a few looms had been collected together, and by the appearance of small factories using power-looms in branches of the trade which produced for export. The exports of silk fabrics (mainly *habutae*) to America increased substantially during the eighties and nineties, though further

---

[1] The Kobe house was closed five years later as the trade became concentrated at Yokohama.

[2] *The Japan Silk Year Book*, 1935-36, pp. 110 *et seq.*

[3] The *tonya* of Kwanto (Eastern Japan) appear as *toiya* in Kwansai (Osaka-Kobe).

growth in this trade was checked by the raising of the American tariff just before the turn of the century. Yet even in 1913 the development of power weaving in factories had not proceeded far enough to effect any significant alteration in the organization of the industry. Thus, in Fukui and Ishikawa prefectures which were the main centres of the production of *habutae* for export, out of 35,000 looms only 15,000 were power driven. Only a small part of this great and expanding industry could be regarded as a factory, even a small factory, trade.

3. *Cotton, Wool and Other Textiles*

Large-scale enterprise had thus scarcely touched the basic activities of Japan during this era of change. New technical methods were introduced, but they were accommodated within the scope of small-scale undertakings, and only through the growing magnitude and complexity of financial relations between producers and merchants had modern capitalism begun to penetrate into these ancient industries. It was otherwise with cotton manufacture. There the modernizing influences were exerted later than in the silk trade, but when they once made themselves felt they soon effected a thorough-going transformation. In the early years of Meiji there were few signs of the changes that were to come. The first result of European contact was to create serious competition with the domestic cotton-spinning industry through the import of yarns finer and cheaper than those produced in the home. The volume of cotton yarn imported rose from 12,000 bales in 1868 to 158,000 bales in 1888, the peak year, and in the first decade of Meiji the ratio of imports of cotton goods to total imports (in value) ranged between 22 per cent and 41 per cent.

The first modern mill in Japan had been founded in 1867 by the lord of Satsuma, who built a second mill in 1870. Mampei, a merchant, set up another mill in 1872 which later passed to Mitsui. Soon afterwards the Government took a hand. It established two modern spinning mills equipped with Western machinery; it imported spinning machinery which it sold to private persons on very favourable terms; and it made loans to others for the same purpose. All these mills were relatively small and most of them were driven by water power. For many years they made little headway against the flood of cheap foreign yarn. A further step was taken in 1882 when Viscount Shibusawa founded the Osaka Spinning Mill (the predecessor of the famous Toyo Spinning Company). This mill was large by the standards of the time, since it had 10,000 spindles, and what is more, it was driven by steam power.[1] Unlike most of the others, from the outset it was a financial success. Despite this progress, however,

[1] K. Seki, *The Cotton Industry of Japan*, pp. 15-16.

the industry was still very small. Even in 1886 the total Japanese spindleage amounted to under 90,000, the equipment of a single fair-sized Lancashire mill. After the depression of the middle eighties had spent itself, several new spinning concerns were founded, including the now famous Kanegafuchi company. This was the herald of a remarkable expansion which began in the last decade of the century and continued for the next forty years.

The timing of this expansion needs some explanation. It was not merely that by then the initial technical difficulties attending the assimilation of a new process had been overcome, or that the Government was prepared to sacrifice the Japanese cotton growers for the benefit of an industry the expansion of which depended on access to cheap Indian materials.[1] There were other causes. The steep rise of prices at that time provided a great stimulus for entrepreneurs, and industrial investment during the nineties was heavy in many branches of activity. Then, after the war with China of 1894-95, Japan succeeded in capturing the Korean market for yarn, and a year later when China placed a ban on Indian goods in consequence of the outbreak of an epidemic in Bombay, she seized her opportunities in that market also. But apart from these fortuitous circumstances, she had an enduring basis for success in this industry in her large supplies of cheap female labour nurtured in a tradition of textile work and in her vigorous leadership. The following table

	Number of Spindles (in thousands)	Output of Yarn (in million lb.)	Number of Spinning Companies
1887	77	—	—
1893	382	88	40
1897	971	220	74
1903	1,381	317	51
1907	1,540	393	42
1913	2,415	607	44

shows how fast spindleage and output increased during the twenty-five years before the First World War.[2] By that time Japan's cotton-spinning industry had been firmly established.

The bulk of the yarn produced consisted of coarse counts (20s and under); but Japan was moving slowly up the scale, and the proportion of coarse yarns to the total output fell from 88 per cent to 80 per cent during the ten years before 1914. It is evident from the above table that the size of the typical concern was growing. During the

---

[1] Import duties on raw cotton were removed in 1896.
[2] Figures of output, mills, spindleage and loomage based on semi-annual reports of Japan Cotton Spinners' Federation (in Japanese) and on an English publication of that body entitled *Cotton Statistics of Japan*.

nineties, the expansion of the industry had been associated mainly with the increase in the number of concerns; but after the depression at the turn of the century many mergers took place, and most of the new mills that came into existence after 1900 were established by the existing companies. Consequently the average number of spindles per company rose from about 27,000 in 1901 to 55,000 in 1913. Even by the latter year, however, the typical concern, and still more the typical mill, were small by British standards.

The industry was built up after 1890 almost entirely on the basis of imported cotton. China, which before this time had supplied the bulk of the import, was superseded by British India as the chief source of supply; while the United States became increasingly important in this respect during the years just before the First World War. The formation in 1892 of the famous Nippon Menkwa with a capital of one million yen marked the beginning of the great cotton-importing business which to the present time has remained concentrated in a few concerns. At this time too there were drawn up (in 1893) the agreements between the Nippon Yusen Kaisha, the Japanese cotton spinners, and the Indian shippers, which provided for a reduction in freight rates on cotton imports from Bombay.[1]

The cotton-weaving industry was differently affected. The domestic producers, having lost the spinning operation first through the competition of imported yarn, and later through the rise of Japanese mills, directed their activities to an increasing extent to the weaving process. In the early years of Meiji the greater part of the narrow cloth for Japanese *kimono* continued to be produced on hand-looms in the home. After 1890, with the growth in the production of cloth, specialized weaving sheds became more important and the power loom made its appearance. But the size of the weaving sheds remained very small, and in 1900 there were over 700,000 hand-looms and only 32,000 power-looms. Meanwhile a new branch of the industry made its appearance. In 1887 a spinning mill at Osaka had established a shed of narrow power-looms to consume part of its yarn output, and this example was followed by a few others.[2] In 1892 there were about 900 power-looms operated by the spinners and the number rapidly increased in subsequent years. In 1903 it reached 5,000 looms and in 1907 9,000. At this time the spinners were beginning to meet with difficulty in their yarn export trade because of Indian and Chinese competition, and they were encouraged to extend their weaving activities more rapidly than before. By 1913 the spinners owned about 24,000 looms and produced 417 million yards of cloth. The bulk of this output consisted of wide piece-goods of a standardized character mainly for export. For example, three-quarters of the

[1] *Golden Jubilee History of Nippon Yusen Kaisha*, pp. 18-22.
[2] *Industrial Japan* (World Engineering Congress, 1929), p. 287.

output was made up of shirtings, sheetings and drills. Most of the exports went to Korea, Manchuria and China Proper.[1]

In the first decade of the twentieth century the several branches of the weaving industry began to be differentiated. There was first the weaving of wide standardized piece-goods, largely for export, a trade which was conducted in large sheds owned by spinners. Secondly, there was the production of piece-goods for the home market by small weaving sheds equipped either with narrow power-looms or hand-looms. Finally, there was the old domestic hand-loom industry. The first two branches of the industry were expanding rapidly; but even in 1913 they had by no means entirely displaced the domestic weaver. In that year 85,000 persons were recorded as being engaged in cotton weaving in factories or mills employing five persons and over. Most of these factories were very small since their total number was 2,087, of which only about half (1,135) had power-driven machinery. At the same time there were probably half a million households in which domestic weaving was still carried on. It is possible to estimate the relative importance of these different branches of the industry. The quantity of yarn used by Japanese weavers as a whole rose from 196 million pounds in 1903 to 420 million pounds in 1913. The proportion consumed in the sheds owned by the spinning concerns rose from 10·6 per cent to 26·5 per cent during this period. But, if the relative importance of this branch of weaving was growing, it was not at the expense of the specialist weaving industry, for the yarn consumption of that branch grew from 175 million pounds to 309 million pounds during the same decade.

The cotton and silk industries grew from ancient roots; but there were some branches of textile manufacture which owed their existence entirely to Western contacts. The most important of these was the woollen and worsted industry. Neither raw wool nor woollen manufactures were produced to any significant extent in Tokugawa Japan, and the industry had to be built up from the very foundations. Its development proceeded from two directions. We have already seen that the Government had set up a factory for making army cloth in 1877.[2] The machinery was imported from Germany and was installed by foreign technicians. Although a few private concerns producing army cloth, blankets and flannels were established during the eighties and nineties, the Government mill remained the most important plant in the industry until the new century. All these concerns depended mainly on Government orders and their output

[1] Exports first exceeded imports in value in 1897 in the case of cotton yarn and in 1909 in the case of piece-goods.

[2] *Industrial Japan*, p. 342. The following account of the growth of this industry is largely based on *The Present Status of the Woollen Industry in Japan* (Nagoya Imperial College of Commerce, 1935).

fluctuated widely. It rose steeply during the Sino-Japanese War and
the Russo-Japanese War; but in peace-time the mills could secure
little business in competition with imported cloth, even though their
products were favoured after 1899 by a 25 per cent *ad valorem* duty
on foreign woollens. At first the mills imported all the yarn required
for their looms. After 1900 some of them began to spin, but even in
1913 they still depended largely on foreign yarn imports.

The heavy woollen branch (except in war-time) made rather slow
progress, and it was soon overshadowed by muslin manufacture.
After the opening of the country to Europeans large quantities of
muslins had been imported for the manufacture of *kimono*, as a
substitute for cotton and silk. These imports averaged about 15
million square yards during the later seventies, about 13 million
square yards in the later eighties, and then rose sharply in the

OUTPUT OF WOOLLEN AND WORSTED TISSUES
(ANNUAL AVERAGES)

Period	Muslin (*in million yards*)	Flannel (*in million yards*)	Serge (for Japanese dress) (*in million yds.*)	Woollens (*in million yards*)	Total Value (including others) (*in million yen*)
1899-1903	8·83	0·90	0·28	0·82	4·36
1904-08	19·61	—	0·49	2·67	11·98
1909-13	51·12	1·30	3·78	1·54	21·66
1913	69·58	3·65	9·65	1·76	23·26

IMPORTS (ANNUAL AVERAGES)

Period	Raw Wool, Greasy (*in million lb.*)	Woollen and Worsted Yarn (*in million lb.*)	Tops (*in million lb.*)	Muslin (*in million sq. yards*)
1899-1903	6·63	1·14	1·24 (1902-03)	16·42
1904-08	11·74	3·68	4·36	7·99
1909-3	10·10	5·66	7·76	2·96
1913	11·61	9·38	9·45	0·16

nineties to over 24 million square yards a year. Up to that time the
Japanese demand was entirely satisfied from foreign sources of
supply. Just before the end of the century, however, a few muslin
mills were established in Japan, and the industry developed so quickly
that the import of foreign muslins was soon affected. The tariff
already mentioned helped the Japanese mills in this competition;
but their chief advantage over the foreign producer lay in the fact

that they were more skilful than he in turning out goods suitable for Japanese tastes. By 1913 imports of muslins were rapidly declining, and an export trade was being worked up. The muslin branch had by then become much the largest branch of the wool-using industry. The manufacture of serge and worsteds was still in its infancy.

As was to be expected in an industry without a long native tradition, production was not widely scattered over a large number of producers, as with cotton and silk. The heavy woollen branch of the industry, being concerned with Government orders for standardized fabrics, was in the hands of a very small number of firms, and even muslin manufacture was conducted in relatively large mills, for it lent itself to standardized production on power-looms. Yet in this industry, as in most Japanese trades, there appeared a fringe of very small producers working to the orders of merchants. The tables on page 75 will serve to illustrate the development of the different branches of production in the 20 years preceding the First World War.[1]

Among the minor textiles the flax and hemp industries, which had a long history in Japan, were reorganized during this period. A hemp factory was founded with Government financial assistance in 1886 and others followed. During the Sino-Japanese War there was an active demand from the army for their products, but the trade decayed subsequently, to be revived during the Russo-Japanese War. In 1907 the industry passed under the control of the Teikoku Seima Kaisha (Imperial Hemp Company), a subsidiary of Yasuda; but it continued up to the war to be dependent on the demand for military goods, and the finer products were imported. In 1913 the spinning branch of the industry had about 27,000 spindles. This branch was conducted in fair-sized mills controlled by a single company, but much of the weaving took place in very small sheds. The hosiery industry also was started during the thirty years before the First World War. It specialized in cotton hosiery, and its equipment consisted of imported knitting machines operated mostly by hand in domestic or very small specialized workshops. The industry had not achieved the rank of an important manufacture in 1913; but it is of interest because it provides an example of a new trade which was organized according to small-scale methods characteristic of the older industries.

At the end of our period the textile industries formed by far the most important section of Japan's manufacturing activity. It is naturally difficult, in a country in which a large proportion of the manufactures is produced either in peasant households or by the part-time work of urban families, to form an accurate estimate of

[1] Sources: Nagoya Imperial College of Commerce, *The Present Status of the Woollen Industry in Japan*; and Oriental Economist, *Foreign Trade of Japan*.

the industrial distribution of the population. Moreover, the vast majority even of the specialized work-places were very small, and there is no reliable statistical information about the numbers employed in workplaces with under five workers in this period. Since 1909, however, figures have been collected of the employment provided by 'factories' with five or more workers. In 1913 nearly three-fifths of the persons so employed were in textile factories.[1] Figures are also available to show the gross output of the various 'factory' industries similarly defined. These, though obviously defective as a guide to the relative importance of the different trades, show that 45 per cent of the total value was attributable to textile factories. Of the total value of textile production about 28 per cent was made up of raw silk and silk yarn, over 10 per cent of silk piece-goods (including mixtures), and 53 per cent of cotton yarn and piece-goods. Thus over nine-tenths of the total output of the textile industry consisted of silk and cotton goods. These formed the major manufactured products of Japan.

The textile trades are of interest for reasons other than their size. Although Government initiative had been an important factor in their development during the early years of Meiji, and although improvements, in the silk industry especially, owed much to official regulation, yet on the whole the expansion of these trades in the new century had depended little either on direct assistance from the Government or on the national economic policy then being worked out. Their rise was the natural consequence of the redistribution of productive resources that resulted from the impact of Western trade and technique on the old Japanese economy. The relative advantages of Japan in these trades depended on her possession of ample supplies of cheap labour with traditions of textile work, and on the technical fact that many of their branches could be satisfactorily conducted in small workplaces and without expensive capital equipment. It was in them, therefore, that the rising entrepreneurial class found the most fruitful field for its operations.

Viewed from another standpoint, the textile trades represent a form of activity where the two major sections of the Japanese economy meet, the traditional peasant economy and the new capitalistic economy. The silk trade, as we have seen, was an outgrowth of the former. Yet even here the new capitalism was intruding by means of the investments of the *tonya* and the city bankers in the large reeling mills, as well as through the working capital which they also provided. The large cotton-spinning mills clearly belong to the new economy. Yet those mills not merely depended for their labour supply on the peasant families, but the whole system of industrial

[1] Excluding miscellaneous labourers, but including employees in Government factories. Source: Department of Commerce and Industry, *Factory Statistics*.

relations that grew up within them was moulded by social conditions peculiar to traditional Japan. At first the daughters of the peasants were reluctant to enter the new factories, and a labour supply had to be attracted by means of factory agents who made contracts with the heads of peasant families about the terms of the girls' employment. As in the workshops of old Japan, the employer housed and fed these workers and even provided for their entertainment. He assumed obligations towards them which were at first the expression of this paternal relationship, but which later came to be regarded by the workers as a right. Among these obligations were the payment of dismissal allowances on the discharge of the workers and also the grant of semi-annual bonuses, which corresponded to the gifts which the employer in old Japan made to his servants at New Year and O-bon. It is true that this relationship might at times be associated with abuses, especially in the novel environment within which it was established; but there can be no question that its origins lie in the assumption by the new industries of a system of relationships derived from the older society. Western industrialism was thus modified by the social environment into which it was imported, and it consequently lost some of its alien character. Indeed, any criticism of the dormitory system in the cotton mills—as distinct from the abuses in that system—is ill-founded if the observer has failed to realize that its roots are to be sought in the social system of the country. Thus, even the large enterprises in the cotton, woollen and silk-spinning trade, had to come to terms with the old society. As for the weaving processs in all the textile industries this was still largely a small-scale or household industry, and by 1913 a technical revolution in this section of manufacture was in its early stages. Much of the trade was located in villages and small towns, and its personnel still had close associations with the farming communities around them.

CHAPTER V

THE HEAVY INDUSTRIES, SHIPPING AND FOREIGN TRADE, 1881–1914

1. *Metals, Mining and Engineering*

Japan inherited a long tradition of skill in metal working as in textiles, and the products of her craftsmen, such as the sword makers, had enjoyed fame for centuries. But she found greater difficulty in adapting her metallurgical trades to Western technical methods than she did her textiles. This is not surprising. Countries in the early stages of modern industrialism have usually concentrated on the re-organization and development of their textile industries whatever their subsequent history may have been. The explanation is not hard to find. For economical production the metal and heavy engineering trades need more expensive capital equipment and more elaborate technical processes than the textile industries, and the scarcity of capital in 'new' countries offers a handicap to development. Further, modern methods of metal manufacture differ greatly from traditional methods. They make heavy demands on scientific knowledge and trained technicians. Traditional aptitudes, therefore, provide a less satisfactory basis for these industries than for textile manufacture. Finally, unless a country offers a large market for a wide variety of metal goods and by-products, it is difficult for each of the special trades that fall within the metal groups to approximate to an optimum scale and so to work with a reasonable degree of economy, Japan suffered a further handicap in the major branch of metal production, namely the iron and steel trades, in that she was deficient both in iron ore and in good coking coal. When the industry began to appear in its modern form, it owed its rise to Government initiative, and for a long time its very existence depended on help from the State. It was in fact typical of those large-scale industries which were called into being by the Government's policy of building up manufacturing resources necessary for national power and security. Political necessity rather than economic advantage supplied the impulse.

In the early years of Meiji the home output of iron was limited to that produced from the sand-iron of the San-in district, and both this industry and the manufacture of finished iron goods suffered from the import of cheap Western products. In 1896 the home output of pig iron amounted to only 26,000 tons, about 40 per cent of the total consumption. The home output of steel was insignificant, and practically all the consumption of 222,000 tons was met by imports. In that year, the Government decided to establish an iron and steel industry equipped with Western plant, and in 1901 a State-owned and operated concern, known as the Yawata Iron works, began production. A few years later several other plants were founded by large private capital interests, and by 1913 the pig iron output reached 243,000 tons and the steel output 255,000 tons, 48 per cent and 34 per cent respectively of the home consumption. Neither the State nor the private undertakings were financially successful, and the contribution of the latter to the total output remained small—in 1913 34 per cent of the pig output and 15 per cent of the steel output. Thus, before the First World War Japan was still largely dependent on foreign countries for the iron and steel which she consumed, and the bulk of her own output was produced by a single State concern. Her finished steel production was naturally confined to a narrow range of products, virtually to bars, rails, plates and wire rods, and for most other kinds of finished steel she relied almost entirely upon imports. Even though her iron output was so small, she could not by any means fully supply her furnaces with domestic ores. In 1913 her ore output was only 153,000 tons, mostly from the Kamaishi mines, about 27 per cent of her ore consumption. The rest came from Korea and China. It is clear that even at the end of this period the Japanese iron and steel industry was of very slight importance.

The mining industries had been more successful. As we have seen, copper, silver and gold had been mined for many centuries, and coal- and oil-mining appear to have developed soon after 1700. Western technical methods were first introduced when the Takashima Colliery in Kyushu was started with foreign capital just before the Restoration. The Meiji Government brought in experts and equipment from overseas, and during the seventies it was itself operating nine undertakings in various branches of the mining industry. These included the largest and most up-to-date mines. After 1880, however, development was left mainly to private enterprise.

Coal-mining soon became the most important branch of the industry. During the Meiji era most of the output came from Kyushu, in spite of the development after 1880 of the Hokkaido field. At first production was small by Western standards, but with the progress of industrialization after 1894 it rose rapidly. By 1913 a hundred mining companies were in existence with an aggregate paid-up capital of 39 million yen and with 172,000 miners in their employment. Many of the undertakings were very small and the bulk of the output was produced by a few large concerns most of which were affiliated to the *zaibatsu*. Efficiency does not appear to have been high. In 1913 production per worker employed was only 123 tons, and the output per man-shift (underground workers only) only

·53 tons. For the low productivity the thickness of the seams as well as the imperfect equipment of the mines was responsible.

On balance Japan had a small export of coal after 1890, and by 1913 it had risen to over 3 million tons a year. At home the largest consumer during the first twenty-five years of Meiji was the salt industry. Then in the nineties, with the increasing use of steam power by the new industries, manufacturing establishments became the largest consumer; while in the decade before the First World War the bunker trade consumed as much as the factories. As the Japanese warmed their dwelling houses with charcoal braziers (*hibachi*), the consumption of house coal was insignificant.

COAL OUTPUT (ANNUAL AVERAGES)[1]

(in million metric tons)

1877-84	0·8
1885-94	2·6
1895-1904	8·0
1905-14	16·8
1914	22·3

The ancient copper-mining and refining industry was also reorganized during these years. Although eclipsed by coal-mining, it continued to expand up to 1914, when Japan ranked as the second largest copper exporter in the world. Both on the mining and the refining side the industry was in the hands of a few great business families. Kuhara, Mitsubishi, Fujita and Furukawa. These also owned factories in which much of the copper was consumed. The bulk of the output came from a small number of mines, over half from the four largest and nearly two-thirds from the eight largest mines. The same is true of the other mining enterprises. Thus, although there was an important fringe of small mining undertakings, the industry as a whole was conducted on a large scale. This had been true even before the Restoration.

Oil-mining was another ancient industry which expanded during the new era. The development became rapid after the establishment in 1888 of the Japan Oil Company, equipped with American apparatus. Later this company established an up-to-date refining works. The output of crude oil in Japan rose from 33,000 barrels in 1887 to over 100,000 barrels in 1893 and to over 1¼ million barrels in 1903. After this time growth was slower because of more intense competition from abroad and the difficulty of exploiting new fields. Foreign

---

[1] Sources of these and other data concerning the mining industry: *Financial and Economic Annual of Japan*; and Mining Bureau of Department of Commerce and Industry, *General Conditions of Mining Industry of Japan* (annual).

F

concerns established refining and storage capacity for imported oils, together with a distributive organization, and after 1908 there was a marked decline in domestic production. The competition from abroad led the Japanese companies to come to an agreement with their foreign rivals, Standard Oil and Rising Sun Oil, who operated in Japan. The various members of the industry were allotted sales quotas, and the foreign companies obtained the right of supplying 65 per cent of the annual consumption. This seems to have been the first international industrial agreement to which Japan was a party.

The engineering industry, although fostered by the Government for political reasons, failed to reach a substantial size during this period. Japan relied until the very last years of Meiji mainly upon foreign shipyards to provide her with the larger ships for her growing mercantile marine. Certain Government yards (notably those of Nagasaki, Kobe, Uraga and Ishikawa), which had been taken over from the Shogunate and the *daimyo*, were transferred to private ownership in the early eighties, and at the same time new private yards were established; for example, the Osaka Iron Works in 1881 and the Ono Shipbuilding Company in 1883. But output remained very small until the end of the century. It was not until the nineties that the first steel ship was built and before 1895 the Japanese yards launched only one steamship of over 1,000 gross tons. A new era began with the Shipbuilding Encouragement Act of 1896. This provided for the granting of official subsidies to builders of iron and steel vessels of over 700 gross tons. The bounty was at the rate of 12 yen a ton for ships of under 1,000 tons and 20 yen a ton for those of over 1,000 tons, while 5 yen per horse-power was given for marine engines manufactured in Japan. As a result several new yards were founded and existing ones extended. But the subsidy was still not large enough to promote a rapid development of the industry; for at that time practically all the materials had to be imported, and Japanese technicians were far inferior to those of other countries. In 1899 further encouragement was given by an amendment of the Navigation Subsidy Law. This law, passed in 1896, had provided for subsidizing the mercantile marine. The amendment entitled owners of Japanese-built ships to claim twice the amount of subsidy granted to owners of foreign-built ships. From this time onwards the leading yards were entrusted with the building of several large ocean-going steamships. In 1909 revised subsidy laws came into force and gave another stimulus to the industry. By then considerable experience in shipbuilding had been gained, and supplies of certain kinds of steel and components were becoming available from domestic manufacturers. In the years immediately preceding the First World War the Japanese yards were able to undertake the building of warships. By 1913 there were six yards capable of building vessels of

1,000 tons and over, besides many small concerns, and the number of workers in the industry was 26,000. The annual average gross tonnage of steamships launched, which had been under 10,000 tons until the late nineties, rose to over 50,000 tons in the period 1909-13.[1] The annual average tonnage of sailing ships launched also increased substantially from the last years of the century and reached about 20,000 tons in the period immediately before the First World War.

By the standards of the leading Western countries the shipbuilding output in 1914 was still unimpressive, and this was true of the production of engineering goods as a whole. The greater part of the equipment needed for the railways, ships, factories, power stations and mines was imported, and the production of engineering goods was limited to a very few factories. Some of these, which were later to become very important, were established towards the end of the nineteenth century, notably the Shibaura Engineering Works, founded in 1887. This firm, besides undertaking general engineering work, began in 1892 to produce electrical machinery and apparatus. Several other firms entered this trade at about the same time. For instance, the Tokyo Electric Company carried on pioneer work in the manufacture of electric bulbs, the Fujikura Electric Wire Company produced wire and cables, and the Oki Electric Company telephone and telegraph apparatus. The first locomotive built in Japan was turned out in 1892. During the period between the Chinese and the Russian wars several new engineering firms were founded by the great business families in association with other enterprises. Furukawa and Sumitomo, which had interests in the copper-mining and refining industry, set up electric wire and cable works where the products of their mines were consumed. The subsidy granted to the builders of marine engines induced Mitsubishi and Kawasaki to create manufacturing plant for that purpose in connection with their shipyards at Kobe. After the nationalization of the railways in 1906 the Government discriminated in favour of domestic producers of rolling stock, and this led to an expansion in that branch of engineering. For instance, the Kawasaki Dockyard Company started its railway workshops in 1908.

During the first decade of the present century there was a marked increase in the use of electricity for lighting, street traction and factory plants. New power stations were built, and Japan began to make use of her great resources of water power for the generation of electricity. In 1907 the production was 115,000 kWh., of which one-third was generated by water power; by 1914 the amount had increased to 716,000 kWh., of which four-sevenths was generated by water power. The spread of electric lighting affected all branches of the electrical engineering and apparatus industries. Foreign capital

[1] Ships of 100 tons and over.

came in to assist in this development. For instance, in 1905 the General Electric Company (of America) acquired interests in and reorganized the Tokyo Electric Company which began to produce the Mazda lamp. It acquired control of the Osaka Electric Lamp Company a year later. In 1905-06 two firms, one of them the Nippon Gaishi of Nagoya, were founded for the manufacture of insulators. The Mitsubishi Shipbuilding and Engineering Company set up a department for making electrical equipment for ships and mines. In 1910 the Kuhara mining interests established the Hidachi Works, now one of the greatest of Japan's engineering firms. The paid-up capitalization of the engineering industry rose from a mere 2·6 million yen in 1893 to 14·6 million yen in 1903 and to 61·1 million yen in 1913. The capital invested in electricity supply companies rose from 2 million yen in 1893 to 12 million yen in 1907 and to nearly 200 million yen in 1913. On the eve of the First World War there were 60,000 persons employed in factories producing machinery, instruments, tools and vehicles, apart from those engaged in ship-building.[1]

There was a considerable number of small workshops engaged in manufacturing parts and working to the orders of the factories; but most of the heavy engineering industry was concentrated in a few large firms, each with a wide range of output. The more important among these firms were owned by the great business families with interests in many branches of large-scale enterprise. For instance, the Hidachi Works was owned by Kuhara, which was dominant in the mining industry; the Shibaura Works was associated with Mitsui; two of the great houses in the copper trade (Furukawa and Sumitomo) controlled the chief electric wire and cable works; Mitsubishi and Kawasaki had important general and electrical engineering activities associated with their shipyards. Many branches of the trade depended mainly on Government orders, such as the firms that produced telegraphic apparatus and rolling stock, or derived great assistance from the subsidy policy, such as the marine engineers. Thus the heavy engineering industry fell almost entirely within the second branch of Japan's economy which was distinguished by a concentration of control in a few capital groups and was moulded and governed by State policy.

A few branches of the light engineering industry, later to become important, were started in the last twenty years of this era; but none of them had become very large. Among them we may mention the

[1] *Industrial Japan*, pp. 245-96; S. Uyehara, *op. cit.*, pp. 213-23; M. Suzuki, *Nihon Zaibatsu Ron* (Essay on the Japanese *Zaibatsu*), *passim*; *The House of Mitsui; An Outline of Mitsubishi Enterprises; Statistical Year-Book of Empire of Japan;* T. Uyeda and T. Inokuchi, *The Electric Lamp Industry* (Institute of Pacific Relations), pp. 3-4.

bicycle industry. The first producers of bicycles were craftsmen formerly engaged in gun manufacturing, especially those situated at Sakai near Osaka. The leading firm in the trade, the Miyata Works, was formerly a rifle manufacturing concern which started making bicycles in 1888 and soon began to specialize in this new industry.[1] In the new century, and especially after the Russo-Japanese War when many gunsmiths turned to bicycle manufacture, the industry expanded. Most of the producers were small men who at first occupied themselves with manufacturing parts needed for repairing bicycles that had been imported. In the years immediately prior to the First World War, however, there was a strong tendency for each small producer to specialize on particular components required for the complete bicycle. These components were made to the orders of merchants who afterwards had the parts assembled. The tendency was accompanied and assisted by a standardization of components, and so the bicycle manufacturing industry began to assume a definite form. Although the output even in 1914 was still small, and although large imports of parts and accessories were needed to satisfy the home demand, this industry is of interest because it provides an early example of certain new trades which were later to become an important feature of Japanese manufacture. These are the industries which turn out light engineering or miscellaneous products and are conducted in small workshops, each specializing on a few processes or components needed for the finished commodity.

2. Other Manufactures

Among other large-scale industries which were formed at this time we can mention the cement, sugar-growing and refining, glass, beer-brewing, paper and chemical fertilizer industries. All these owe their inception to the great business families who were often assisted by the State to launch the new enterprises. For example, the manufacture of foreign-style paper had begun with the formation of the Oji Company by Mitsui and Shimada in 1871 on the advice of the Government. Several other concerns were founded during the last decade of the century, and by 1913 the annual output of paper amounted to about 500 million pounds. This figure includes Japanese-style paper which was organized in an entirely different way from the foreign-style paper-making industry. Japanese paper continued to be produced, as it had been for centuries, in small workshops or in peasant households, whereas foreign-style paper was manufactured in large mills equipped with massive Western machinery.

[1] Pamphlet issued by Miyata Works, Tokyo.
This affords an interesting parallel to the development of the industry in England. Rifle manufacturers, notably the B.S.A. Co., were among the first English firms to take up the manufacture of bicycles on a large scale.

The contrast between the old and new branches was to be observed in many industries. In brewing, for example, the production of *sakē* was conducted in very small establishments; but the new beer industry from the first was in the hands of a small number of large concerns. It had begun in the seventies when the Kirin Company, and also a Government brewery in Hokkaido, were set up. In the eighties the latter passed to the Dai Nippon Brewery Company, and at the end of that decade the Ebisu and Asahi Companies were formed. Up to the First World War, and indeed for long after, practically the whole trade was controlled by four concerns in which the *zaibatsu* had important interests.[1]

The sugar industry provides a particularly good example of the co-operation of the State and the *zaibatsu* in the creation of large-scale enterprises. Cane sugar had been produced in Japan before the Restoration; but the industry declined during the early part of the Meiji era in consequence of the imports of cheap foreign sugar. The annexation of Formosa, gave Japan extensive territories climatically suited to cane-sugar growing. Even so, the trade would have made little headway against imports of cheap Java sugar if the Government had not given substantial subsidies to the Formosan companies and if high import duties on foreign sugar had not been imposed. These duties and subsidies date from 1902, and production was trebled during the next ten years. Meanwhile, a sugar-refining industry had grown up in Japan. From the middle nineties the Dai Nippon Seito began to refine imported Javanese sugar, and although the duties of 1902 damaged this trade, a system of drawbacks was instituted and made possible the growth of an export trade in refined sugar produced from Javanese raw sugar. Both branches of the industry were controlled by a very few concerns. From 1902 the Dai Nippon Seito monopolized the home market until it was joined in 1908 by two others. In 1914 it owned three out of the five sugar-refining factories of Japan.

The interests of the raw-sugar producers and the refiners came into conflict in connection with the Javanese imports which the former wished entirely to exclude. The conflict was ultimately resolved by vertical integration. The Dai Nippon Seito in 1911 entered the raw-sugar trade, and the two leading raw-sugar companies, the Meiji and Taiwan, bought sugar refineries in Japan. Both Mitsui and Mitsubishi were closely associated with the development of this industry, and each controlled one of the leading concerns.[2] In this field, as in many others, they acted in a sense as agents of the Government in the execution of its economic policy.

In the cement industry, also, *zaibatsu* capital was present but

[1] Information supplied by *Oriental Economist* in 1936.
[2] Information supplied by *Oriental Economist* in 1936.

scarcely so dominant as in the sugar trade, partly no doubt because the scale of enterprise was smaller, and partly because Governmental policy was not so closely involved in its development. Japan has abundant clay and limestone and fair coal supplies, and so she was well fitted for this industry. A Government factory, established in 1871, was turned over to S. Asano in 1884, who was a typical 'self-made' industrialist of the Meiji era. Just after the Restoration he had supported himself in Tokyo as a hawker. He later began to trade in the by-products of the Yokohama Gas Works, and after purchasing the Government's cement factory, he soon built up an important business in that industry as well as in the oil, shipping and ship-building trades. In the early eighties the Onoda Cement Company was formed, and this later passed under the control of Mitsui.[1] It was not, however, until Western technical methods were introduced during the nineties that output became at all substantial. With the industrialization of the country and with the development of communications in the fifteen years before the First World War, the demand for cement greatly increased, and output rose from 87,000 tons in 1896 to 645,000 in 1913. In that year the industry was in the hands of eighteen companies, which together operated twenty-one factories.

Another new large-scale industry which was started in the later years of Meiji was glass manufacture. Several firms engaged in producing bottle and lamp glass were established in the nineties, and there was some small production of sheet and plate glass. This last branch of the trade became more important after 1907, when the Asahi Glass Company was reorganized with Mitsubishi capital. Even in 1913, however, the bulk of Japanese requirements depended upon imports, and the trade was still in its infancy. This could be said of several branches of manufacture which were later to become great industries, such as the chemical industry and the rubber trade. The latter industry had scarcely existed before 1900, and only began to develop rapidly after 1909 when the Dunlop Company built their factory at Kobe for manufacturing bicycle tyres. About the same time the manufacture of rubber shoes began to grow up, and this industry took over many of the small workplaces and part of the labour force formerly engaged in the Kobe match trade, then fallen on bad times. This branch of the rubber industry was typical of a number of trades that made their appearance in the decade before the First World War. These were industries producing small miscellaneous goods of a Western kind which lent themselves to manufacture in small workplaces. Japan possessed in her abundance of cheap, assiduous and docile labour a relative advantage over other nations in this type of industry, an advantage which she could not

[1] M. Suzuki, *op. cit.*, pp. 217 *et seq.* and *passim.*

claim in trades where for technical reasons efficient production required highly mechanized factories. Once the labour force had become sufficiently experienced and entrepreneurs had become alive to their advantages, these trades were bound to expand along with the rise among Japanese consumers of a demand for Western-style goods.

While some of these small-scale industries had slender connections with the traditional activities of the country, others gradually developed from roots that went far into the past. The pottery trade, for example, was of ancient origin, and was conducted by small potters in several regions, each with its own speciality. Some branches of it, such as the Kyoto trade, were concerned with high-grade wares made by artist-craftsmen; other branches were in the hands of peasants. These producers continued to manufacture goods for the home market throughout the new era. The potters of other districts, however, turned to the manufacture of foreign-style goods for export. In the main the organization of the industry changed but little, even in the export branch. The working potters generally produced their wares to the orders of local merchants, and these supplied the export houses which had originally furnished the patterns. At Seto, near Nagoya, an important centre of the trade in both Japanese and foreign-style goods, there were in 1893 434 master potters and decorators, 109 glost kilns and about 3,000 workers. Just before the First World War one or two fairly large factories were established in the foreign-style china trade; but these were exceptions to the prevailing industrial pattern. By 1914 there were no less than 5,540 workplaces engaged in pottery and china manufacture, and about a third of the output (in value) was exported. The lacquer-ware trade was another manufacture which continued to work according to the old methods but which developed new varieties of goods. In both of these industries the superb aesthetic traditions of the Japanese served them well.

Agriculture and the staple manufacturing industries, especially those modelled on the West or engaged in providing export goods, attract the imagination and have received most attention from Western writers. But we should gain a distorted view of the Japanese economy if we failed to observe another sector which was, and still is, exceedingly important, though difficult to measure. The Japanese, even today, preserve to a remarkable extent the habits of domestic life handed down from past times. They live in wooden houses of traditional design; their furniture, domestic utensils, and food are still in the main peculiar to themselves, although of course by no means unaffected by Western influences. Up to 1914 these influences on domestic life were slight. Then, and for many years afterwards, even the traditional national dress was commonly worn. Consequently, a great mass of trades existed to provide the goods and services of which there were no counterparts abroad. In every centre of population there were large numbers of people who prepared various kinds of Japanese food and who either sold their products in little shops attached to their houses or peddled them round the neighbourhood. In the same way, *geta* (wooden footwear) were then for the most part turned out by craftsmen who sold direct to local customers; while the coloured thongs which attached the *geta* to the feet were produced by domestic workers in their spare time. The Japanese, though their life has always been simple, demand a high standard of artistic merit in articles of everyday use. So not merely their furniture and ornaments, but even some of their common domestic utensils have to be made by craftsmen, and these can work most effectively in little domestic workshops. The very small producing units which, as we have seen, remained typical of much of the weaving trade, were well adapted to serving a market composed of consumers who insisted on individuality in the design of their dress materials. Finally, the building trade, in Japan as elsewhere, was conducted by small firms. These trades which catered for the home market accounted in the aggregate for a very large proportion of the industrial population. It is impossible to estimate numbers, because many of the industries could scarcely claim a separate identity. Some of them were in the hands of part-time workers whose main job was farming; others were not differentiated from the retail trade. The number of retail establishments was immense. Kaempfer in the eighteenth century had been impressed by the number of shops in Japan, and they certainly did not become less numerous in the new era. It would, however, be a mistake to think that all of them were small shops attached to dwelling-houses. We have referred to the large stores which had existed from the eighteenth century; many of these were reorganized and expanded after the Restoration. Notable among them was the old retail store of Mitsui, which, in 1904, was separated from the parent firm and became the famous Mitsukoshi Departmental Store.

Recent work on the development of the Japanese economy has thrown up some statistical estimates of rates of growth.[1] The gainfully occupied population in secondary industry is believed to have risen from 1·1 million persons in 1878-82 to 2·9 million at the turn of the century and to 3·9 million in 1908-12. The index of the real national income produced by secondary industry is estimated to have risen from 4·4 in 1878-82 (1928-32=100) to 15·7 in 1898-1903 to 30·7 in 1908-12. These estimates must all be treated with caution. The growth is obviously difficult to measure because the composition of the

[1] See especially K. Ohkawa, *op. cit.*, pp. 27, 245; also W. W. Lockwood, *op. cit.*, pp. 115, 137, 462.

industrial output was changing rapidly during the whole of the earlier period and because the output of the large small-scale sector was very difficult to ascertain. Certainly the development was rapid. Yet even in 1914 the total number of operatives in factories that employed five or more persons was only 950,000, of whom 560,000 were females. The large technical unit in industry was still exceptional.

3. *Transport*

Everywhere during the nineteenth century improvements in transport were the concomitant of industrialization, and the Japanese Government was fully alive to the necessity of effecting such improvements in its own country. In the early years of Meiji it was recognized that one of the chief obstacles to growth lay in the high cost of transport, and the removal of this obstacle by the construction of railways and roads, the introduction of wheeled vehicles and the development of coastal shipping services was a task to which governments and private persons soon directed their energies. Up to the early eighties the Government was responsible for nearly all railway construction. It was then joined in this enterprise by private firms, and during the next few decades a large expansion of the system took place. In 1906, when the railways were nationalized, the mileage was about 6,000; it rose to some 7,000 in 1913. The tonnage of freight traffic grew even more impressively. Between 1888 and 1910 it rose from 850,000 to over 40 million.[1]

The development of the shipping industry was on a corresponding scale. For shipping Japan was well favoured. Her traditions of seamanship, though deprived of full expression by the restrictions of the Tokugawa period, and her geographical position and structure were factors favourable to the development of a mercantile marine. Experience in operating ocean-going ships alone had to be acquired. To this end the Government set up in 1875 schools of navigation and marine engineering, and it engaged British experts to staff them. Foreign captains and officers also were taken into the service of the shipping firms. Until the end of the nineteenth century these foreigners formed a high proportion of the officers employed by the mercantile marine, and their numbers remained significant until 1914.[2] As with other industries, the Government chose to work out its policy through the medium of a few financial groups which it assisted and guided but did not directly control.

The history of the modern mercantile marine begins with the estab-

[1] W. W. Lockwood, *op. cit.*, p. 106.
[2] In 1895 about two-fifths of the masters, navigating officers and engineers employed by the NYK were foreigners. Even in 1910 more than a quarter of the masters were foreigners (*Golden Jubilee History of Nippon Yusen Kaisha*, p. 166).

lishment in 1870 of the Kaiso Kaisha (Transport Company) which owned vessels formerly belonging to a clan government and was capitalized jointly by the State and by private interests. In 1872 this company, after reorganization, began to operate a subsidized service between Tokyo and Osaka. Two years earlier a *samurai* named Iwasaki acquired three steamers, previously the property of his *daimyo*, and employed them in the coastal trade. In 1873 his business became known as the Mitsubishi Shokai, a name of significance in modern Japan. When the Government in 1874 needed ships in connection with the expedition to Formosa, it bought them from abroad and entrusted them for operation to Mitsubishi which was given charge of military transport. By 1875 Mitsubishi, having absorbed the Kaiso Kaisha, owned 37 vessels with a tonnage of 23,000. It then founded a marine school, which received a Government subsidy, and it started a service to Shanghai. During the Satsuma Rebellion of 1877 Mitsubishi ships were again required for military transport, and the concern was able to extend the size of its fleet through official financial assistance. In 1879 its ships began to run to Hong Kong, and in 1881 to Vladivostock. Mitsubishi's shipping activities in this decade were thus closely bound up with its associations with the Government.

Other small concerns were started after 1877, also with Government aid, and these amalgamated to form the Kyodo Unyu Kaisha (United Transport Company) in 1882. Keen competition appeared between Mitsubishi and this new company in the coastal trade during the early eighties, and pressure from the Government led to their amalgamation in 1885 and to the formation of what has since become the chief Japanese shipping line, the Nippon Yusen Kaisha. At the beginning of its career the new company had fifty-eight ships and a total tonnage of 65,000, apart from sailing ships. Close associations with the Government were maintained. The State guaranteed dividends of 8 per cent on the company's capital for fifteen years, and it also supervised its business and designated routes on which its ships were to run. In the meantime a number of small shipowners engaged in the coastal trade from Osaka joined together to form the Osaka Shosen Kaisha (1883), which from this time constituted the second largest shipping company.

During the eighties Japanese ships were engaged merely in coastal trading or in services to the China coast. In the early nineties they began to run to Hawaii. Then, with the outbreak of the Sino-Japanese War, new carrying-capacity was needed, and many new ships were added to the mercantile marine. After the war a new era in Japanese shipping began. Governmental policy was crystallized in the Navigation Subsidy Act of 1896, under which State subsidies were granted to Japanese shipowners on ships of 1,000 tons and over and of ten knots and upwards employed in foreign trade.[1] As a result of this encouragement, the shipping companies began to acquire larger ships and to extend their operations to distant parts of the world. The NYK started its services to Europe, Australia and North America before the end of the century; and, as the Shimo-noseki Treaty gave Japan navigation rights in Chinese waters (especially on the Yangtse), several companies began to operate services there.

The Russo-Japanese War proved another starting-point for a rapid advance in tonnage, as ships had to be bought for military transport. After the war these ships were employed on new routes, and several new companies were formed. For instance, the OSK started its Takoma service in 1910; the Nanyo Yusen Kaisha was founded to trade with Java and the South Seas; and new services were operated to Dairen, Saghalien and other parts of North Asia. In 1909 the Government replaced the legislation of 1896 and 1899 by a new Act which empowered it to select and to subsidize mail steamship routes. The years immediately preceding the First World War saw the amalgamation of several concerns. In 1907 a number of companies operating services in Chinese waters formed a new concern, the Nisshin Kisen Kaisha, which then took charge of this section of their interests, and in 1911 the Chosen Kisen Kaisha was established in the same way for the Korean service. The rise in the importance of Japanese shipping is shown by the growth in the proportion of the country's foreign trade carried by it. In 1893 about 14 per cent of the ships entering the ports were Japanese, and these carried only 7 per cent of the country's exports and under 9 per cent of her imports. By 1903 the proportions had risen to 38 per cent, 40 per cent and 34 per cent, and by 1913 to 51 per cent, 52 per cent and 47 per cent. In shipping as in most of the modern industries it was only after the middle nineties that Japan began to achieve a position of any importance, but once progress had begun it was extremely rapid.

MERCANTILE MARINE

	Steamships[2] (in thousand gross tons)	Sailing Ships (in thousand tons)
1873	26	8
1894	169	45
1904	797	327
1913	1,514	828

[1] The annual amount of subsidy paid to Japanese shipowners rose from about 1 million yen before 1896 to nearly 6 million yen in 1899-1900. The Act was amended in 1899; see, *supra*, p. 82.

[2] Twenty gross tons and over.

4. *Foreign Trade*

The broad changes in Japan's foreign trade between 1881 and 1913, on which the discussion of industrial development has already thrown some light, are shown in Tables XXII, XXIV and XXVII of Appendix B. The trade, it will be seen, was of little significance until the later nineties, but from then on it grew fast, and by 1913 could be considered substantial. The alterations in the value of the monetary unit in which the trade is measured tend to exaggerate the rise which occurred; but estimates suggest that there was a tenfold increase in volume during these thirty years. In the first part of the period, from 1881 to 1893, almost every year showed a favourable trade balance; but after the Sino-Japanese War of 1894-95 there were heavy imports of capital and a large adverse balance in the visible trade.

The industrialization of the country, which at the beginning of this era was almost wholly agricultural, naturally affected the composition of the foreign trade. On the import side there was a decrease in the importance of finished manufactured goods and among the exports a decline in the importance of foodstuffs and raw materials. Throughout the period the chief exports consisted of semi-manufactured commodities and the proportion of these goods to the total tended to increase. These changes require a more detailed examination. In the early eighties the three major exports consisted of raw silk (a semi-manufactured commodity), tea and rice, and these together accounted for nearly two-thirds of the total. Raw silk was by far the most important of them, and tea came second. The few manufactured exports still consisted, as they had done in earlier decades, of pottery and other products of the old domestic trades, and there was in addition a small trade in copper, an export of long standing. Little alteration in the structure of the export trade occurred in the next decade and a half. By 1894 the share taken by raw silk had slightly increased, while that of rice and tea had diminished. The importance of copper had risen, and a new trade had developed in coal. These agricultural and mineral products (raw silk, tea, rice, copper and coal) in 1894 accounted for well over three-fifths of the total exports. A few additional manufactured goods had by this time entered the export list. The most important of these was silk piece-goods, while an export of matches had also been developed. The former trade was the result of the successful adaptation of an ancient Japanese industry to the requirements of foreign (chiefly American) markets; the latter was a Western industry for which Japan's ample supplies of cheap unskilled labour suited her. In 1894 Japan's exports still depended mainly on her native raw materials and her traditional small-scale industries.

In the next few years the effects of industrialization began to reveal themselves. A large new trade in cotton yarn was built up and a smaller export of cotton piece-goods appeared. Silk piece-goods continued to grow in importance, and in 1900 manufactured textiles (including cotton yarn) were responsible for 22 per cent of the total exports. With this enlargement in the scope of the export trade, the share taken by raw silk declined, in spite of a considerable absolute increase. The importance of copper and coal was maintained; while the agricultural exports, tea and rice, suffered a relative decline.

Between 1900 and 1913 there was a steep rise in exports, attributable mainly to the expansion of trade in raw silk, silk piece-goods and cotton yarn and piece-goods. On the eve of the First World War these four commodities accounted for well over half the total exports; raw silk alone provided 30 per cent. The specialization on textiles or textile materials which was to be the most prominent feature of Japan's trade for the next two decades had thus come into being. Exports of mineral and agricultural products, which had been so important in the nineteenth century, had by this time fallen away.

The import trade underwent corresponding changes. In the early eighties nearly half the imports consisted of manufactured goods, and there were few industrial raw materials. By 1913 the finished manufactured imports had fallen to under a fifth of the total trade, while over a third consisted of raw materials and about a sixth of semi-manufactured goods. Perhaps the most surprising feature of the trade was that in spite of the large growth in the population, food and drink imports formed a smaller proportion of the total in the years just before the First World War than they did in the early eighties. This demonstrates the success of Japan in raising her food production from agriculture and fisheries to supply her growing needs. A glance at the trade in particular commodities is illuminating. In 1881 imports of cotton yarn accounted for about a quarter of the total, and imports of cotton yarn and of cotton and woollen piece-goods for about three-fifths. The other chief imports were sugar, mineral oil, and iron and steel products. By 1894 the structure to the trade was already changing, for a large import of raw cotton had appeared and machinery, tools, instruments and vehicles occupied a prominent place. Textile imports had suffered a relative decline, and cotton yarn and piece-goods and woollen piece-goods by this time accounted for under a fifth of the total. Among the foodstuffs sugar retained its importance (with about 12 per cent of the total), and imports of rice began to exceed exports. These tendencies continued during the later nineties and into the new century. By 1913 nearly a third of the imports were of raw cotton, and imports of other textile materials, such as wool, had also achieved some significance. Iron and steel and other metals had a larger share of the trade than in 1900 and 1894, and the importance of machinery and tools had risen. On the other hand, imports of cotton yarn and textile piece-goods had by this time become very small. These changes were symptomatic of a country that had created flourishing textile industries and was rapidly building up its equipment for its manufacturing trades as a whole.

Although foreign technical experts had made an important contribution to the development of the Japanese economy, entrepreneurial initiative in *industry* came almost entirely from native sources. It was otherwise with Japan's international trade. From the time of the opening of the country until the later years of the nineteenth century most of the import and export trade was in the hands of foreign merchants. This was not surprising. The old Japanese business houses had long been skilled in the conduct of domestic commerce, but they lacked experience in the technique of international trade and they had no acquaintance with foreign markets and sources of supply. Even when this knowledge was acquired, the goodwill enjoyed by the foreign houses among customers and suppliers overseas preserved their dominance. As a British consular report stated in 1897: 'The trade of Japan would never have reached its present proportions had it not been for foreign resident merchants; and what is true of the past will remain true for a considerable time to come until the Japanese obtain the knowledge and foresight in business transactions which can only be acquired by experience, and succeed in inspiring the commercial world with confidence. Their credit at present is not sufficiently high for success in direct dealings with foreign countries ... no foreign bank would buy a bill drawn on a Japanese firm unless the firm had previously opened credit, and before it could do so it would have to be guaranteed by a Japanese bank of good standing.'[1]

Although the Japanese had to accept the predominance of the foreigner in this business it was not long before they ventured to participate. Mitsui who in Tokugawa times had set up agencies at Nagasaki for buying goods from the Dutch were among the first to try their hand. In 1876 they founded the famous Mitsui Bussan Kaisha, which soon obtained a share in raw silk exports. Several other concerns followed this example, but for many years it was only in trade with China that Japanese merchants made much headway. In 1887, so it was estimated, nearly nine-tenths of the foreign trade was handled by foreign merchants. During the next decade the Japanese had more successes. Mitsui began to handle the import of Indian cotton and established a branch at Bombay. They developed their silk trade and undertook the import of sugar from Java. By 1900 the foreigners' share in the trade was falling rapidly. The tendency was strengthened by changes in the structure of the trade.

[1] *British Consular Reports*, Miscellaneous Series, No. 440, 1897; on this subject, see G. C. Allen and A. G. Donnithorne, *op. cit.*, pp. 197-8.

Japanese houses obtained a large share in the new export of cotton goods and in the rapidly increasing import trade in raw cotton. At the same time the growing power of the *zaibatsu,* with their wide range of integrated interests, presented the foreigner with formidable competition. Gradually, therefore, the part of the Western merchant became confined to dealings in specialities and 'technical' imports. Most of the bulk good trade was lost to them. The process, however, was not completed until well after the First World War, and as late as the thirties foreign merchants took a notable part in the expansion of Japan's exports of miscellaneous manufactured goods.

Even in the early years of the present century, European observers were still sceptical of Japan's capacity for industrial expansion, and most of them thought little of her chances of ever competing effectively with other countries in the world markets for manufactured goods. A typical opinion was that of a French observer 'En somme il faut dire . . . que l'industrie japonaise semble incapable d'entrer en concurrence sérieuse, sur les marchés européens, avec nos usines. Le Japon n'a qu'un moyen de faire quelque chose, c'est de réserver pour les marchés d'Europe et d'Amérique les productions spéciales dans lesquelles il excelle, telles que les soieries, les objets d'art, c'est à dire les articles dont la confection dérive du travail manuel; . . . il ne doit guère songer à lutter avec les nations européennes en ce qui concerne les objets manufacturés même avec les avantages de main d'œuvre à bon marché . . . . Au point de vue industriel ,il ne fera toujours que de mauvaises contrefaçons des produits européens dignes au plus, par leur bas prix, d'approvisionner les marchés d'Extrême-Asie.'[1] In spite of the great expansion that had occurred in the preceding forty years, this was not an unreasonable judgment to make in 1905, or even in 1913; for Japan's export trade was highly specialized to raw silk, which she supplied to the United States, and relatively small quantities of cotton goods which she sent mainly to China. But the qualification which this commentator had thought fit to introduce in the last sentence of the quotation might have led him to further reflection. He might have considered that the development of the natural resources of East Asia and the South Seas—and indeed of other raw material producing areas—might well present great opportunities to a country that was capable of supplying the vast and still impoverished population of those regions with cheap manufactured goods, even if the quality of those goods might not always compare favourably with that of similar products of Western industry.

[1] H. Dumolard, *Le Japon, politique, économique et social* (1905), p. 163.

CHAPTER VI

THE FIRST WORLD WAR AND
THE POST-WAR DECADE

The Meiji era coincided with the period in which Japan laid the economic foundations of a modern State. The accession of the new Emperor, Taisho, came only two years before the outbreak of the World War of 1914-18, which marked for Japan, as for other countries, a great dividing line in economic history. During the whole of the Taisho era, which ended in 1926, Japan was concerned with urgent financial, industrial and social problems which were the result of the impact of the war on an economy which for other reasons was in a stage of rapid growth and change. Shortly after the end of that era, just when the problems of adjustment seemed to be approaching solution, Japan was overwhelmed by the world depression of 1930-31, and her efforts to free herself from its effects brought about profound modifications in economic policy and in the trend of industrial development. Let us first survey briefly the proximate effects of the First World War on Japan. Then we can pass to a more detailed study of her financial, industrial and commercial history during the twenties.

The immediate effect of the war was to accentuate the financial difficulties with which Japan was already struggling; for it not merely interrupted some of her more important channels of trade but also disorganized her arrangements for financial settlements through London. In the early months of 1915, however, it became clear that the country was on the threshold of a period of unexampled prosperity. Markets, especially Oriental markets, were thrown open to her through the inability of the former suppliers to meet current demands; contracts for munitions began to be placed with Japanese manufacturers by Allied Governments; and there arose a strong demand for Japanese shipping. These conditions persisted until the end of the war; indeed, the industrial boom lasted until the break in the spring of 1920. Important new enterprises were established in many branches of industry; existing enterprises were enlarged; and between 1914 and 1919 the number of workers in factories that employed 5 persons and over grew from 948,000 to 1,612,000.[1] Some details of this industrial expansion will be given in the next chapter,

[1] *Factory Statistics*, issued by the Department of Commerce and Industry. The figures are for the end of the year in each case.

G

and here attention will be concentrated on developments in finance and foreign trade.

The buoyant demand for Japan's goods, at a time when she could not secure equivalent imports, led to the appearance of an impressively large export surplus. Whereas in 1911-14 the average annual excess of imports over exports amounted to 65 million yen, in 1915-18 the annual excess of exports averaged 352 million yen. In value the exports of 1918 were three times those of 1913; in volume it has been estimated that they were 47 per cent greater. At the same time, her invisible exports greatly expanded. In 1914 her steamship tonnage stood at $1\frac{1}{2}$ million; in 1918 she had over 3 million tons. Japan's net income from freights rose from under 40 million yen in 1914 to over 450 million yen in 1918. Even in 1919, when there was a return to a small import surplus in her visible trade, the shipping boom continued. The result has been summed up by saying that Japan's net credits on international account from trade and services aggregated over 3,000 million yen between 1914 and 1919. This was 1,000 million yen more than her total foreign indebtedness in 1913 and about 1,700 million yen more than her net foreign indebtedness at that time.

The financial circumstances attending such a complete and rapid transformation are interesting in themselves, besides being of great significance for an understanding of the subsequent development of Japan's economy. It might have been expected that the huge surplus earned by Japan on income account would have been applied to the redemption of her outstanding foreign debt, to profitable foreign investment, and to the strengthening of her gold reserves. The first expedient was attempted only on a small scale, partly because the Government objected to issuing domestic loans for this purpose, and partly because Japanese securities rose in price during the war. The second expedient was tried fairly extensively, but very unwisely. Of the total of over 1,000 million yen of foreign investment made during this period, more than half was in short-dated securities issued by Allied Governments. None of these gave rise to a permanent source of foreign income, since they were redeemed soon after the war, with the exception of a loan to the Czarist Government which was repudiated. Other very large loans were made to the Chinese local and provincial governments for political reasons, notably the Nishihara loans to the Anfu 'war-lords'; and most of these were never repaid. Thus, Japan's war-time incursions into the field of long-term foreign investment were extremely unfortunate; even so, that investment represented but a small part of the surplus which she accumulated.

The result was that in the early years of the war Japan imported gold on a large scale, and the Bank of Japan's gold reserves held in Japan, together with the gold holdings of the Government in Japan, increased very substantially. After the United States imposed her embargo on gold in September 1917, however, the balance of indebtedness to Japan could not be settled by gold movements, and there was a heavy accumulation of funds in New York. Even before the war, as was described in Chapter III, it was customary for the Government and the Bank of Japan to hold balances abroad (mainly in London), and the foreign holdings of the latter counted as part of the gold reserve against the note issue. These foreign balances were now swollen enormously. By December 1919 they reached 1,343 million yen, compared with 213 million yen before the war. After the United States lifted the gold embargo (in May 1919) there was a resumption of gold imports, but at the end of 1920 the foreign balances were still nearly 1,100 million yen. The results of war-time financial operations may be conveniently summarized in the following table—

GOLD RESERVES OF BANK OF JAPAN AND JAPANESE GOVERNMENT

(in million yen)

Date	Held at Home	Held Abroad	Total
December 1914	129	213	342
December 1920	1,116	1,062	2,178

The financial machinery of Japan was incapable of dealing successfully with the profound changes in her international trading position. Before the war Japan's international accounts had been mainly settled through London,[1] and the financial experience and resources of that centre were denied to her at a moment of unexampled financial strain. The financing of foreign trade in Japan, as we have seen, was largely in the hands of a specialized exchange bank, the Yokohama Specie Bank. In the absence of a discount market and of the bank acceptance, the funds of the ordinary banks were not available for the financing of foreign trade. Consequently, the Yokohama Specie Bank was left to rely on its own resources and on borrowings from the Bank of Japan, which again had established no close connections with the ordinary banks. After the American gold embargo had been imposed, the Yokohama Specie Bank could not transmit the proceeds of its export bills to Japan, and it could find funds to take up the growing offerings of those bills only by selling its foreign holdings to the central bank or the Government and by borrowing from the central bank. It was by these processes that the foreign holdings of the Bank of Japan were augmented and that the

[1] Practically all export bills were sent to London for discount.

Bank's loans to the exchange banks grew from 20 million yen in December 1915 to 440 million yen in June 1918. These operations were accompanied by a large increase in the Bank's note issue, which rose from 385 million yen in December 1914 to 1,555 million yen in December 1919, and by a steep rise in prices; in March 1920 the wholesale price index reached 322 (1913=100).[1] The rise in prices stimulated industrial activity, but at the same time provoked social unrest; for the profit-inflation was accompanied by a fall of real wages, in spite of a rise in money wages. The famous 'rice riots' of 1919 showed how incensed the urban population had become because of the fall in its standard of life. During the war, then, Japan had succeeded in making a substantial economic advance, and had converted herself from a debtor to a creditor country; but her cost and price structure had been distorted and the war had thrown into relief serious weaknesses in her financial organization.

The post-war boom collapsed in Japan in March 1920. The wholesale price index fell from 322 in that month to 190 in April 1921. The collapse was particularly pronounced in raw silk and rice prices, and the Government supported a silk valorization scheme and introduced the Rice Control Act in an effort to arrest the decline. By 1922 Japan was climbing out of the depression, although certain of her industries, particularly those which had expanded very quickly as a result of the war-time demands, failed to recover; notably, shipbuilding and coal-mining. In the sphere of foreign trade, the immediate post-war years saw the reappearance of an import surplus. In 1919 and 1920, while exports were practically stationary, imports grew very fast, and in the next two years declined more slowly than exports. For the period 1919-22 the aggregate excess of imports amounted to 824 million yen, and the net favourable balance on invisible items, which had grown so large during the war, also greatly diminished.

The reasons for the growth of this unfavourable balance deserve examination. In the first place, it is clear that post-war deflation in Japan was not carried as far as in the main financial centres abroad. After the steep fall in Japanese prices during the first year of the depression, there was a slight up-turn, in contrast to the movements in England and the United States where the decline went further, and by August 1923 Japanese prices appeared to be out of line with those abroad. The table on p. 101 demonstrates this.

The causes of this failure to carry deflation as far as it had gone in other countries throw light on certain characteristics of Japan's economy as a whole. The expansion of business during the war and the post-war boom had been made possible by the heavy extension of credit on the part of the ordinary banks of the country. The

---

[1] This is the Bank of Japan's Wholesale Price Index, 1900=100, converted from the original base. See Appendix B, Table XXX.

collapse of the boom in 1920 meant the 'freezing' of many of these advances, and further deflation would have increased the crop of industrial and banking failures to the point of economic disaster. The Government, reluctant to push things through to a crisis, preferred to temporize rather than to incur the social consequences of a violent, deliberate deflation. Moreover, it had to take account not merely of the general public reaction to such a policy, but also of the influence of powerful organized groups. The *zaibatsu*, in particular, who controlled some of the chief ordinary banks, were unlikely to look with favour on a policy which would be detrimental to their far greater industrial interests. In other words, the close links between industry and banking in Japan meant that economic policy was unlikely to be determined by technical financial considerations.

INDEX NUMBERS OF WHOLESALE PRICES [1]

Date	Japan (Bank of Japan)	United Kingdom (Sauerbeck-Statist)	United States (Bureau of Labour)
March 1920	322	307	227
April 1921	190	199	142
December 1921	209	157	133
December 1922	183	152	144
August 1923	190	147	140

Even had the Government attempted to enforce a policy of deflation, it is doubtful if there existed on that occasion the means for carrying it out. It has already been shown that the Bank of Japan had little control over the banking system of the country, and that its bank rate was ineffective in its influence on the credit policy of the numerous ordinary banks. But, while it could not check their rashness during the boom, it was required to make large advances to them on several occasions after 1920 in order to avoid a panic. As, at the same time, the Government was giving financial support to schemes for checking the slump in rice and silk prices, and as this meant an increase in borrowing, the deflation was arrested at an early stage. Yet, although Japanese prices did not fall so far as British and American prices in the period from 1920 to 1923, the exchange value of the yen was maintained in the neighbourhood of dollar parity. This was achieved through the re-sale by the Government of the foreign balances accumulated during the war to the exchange banks which were thus enabled to meet their import bills. Thus,

[1] The price indices have been converted to a common base year; 1913 = 100.

from 1921 to the end of 1923 the yen was over-valued on the exchanges, and it was because of this that the import surplus became so large. The policy came to an end with the earthquake of 1923, for that disaster necessitated the import of huge quantities of reconstruction materials, and it so seriously reduced the foreign balances that further support of the exchange became impracticable. The yen was allowed to fall, and until the end of 1925 it remained almost 20 per cent depreciated. The decline in the exchange was accompanied by a rise in exports, and in 1925 these attained a level which was not reached again for ten years.

Meanwhile the earthquake led to a further period of inflationary finance. The Bank of Japan adopted an easy credit policy and, in order to relieve financial institutions whose loans had become frozen as a result of the earthquake, it was authorized to discount specified bills (Earthquake Bills) under a Government guarantee against loss up to 100 million yen. Further, the Industrial Bank of Japan and the Hypothec Bank made loans on easy terms to facilitate reconstruction. Government expenditure also increased as a result of the earthquake, and this was financed mainly by borrowing. There was, moreover, at this time a growth in local and colonial government indebtedness for reconstruction and development purposes, and public utility companies raised large amounts of new capital. Some of the borrowing was in foreign capital markets. The consequence was a 'reconstruction boom'. The whole sale price index, which had stood at 190 in August 1923, rose to 214 at the end of 1924, but afterwards fell back a little.

The Government was disquieted. It was anxious to restore financial stability and, after the British return to the gold standard in 1925, it began to take measures which were believed to herald the removal of the embargo on gold exports. Economies were effected in expenditure, and new taxes imposed with a view to balancing the budget. Substantial shipments of gold from Japan were permitted in the autumn of 1925, and this led to bull speculation in the yen which carried it by the later months of 1926 to the neighbourhood of par. The rise in the exchange led to a fall in exports and disorganized particularly the raw-silk producers. Prices fell steadily.[1] These conditions intensified the strain on the Japanese banks, burdened as they were with 'frozen' advances. In the spring of 1927 discussions in the Diet on the question of postponing the settlement of the Earthquake Bills revealed the unsoundness of many financial institutions. A crisis developed during which the Bank of Taiwan, the 15th Bank (the Peers' Bank, one of the largest ordinary banks in Japan) and thirty-four others closed their doors. A moratorium had to be proclaimed, and the Government authorized the central bank to give

[1] Wholesale prices fell from 200 in October 1925 to 170 in December 1926.

accommodation to other banks, including the Bank of Taiwan,[1] under an official guarantee of 700 million yen. These measures brought the crisis to an end; but the effect of it was to postpone the return to the gold standard and the deflation that was necessary before a return could be contemplated.

Nevertheless the financial crisis of 1927 was of great importance for the future economic development of Japan. For reasons that have already been described, the liquidation of unsound undertakings which owed their rise to the war-time boom, and the adaptation of the economy as a whole to peace-time conditions of trade had not occurred on the same scale in Japan as in other industrial countries during the early post-war years. In the crisis of 1927 this readjustment was at last achieved. Unsound industrial and trading concerns were weeded out, or passed, after decapitalization, under new and more efficient control; many of the Suzuki interests, for instance, passed to Mitsui. The same is true of the banking system. The eighteen months after June 1927 were a period of consolidation during which the number of ordinary banks was reduced from 1,359 to 1,030. This period saw the beginning of efforts to improve efficiency in the textile industries which were later to bear fruit.

When the Minseito party returned to office in the summer of 1929 they began to prepare for a removal of the gold embargo.[2] The Finance Minister, Mr J. Inouye, had long advocated a policy of balanced budgets and free gold movements. He recorded his views on Japanese financial policy in a book which has been translated into English[3] and reveals a mind firmly convinced of the correctness of what was then regarded as 'orthodox' financial policy. Like the old-fashioned Liberal finance ministers, he believed that it was of first-rate importance that a country should honour its financial obligations, should preserve stability in its exchanges, and should adhere to an international gold standard for reasons of national prestige as well as of convenience. Mr Inouye had convinced his colleagues and the business world that exchange fluctuations were more detrimental to Japan's future development than any temporary inconveniences that might attend a return to the gold standard. He aimed at balancing the budget without resort to loans, and in 1929 the moment

---

[1] The Bank of Taiwan had lent heavily to Suzuki, a large Japanese concern engaged, *inter alia*, in the sugar industry. This bank had borrowed from other banks, and from the Bank of Japan, in order to maintain solvency, but when the Bank of Japan refused to continue advances without a Government guarantee, it failed.

[2] The two chief political parties at this time were the Minseito and the Seiyukai. The Minseito had developed from the older Kenseikai. See R. K. Reischauer, *Japan: Government—Politics*, especially Chap. VI, for an excellent short description of the political system.

[3] *Problems of the Japanese Exchange, 1914-1926.*

seemed propitious. 'American prosperity' was causing an exceptionally rapid expansion in the demand for raw silk; India was buying increased quantities of Japanese cottons; and the general buoyancy of world trade was having its influence on other Japanese exporting industries and on the mercantile marine. (In 1929 the balance of payments on current account appears to have been favourable for the first time since 1919.) The announcement in June 1929 of the new Government's policy led to a movement of short funds into Japan and a sharp rise in the exchange. The gold embargo was lifted in January 1930.

No more unfortunate moment could have been chosen for the operation of this new policy. It is generally recognized that Japanese prices before 1929 were too high in relation to American prices to make it possible for her to maintain dollar parity without exporting gold or borrowing abroad. Thus, even had the world prosperity continued after 1929, it is likely that some fall of domestic prices would have been necessary in order to maintain the yen at par. This fall would have placed a strain on the economic system, since price- and cost-relations had for a long period been consolidated at a level well above that in the rest of the world. The onset of the depression, just when the yen had been restored to par, and the consequent heavy fall in world prices, greatly increased the difficulties of adjustment. The movements of Japanese prices during this period are given in the table on page 105, which also shows the movements in American prices. It will be seen that the decline in the former was no less than 35 per cent, compared with the American decline of 27 per cent.

It was thought by some Japanese that this steep fall in their prices was an indication that their country's price structure had been adjusted to the new conditions; but they overlooked the lamentable social consequences of the decline and had no vision of the political upheaval that was to be the heir of the depression. Moreover, the rise in the exchange during the latter half of 1929 had been associated with an inward movement of funds. Some of these were withdrawn when the gold embargo was lifted, and in the course of 1931 the Bank lost 260 million yen from its gold reserve, almost a quarter of it.

The chief source of the economic difficulties which now faced Japan was the fall in raw silk prices that accompanied the collapse of 'American prosperity'. During 1930 raw silk prices declined by 50 per cent, and silk exports in that year were only 53 per cent in value (though 82 per cent in weight) of those of 1929. Exports of cotton goods also fell off, and the export trade as a whole was some 27 per cent less than in the previous year. The slump struck a serious blow at one of the largest and most vulnerable sections of the

Japanese economy, the peasant farmers. The fall in silk prices ruined many of these farmers, while the decline in the cotton trade reduced the opportunities for employment offered to their daughters by the textile mills. In 1931 the situation deteriorated. Silk prices and the value of silk exports declined further, and exports of manufactured

INDEX NUMBERS OF WHOLESALE PRICES

(1913 = 100)

	Japan (Bank of Japan)	United States (Bureau of Labour)
April 1929	170	139
December 1929	155	135
December 1930	122	112
October 1931	110	101

goods met with additional obstacles from the higher Indian tariff and from a Chinese boycott. For some years, moreover, the price of rice had been low because of a series of good harvests, and in 1930 the crops were exceptionally heavy both in Japan Proper and in Korea. The price of rice in Tokyo, which had averaged 29 yen a koku during 1929 fell to 17 yen in November 1930, and although in 1931 the harvest was small, prices showed little recovery. The peasantry faced ruin.

The Government had to modify its 'no loan' policy to meet the distress in agricultural areas. In the spring of 1930 it launched a silk valorization scheme; it incurred additional expenditure for relief works; and it disbursed large sums as loans to the distressed classes of producers. Yet it still persisted in its efforts to carry through deflation. It set up elaborate machinery for encouraging rationalization and technical improvements in industry; and it proposed to reduce a number of industrial subsidies. In the summer of 1931 Mr Inouye pressed for a lowering of military and naval expenditure, as this alone could enable him to reduce substantially his budgetary deficit. The proposal met with bitter opposition from the military groups, and from that moment the Government was doomed. During the twenties the militarists had been losing their political influence, and power had been passing to the commercial classes and the Diet. The collapse of 'American prosperity' discredited these new leaders and, indeed, parliamentary government as a whole. The unrest of the peasantry was communicated to the Army, which was recruited largely from that source, and the military made plans to re-assert their authority. In the meantime the turn of events was leading speculators to buy dollars in anticipation of the fall in the yen, and gold shipments continued on a large scale. The final blow was given when Great Britain left gold. Japan was now exposed to renewed British competition both in manufactured exports and in the carrying trade, while her banks sustained losses through the depreciation of their funds in London. When the Army launched itself, almost at the same time, on its Manchurian campaign, the end was very near. The flight from the yen proceeded still faster, and by the end of 1931 the gold reserves of the Bank of Japan were only 470 million yen compared with 1,072 million yen two years before. In December the Government fell and the embargo on gold exports was re-imposed. This was the end of the deflationary policy, and indeed of a decade of uncertain and, on the whole, mistaken, financial policy. Like many other countries, Japan had been torn between a desire to return to 'orthodox' finance and a desire to avoid the measures that were its logical consequence. She was able for a time to avoid the results of her inconsistent policy because of the reserves which she had accumulated during the war. When she had reached the point of being willing to accept the logic of her choice it was too late.

It is easy for the critic to argue, in the light of later events, that she should have invested her reserves accumulated during the war, and that she should have allowed the yen to fall to its 'natural' level in the early twenties. It is also easy for him to claim that it was foolish for her to return to gold when she did, and at the pre-war dollar parity. But that those who were responsible for the deflationary policies of 1926 and 1929 were entirely mistaken in their efforts is not beyond question. For one result was certainly to stimulate improvements in manufacturing methods; and on this, in part, was based the striking industrial advance of Japan in the next decade. A final judgment, however, must take into account the political effects of economic policy, and this is no place to consider how far the transference of power to the barbarous elements in the Japanese governing classes was dependent on the consequences of the economic policy just examined, nor, indeed, how far those consequences could have been avoided in the existing economic situation in the outside world.

The financial difficulties of the twenties revealed deficiencies in the banking system and led to some important modifications. During this period large numbers of the smaller banks failed, especially after the financial crisis of 1927, or were absorbed by the larger banks. A revision of the banking law which took effect in 1928 was partly responsible for the amalgamations. The capital requirement of banks in Tokyo and Osaka was raised to 2 million yen and of other banks to 1 million yen—double the previous requirement—and the Government's power of inspection was strengthened. The result was that the number of banks declined from 2,285 in 1918 to 913 in 1930, and outside the special banks, a high proportion of the total business came to be conducted by a very few great banks working with a number of branches. Thus the 'big five' banks (Mitsui, Mitsubishi, Dai-ichi, Sumitomo and Yasuda) held by the end of 1928 26 per cent of all deposits, or 34 per cent of the deposits of the ordinary banks. If to the deposits of the 'big five' are added the deposits of the nine next largest ordinary banks, the proportion of all ordinary bank deposits held by this group of fourteen banks was 55 per cent. It should be observed that four out of the five greatest banks were controlled by the *zaibatsu*, whose financial power was greatly increased by this process of consolidation.

While these large banks were engaged to some extent in commercial banking, as it is understood in the West, the smaller banks— chiefly country banks—were concerned with mortgages and industrial and agricultural financing. This brought them within the sphere for which certain of the special banks, and in particular the Industrial Bank of Japan, had been designed. Frequent failures attended concentration upon this hazardous form of business for which they were generally ill-equipped. Even among the large banks, business was very different in character from that of the great English joint stock banks. A cheque currency developed slowly in Japan, and the greater part of the advances of the banks took the form not of overdrafts but of loans, against promissory notes, on the security of stocks or the properties of the borrowing concerns. The shortage of first-rate marketable shares or bonds that might serve as security for loans persisted, largely because of the concentration of the chief business undertakings in the hands of the *zaibatsu* which had little to do with the security market. Further, efforts that were made to develop the bank acceptance and a discount market shortly after the First World War ended in failure. The banks could not dispose of their 'call funds' to the bill market, which, indeed, in the absence of bank acceptances and Treasury Bills, hardly existed. So most of these funds, as previously, flowed to the special banks, especially the Yokohama Specie Bank, while certain of the 'big five' began to take part directly in foreign exchange business. Thus the assets of the ordinary banks consisted mainly of promissory notes, backed by collateral not easily realizable, loans to special banks, advances on mortgages of land and buildings, and foreign bills which they had little chance of re-discounting.[1] The liabilities side of their accounts were likewise in sharp contrast to that of ordinary commercial banks in Western countries. A high proportion of their deposits consisted of fixed deposits, to be withdrawn at long notice.

The special banks naturally declined in importance with the development of the private banks, but the absolute volume of their business nevertheless extended considerably. The Hypothec Bank,

[1] In the years 1928-30 over a quarter of the loans of the ordinary banks were made on the security of land and buildings.

which specialized on granting long-term loans largely to agriculturists and to small country manufacturers on the security of immoveable property, raised the amount of its loans of that character by two and a half times between 1921 and 1931. It played an important part in relieving the difficulties of the small country banks during the crisis of 1927. The process of banking consolidation affected this field of finance also; for after 1921 the Hypothec Bank began to absorb the prefectural Agricultural and Industrial Banks and to operate them as its branches.

The Industrial Bank of Japan's business underwent some important changes. It was first established to make long-terms loans to industry on the security of moveable property, and it also played an important part in introducing foreign capital into Japan.[1] During and after the First World War it became an agent for Japanese investment in China and the South Seas, and it co-operated with the *zaibatsu* in investing in continental and other enterprises deemed to be of national importance. Some of this continental investment was unprofitable, and was inspired largely by political motives. Up to 1927 it does not seem that the Industrial Bank did much to help smaller industrial enterprises in Japan; for the greater part of its loans and investments were in large concerns, many of them of a public and semi-public character. After the financial crisis of 1927, however, it adopted a policy of extending help to smaller borrowers and obtained additional funds for this purpose from the Treasury Deposits Bureau.

In spite of the development of foreign exchange business by certain of the ordinary banks, the Yokohama Specie Bank continued to be responsible for the financing of the greater part of Japan's foreign trade, although in the import trade the Japanese branches of foreign banks still remained important. The Specie Bank became, after the failure of the Taiwan Bank in 1927, about the only market for call loans available to the ordinary banks, and in acquiring the resources for its operations it relied heavily on advances from the Bank of Japan or on the rediscounting of its bills with that institution. As the ordinary banks did not rediscount with the central bank, except in times of financial emergency, the central bank's holdings of foreign bills, which formed at this time a considerable proportion of its assets, came almost entirely from the Yokohama Specie Bank. Thus the Yokohama Specie Bank constituted almost the sole link connect-

[1] To a very large extent Japan financed her industrial expansion out of her own savings. But foreign loans were of critical importance in two periods—in the first decade of the present century when she needed capital for armaments and territorial expansion as well as for rapid industrial development, and in the twenties when capital was required for reconstruction after the Great Earthquake and for electric power development. On this question, see G. C. Allen and A. G. Donnithorne, *op. cit.*, pp. 232-7 and 264.

ing the Bank of Japan with the credit market. Most of the bills were single-name bills (or at most two-name bills) secured by collateral.

From what has been said above, it is clear that the relations of the Bank of Japan and the rest of the banking system altered but little during the twenties. The bank still remained merely an institution for conducting Government business and for supporting the exchange bank; and only in times of crisis (as in 1927) did it make close contacts with the credit market as a whole. Its rate was ineffective, and its so-called open-market policy was directed towards creating favourable conditions for Government issues rather than towards controlling credit creation by the other banks. In fact, the policy of the ordinary banks remained little affected by the decisions of the central bank. If it failed to secure control of credit policy in Japan itself, it could also do little to affect movements of funds between Japan and other centres. In this respect, movements of the bank rate had little or no effect, and temporary difficulties could not be met by drawing on international short-term funds. Japan's financial system was to this extent insulated from the rest of the world, a condition which had both advantages and disadvantages.

The continued weakness of the Bank of Japan may seem rather surprising, since one cause of this, namely the existence of very large numbers of small independent banks, was being removed during the twenties by process of banking consolidation. This consolidation, however, had the effect of strengthening the great banks associated with the *zaibatsu*, which were themselves vast concentrations of economic power and had huge resources apart from those associated with their banking interests. These great banks became increasingly independent of the central bank, and were more than ever inclined to follow autonomous policies. While the Bank of Japan was an exceedingly imperfect instrument for exercising centralized control over the financial system, the Government could sometimes affect the policy of the other banks through its control over the vast volume of postal savings that were administered by the Treasury Deposits Bureau. Changes in the savings-deposit rate sometimes caused the other banks to modify their rates in a similar direction, since they were competitors for small and medium deposits. There were, however, narrow limits to the application of control in this way. Whether attempts were made, by the use of powers conferred by the bank-inspection legislation, to bring the banks into line with Governmental policy, it is difficult to say; the powers do not seem to have been widely used.

The growth of the *zaibatsu* also affected the capital market, since a large proportion of the sounder concerns was owned by great houses which were not obliged to raise capital through public issues. The number of persons prepared to invest directly in industrial securities remained very small. The vast majority still preferred to entrust their savings to banks, savings banks, or the post office, and much of the capital for industry was provided by these institutions or by the official Industrial and Hypothec Banks which raised money on debenture issues for this purpose. After 1927 there was an important development. The crisis of that year caused widespread distrust of the ordinary banks which were caught with many 'frozen' advances to industrial concerns. Depositors looked for other outlets for their savings, and found them partly in trust companies which had hitherto been of small importance. The additional resources thus placed at their disposal enabled the trust companies to play a much bigger part than before in underwriting and taking up issues of capital. The most important of these trust companies were owned by the *zaibatsu*, which operated them in close association with their banks and insurance companies. Thus this development also increased the concentration of economic power in the great economic enterprises of Mitsui, Mitsubishi, Sumitomo and Yasuda.

The general course of foreign trade in the period from 1914 to 1930 has already been sketched, but it is convenient at this point to sum up the results of this period of development and to examine the changes in the composition of the trade that took place.

The figures of foreign trade show an increase between 1913 and 1929 of well over three times in value and twice in volume. The

FOREIGN TRADE OF JAPAN PROPER

(in million yen)

Year	Trade with Foreign Countries				Trade with Foreign Countries and the Japanese Colonies Together	
	Imports		Exports		Imports	Exports
	Value	Volume	Value	Volume	Value	Value
1900	287	—	204	—	292	213
1913	729	100	632	100	795	715
1919	2,173	126	2,099	127	2,516	2,374
1925	2,573	174	2,306	159	3,109	2,676
1928	2,196	190	1,972	184	2,749	2,409
1929	2,216	199	2,149	205	2,765	2,604

increase in total overseas trade, including trade between Japan Proper and her colonies, was even greater. Before 1914 this colonial trade was of little significance, and even at the end of the First World War it represented only about 12 per cent of Japan's overseas trade.

During the twenties there was a rapid expansion, and by 1929 colonial trade represented nearly one-fifth of the total. This trade, it should be noted, was not handicapped by import duties or restrictions; while colonial tariffs on foreign goods were on the same scale as those of the mother country. Japan's trade with her colonies was typical of the classical relations between a home country and her empire. Exports consisted of manufactured goods, including capital goods for building up their resources; while imports consisted almost entirely of foodstuffs and raw materials. Korea sent mainly rice (which formed an increasing part of the Japanese home supply), beans, marine products and fertilizers; Formosa sent mainly sugar and rice.

If we turn to the composition of Japan's trade with the outside world over this period, we find, as we should expect in a country in process of industrialization, that the proportion of finished manufactures to her total exports rose substantially. In 1913 it was 29 per cent; in 1929 it was 44 per cent. About the same percentage in 1929 consisted of semi-finished goods, mainly raw silk. In 1913 there was already a predominance of textiles among the exports. Cotton yarn and cloth, raw silk and silk manufactures, together accounted for nearly 53 per cent of the total exports. Raw silk alone made up 30 per cent. By 1929 the trade had become even more highly specialized. In that year this group of textiles accounted for 65 per cent of the total exports; raw silk alone made up 37 per cent. Cotton exports had changed their character. In 1913 the bulk of them had consisted of yarn. By 1929 yarn exports had declined absolutely; but a great trade in cotton piece-goods, amounting to over 19 per cent of Japan's total export trade, had been built up. The export trade was specialized in markets as in commodities, and this specialization had also increased in the period now being considered. In 1913 China (including Manchuria, Hong Kong and Kwantung) and the United States, took 64 per cent of the total exports; in 1929 the proportion was 67 per cent. The United States took no less than 43 per cent of the exports in 1929 and her importance had risen, while China's had fallen. British India had come to the front as a market in this period and took 9 per cent of the exports in 1929, and South East Asia was also becoming a substantial market. The types of exports taken by the Asian markets on the one hand and the United States on the other differed greatly, for the United States took mainly a semi-manufactured commodity, raw silk, while Asia took manufactured goods, chiefly cotton goods. This was the pattern of the export trade which had been forming in the early years of the century and seemed to be firmly set by the late twenties.

CHAPTER VII

INDUSTRY AND AGRICULTURE, 1914–32

The unbalanced development that occurred between 1914 and 1919 left Japanese industry with serious problems of adjustment, which the financial troubles of the early twenties did not help to overcome. Japanese industrialists were inclined in subsequent years to look back on the whole decade as one of stagnation. Yet, in fact, progress was substantial, even if it was irregular and not equally evident in all fields of activity. Furthermore, there were changes in technique and organization which held promise for the future. In some fields, the post-war decade was one of great development; in others, of preparation for advances to come. From this time onwards, statistical information is more abundant than in the pre-Taisho era. The censuses of 1920 and 1930 provide us, for the first time, with adequate data about the occupational distribution of the population, and attempts have also been made to measure the general economic progress that was achieved during the period. It is convenient to begin this chapter by a reference to the more important facts disclosed by these inquiries.

Between 1914 and 1930 the total population of Japan Proper grew from 51 millions to 64 millions, more than 25 per cent. The national income, if we ignore changes in the value of money, increased more than fourfold over this period. In real terms it was probably well over twice as great; an estimate shows the change to have been from 5·67 thousand million yen in 1914 to 12·72 thousand million yen in 1930 at 1928-32 prices.[1] It is not easy to measure the way in which the different classes in the community were affected by this growth. Japan was applying herself throughout this period to building up her industrial equipment, and the proportion of the national income that was annually invested was therefore high; while governmental expenditure on the armed forces, though it did not increase in proportion to the rise in the national income as a whole, remained considerable.[2] Nevertheless, there is no doubt that the real income of the workers grew substantially. Professor Uyeda has estimated that the real wages of the industrial workers throughout the country

[1] K. Ohkawa, *op. cit.*, p. 248.
[2] In most of the years 1914-30 the ratio of gross capital formation to national income was in the range of 16 per cent to 23 per cent. See K. Ohkawa, *op. cit.*, p. 199.

as a whole were in 1929 50 or 60 per cent above the 1914 level. The real incomes of the peasants certainly rose to a much less extent; but even the peasants, especially those in the neighbourhood of the industrial centres, were better off than they had been in 1914, except in the bad years.

In which parts of the economy did the expansion occur? Koide's estimates of raw material production show a rise of about 46 per cent between 1914 and 1930, or about 19 per cent per capita; the greater part of this rise took place before 1924.[1] The increase was particularly marked in fishery products, cocoons and agricultural raw materials as a whole; while in cereal production it was comparatively small. Industrial production rose much faster. It was estimated that in the period from just before the First World War to the late twenties the physical volume of manufacturing production more than trebled.[2] Available figures of particular manufactured commodities indicate a very rapid expansion—often, of course, from small beginnings—over this period 1914-29. Some of them are given below.

	Cotton Yarn (million lb.)	Raw Silk (thousand kwan)	Woollen and Worsted Tissues (million yards)
1913	607·2	3,741	81·2
1920	726·8	5,834	70·5
1925	974·7	8,284	161·3
1929	1,117·0	11,292	222·2

	Coal (million tons)	Finished Steel (thousand tons)	Cement (thousand tons)	Chemical Fertilizer (thousand tons) Superphosphate of Lime	Sulphate of Ammonia	Electric Power Capacity (thousand kilowatts)
1913	21·3	255	645	—	—	504
1920	29·2	533	1,353	509	80	1,214
1925	31·5	1,043	2,508	674	131	2,768
1929	34·3	2,034	4,349	947	234	4,194

It is clear from these figures that those manufacturing industries which before 1914 had begun to occupy a prominent place in Japan's new industrial system, namely cotton and silk, were immensely enlarged. A number of other industries imported from the West also began to reach substantial proportions at this time. These included not only consumer-goods industries such as woollen and worsted, but also chemicals, engineering, iron and steel. The relative importance of these latter industries in Japan's economy still remained small, but their absolute growth was a reflection of the rapid rate of

[1] See, Table VIII in Appendix B.
[2] W. W. Lockwood, *op. cit.*, pp. 115, 117.

H

capital construction. The steep increase in electricity-generating capacity, to which much new investment was applied during the twenties, provides a good index both of the increasing use of power-driven machinery and of the rate of growth of the economy in general. This rapid industrial advance must, of course, be viewed against Japan's economic background as a whole. Secondary industry had increased in relative importance during this period, and in the late twenties its contribution to the national income had become as high or higher than that of primary industry. But manufacturing, including building, still engaged less than one-fifth of the occupied population, while agriculture occupied nearly half of it.

We must turn, therefore, to consider what happened during those years to the peasantry, before studying in detail the character of the more striking developments in manufacturing industry. The number of farming families was practically stationary over this period at about 5½ million. The change in the size-distribution of the farms, as the table below shows, was small, the trend being slightly against both the very smallest type of farm and the large farm.

NUMBER OF FARMS

(*in thousands*)

Year	Under 5 tan	5 tan-1 cho	Over 1 cho-2 cho	Over 2 cho	Total
1913	2,003	1,816	1,079	546	5,444
1930	1,939	1,916	1,227	517	5,600

Further, the system of land tenure altered little, though there was a tendency for the number of tenant farmers to decline, while those who owned part of their land and rented the rest grew in numbers. Rice remained the chief food crop grown, and well over half the cultivated area was under that cereal. The annual production of rice in the later twenties was only slightly above the pre-war average, and by then Japan was relying to a steadily growing extent on imports of rice from Korea and Formosa to supply her rising population. There was also a much smaller and declining import of foreign rice, a product which is not congenial to the Japanese taste. After rice, the next most important cereal crops were wheat and barley; but the output of these taken together was only one-sixth as valuable as the rice production. Barley and certain other cereals, such as millet, actually declined during the twenties. On the other hand, both the area under wheat and its production, after falling until the middle twenties, rose in the later years of the decade. To a large extent barley and wheat were competitive for the same soil, though neither

[1] 1 cho=10 tan=2·45 acres.

was competitive in that sense with rice, since they were grown as winter crops on the rice land. Barley was largely consumed by the poorer people who could not afford Japanese-type rice; it was competitive with foreign imported rice rather than with Japanese rice; and the decline in its production during this period was indicative of improvement in the standard of life. Agriculture extended considerably its range of products between 1914 and 1930. More vegetables were grown and different varieties introduced, and there was an extension of fruit farming and of poultry farming. Compared with rice these new crops played a small part in Japanese agriculture, but their growing importance was symptomatic of the rise in the incomes of the people. The main technical change introduced into Japanese agriculture, so far as the main cereal crops were concerned, was the increased use of manures. Foreign trade had given the farmers access to additional supplies, soya beans from Manchuria, phosphates from the South Seas and ammonium sulphate from the West. After the First World War the expansion of Japan's own chemical industry produced a local supply of nitrogenous fertilisers.

It might have been expected that the improvement in the economic position of the peasantry would have been substantial during this period in which the urban population, with its still highly specialized diet, was increasing very fast. During the First World War, the price of rice rose to high levels; but with the end of the boom the price collapsed, dropping from 55 yen a koku in January 1920 to 25·5 yen a koku in March 1921. The Government then introduced the Rice Act, which gave power to the Minister of Agriculture to 'adjust supply and demand' by storing rice when prices fell very low and selling it when prices rose high. He was provided with a fund of 200 million yen for this purpose. The recurrence of several poor harvests and the absence of any exceptionally good ones caused prices to run at fairly high levels until 1927. In that year and subsequently four large crops occurred in succession; the 1930 crop was exceptionally heavy. In spite of Government purchasing under the valorization scheme, prices which had been falling steadily since 1927 collapsed. In August 1930 they stood at 31 yen a koku; in the next four months at 18 yen a koku. The peasants thus sustained a serious blow to their interests just when the world depression was about to destroy their other main source of income, raw silk. Even before this disaster, discontent among the peasantry was growing. The tenants, in particular, were protesting vigorously against their heavy burden of rent, and unions for the protection of their interests increased in membership and activity. Now the flames spread.

A new factor intruded into the rice-growing industry during the first post-war decade. This was the extension of Japanese-style rice production in Korea and Formosa and the import of large quantities of that rice into Japan Proper. When Korea was annexed in 1910 her exports of rice were negligible, but, with encouragement from the Japanese Government, which had its eye on the future of the food supply, improvements were effected in methods of cultivation, especially by advances in irrigation, and there was an increased use of fertilizers. The cost of production fell; the area under cultivation increased, and, between 1910 and 1929, output grew by 30 per cent. Exports to Japan became important during the First World War and advanced steadily throughout the twenties. Similar developments took place, though on a smaller scale, in Formosa, and in 1927-29 these two colonies exported to Japan a quantity equivalent to between 12 and 14 per cent of her domestic production. The colonial import enabled Japan to meet the demands of the increasing population, and consumption per head was maintained throughout the twenties. There was a strategic as well as an economic advantage for Japan in fostering food production within her own Empire. But the effect on the Japanese farmers themselves was less agreeable. They gained little advantage from the rising demand for rice, and certain groups[1] agitated in favour of restricting imports from the colonies so as to preserve the farming community, which was regarded as 'the backbone of the nation, the source of its military strength and the guardians of traditional virtues against alien influences'.[2] For the Government to have listened to such demands would, however, have produced trouble among the urban population, besides endangering both industrial progress and strategic advantages.

For the second most important agricultural product of Japan, raw silk, the period between 1914 and 1929 saw a most remarkable development—indeed a threefold increase—in production. The growth had important repercussions on the farming industry, for it led to a corresponding rise in the demand for cocoons as well as for mulberry leaves. The number of farms raising cocoons grew steadily, and by 1929 two-fifths of all farming families were engaged in this occupation as a secondary employment. At the same time, since the reeling mills have to be located in the neighbourhood of raw material supplies, an additional demand was created for female workers. These came mainly from the peasants' families. The sale of cocoons, and the wages earned by his daughters in the reeling mills, contributed a very important part of the farmer's cash income, since much of his rice production was kept for his own use or, in the case of tenants, was passed to the landlords as rent. Cocoon-raising was particularly well adapted to Japanese agriculture, for it requires much skilled labour and little capital or material resources. At a time when

[1] Notably the Imperial Agricultural Society (*Teikoku Nokwai*).
[2] E. F. Penrose in *The Industrialization of Japan and Manchukuo* (ed. Schumpeter), p. 145.

very little additional land was available for cereal cultivation, this outlet was most valuable to the peasants. Such improvements in their standard of living as occurred in this period—and they can hardly be considered substantial—are attributable largely to fresh opportunities to engage in industrial occupations and, in particular, to participate in the rapidly growing silk trade. Any disturbance to the growth of that trade was bound to have disastrous consequences for them.

During the war prices rose very steeply, and in 1920 the average export price per 100 kin was 1,191 yen. Although there was a sharp fall when the post-war slump came, recovery was rapid, and in 1923 it stood at 2,150 yen. After 1925, with the rise in the exchange value of the yen, prices fell, and in April 1929 the export price was 1,420 yen. This still compared favourably with an average of 800 to 900 yen in the years before the war. Then came the collapse of the American market, and by October 1930 the price was down to 540 yen. It fell to still lower levels in the next two years, and in June 1932 stood at 390 yen. The result was that the farmers found their cash incomes greatly diminished, just at a time when there had been a collapse of rice prices. Their distress had unfortunate political consequences. They attributed responsibility for it to the politicians and the *zaibatsu*, and their discontent, in which their landlords shared, was communicated to the Army, largely recruited from the agricultural community, and undoubtedly contributed to the overthrow of the 'liberal' Government and the transference of power to those who favoured military aggression.

One of the most considerable advances in food production was made by the fishing industry, which has long supplied Japan with her main animal foodstuffs. Koide's index of aquatic production (1921-1925=100) rose from 43 in 1914 to 127 in 1929. All branches of the industry expanded; but the most striking development occurred through the introduction of floating canneries which operated in the distant waters of the northern Pacific and the Behring Sea. The canneries were controlled by a few very great concerns, and presented a contrast in organization to the coastal fisheries which were in large part conducted by peasants as a subsidiary occupation. Even in that branch of the industry, however, there were technical changes that brought economies, for example, the introduction of oil marine engines.

From agriculture and fishing we may now turn to manufacturing industry, and, in particular, to the technical advances in that field. Here the most obvious development between 1914 and 1929 was the extension of the silk and cotton industries; but there was also a considerable enlargement in the scope of Japan's industrial activities, the significance of which did not become clear until the next decade. The great expansion of raw silk production has already been referred to. It was associated on the demand side with the growth of the American demand for silk for the manufacture of fully fashioned hosiery. On the supply side, the industry in this period reaped the fruits of improved methods of production and of scientific research which had been introduced in an earlier time under the fostering care of the Government. These improvements covered the cultivation of mulberry trees, the production of superior breeds of silkworms, new processes of egg-production and treatment, the introduction of multiple-thread reeling machines, and other detailed improvements in filature processes and organization. The general adoption of the practice of producing a summer-autumn cocoon crop, in addition to the traditional spring crop, meant that mills could work more regularly, while success in producing cocoons of standardized quality made possible the more rapid output of silk in the reeling mills as well as a rise in the quality of the reeled products. The output per reeling basin in the filatures increased by two and a half times in this period as a result of these improvements. The transformation of the reeling industry into a factory trade, which had gone a long way in the twenty years before the war, was carried further. By 1929-32, hand-reels were responsible for only about 4 per cent of the total production. In the filatures themselves a fourfold rise in output had been accompanied by an increase in their size, and a reduction in their numbers. The number of reeling basins per filature rose from thirty-six to ninety between 1911 and 1928.[1]

There was an expansion also in the silk-weaving industry. The narrow silk fabrics for Japanese dress continued to be woven on hand-looms installed, for the most part, in very small establishments, although during the twenties for some lines of product hand-looms were replaced by narrow power-looms. Meanwhile, the section of the trade that catered for export and used broad looms not only expanded but also became more highly diversified. The earlier specialization on *habutae* disappeared, and new varieties of cloth, such as Fuji silk (made of spun silk) and crepe grew in importance. This section of the trade worked on a larger scale than that catering for the home market, and mills with over fifty looms appeared.

In the cotton industry the pre-war growth continued. The number of spindles rose from 2,415,000 in 1914 to 3,814,000 in 1920, and after a setback through the destruction of some 900,000 spindles in the Kwanto earthquake of 1923, to 6,650,000 spindles in 1929. The increase in the number of mills and firms was not in proportion to this

---

[1] This applies to filatures with ten basins and over. The number of filatures with less than ten basins fell from 2,172 in 1913 to 294 in 1928, while the number with ten basins and over rose from 2,529 to 3,215. In addition, there were still in 1928 62,000 hand-reeling mills with 85,000 basins. This compares with 142,000 mills with 175,000 basins in 1924 and 285,000 mills with about 350,000 basins in 1913.

rise in capacity. In other words, the typical mill and firm became much larger.[1] Moreover, there was a pronounced tendency towards consolidation, and by 1929 56 per cent of the spindles were in the hands of seven large concerns. The spinners, as we have seen, had originally supplied yarn for export to the domestic hand-loom weavers, and to small specialist weaving sheds. Later some of them established weaving sheds of their own to weave the yarn spun in their mills. Between 1913 and 1929 this tendency was carried much further, and the combined spinning-weaving mill became characteristic of a large section of the Japanese cotton industry. The looms owned by the spinners rose from 24,000 in 1913 to 74,000 in 1929, and their cloth output increased nearly fourfold, compared with a yarn increase of under twofold. This development was associated with the falling off of yarn exports to Asia and with the rise of the export trade in piece-goods. The industry had now moved to a new plane of production. In 1914 four-fifths of the yarn produced consisted of low counts (20's and under). During the next decade and a half, while the production of the coarsest types (under 20's) actually declined, the production of medium yarns greatly expanded, with the result that in 1929 yarn classed as 20's and under accounted for only three-fifths of the total.

Meanwhile there had been changes in other sections of the Japanese cotton industry. The domestic weaving section, which used hand-looms for the production of narrow fabric for Japanese consumption, declined rapidly throughout this period; while the section composed of specialist weaving sheds was transformed. At the beginning of the period the smaller specialist weavers used either narrow power-looms or hand-looms. By the middle twenties narrow power-looms had largely replaced hand-looms in the manufacture of narrow cloth. The most significant development was the appearance of larger specialist sheds (with fifty looms or over) equipped with wide power-looms for the manufacture of cloth for foreign markets. This section grew substantially throughout the twenties. Whereas the combined spinning-weaving mill concentrated largely on standardized fabrics, especially shirtings and sheetings, the specialist sheds used their wide looms for fancy goods. This dichotomy became more pronounced in the subsequent decade. Even in 1928-29, however, the specialist weaving sheds were responsible for just under two-fifths of the piece-goods exports in quantity and well over two-fifths in value.

Broadly speaking, then, the structure of the industry by 1929 was

---

[1] In 1913 there were forty-four companies with 152 mills; in 1929 there were fifty-nine companies with 247 mills. The average number of spindles per mill rose from 16,000 in 1913 to 27,000 in 1929, and the average number per company from 55,000 to 113,000.

composed of (1) spinning mills, producing yarn for specialist weavers and to a diminishing extent for export; (2) large spinning-weaving mills which consumed a high proportion of their yarn output in the manufacture of standardized piece-goods, mainly for export; (3) medium-sized specialist weaving sheds producing fabrics for export on wide power-looms; (4) small weaving sheds with under fifty looms, equipped mainly with narrow power-looms and catering for the home market; and (5) the dwindling domestic industry, equipped with hand-looms.

Between 1913 and 1926 the technical efficiency of the Japanese cotton industry on its spinning side, as measured by the weight of output per operative, failed to show any notable improvement. In the weaving sheds progress was more substantial because of the changes already described. After 1926, however, the most remarkable growth in efficiency occurred in both spinning and weaving. Although the improvement had gone some distance even by 1929, the full story of this rise in technical efficiency belongs to the subsequent period, and will be discussed later.

The woollen and worsted industry was of small account in 1914 except for the muslin branch which produced cloth for kimono. Even that branch then depended on imports of yarns and tops, which were increasing steadily. The war gave a sharp stimulus to the industry as a whole. The demand for woollen cloth for military uniforms increased, and so the heavy woollen section expanded. At the same time, imports both of cloth and of yarns and tops were restricted. Hence the combing and worsted spinning branches, which had only just been created before the war, were given an opportunity to develop. When foreign sources of supply were restored after the war, the growth was interrupted. But after 1925 it was resumed on a greater scale than before. The rising demand of the Japanese for Western dress stimulated the manufacture of serges and woollen cloth, while the manufacture of muslin for kimono continued to grow until 1927. The rise in the output of the main types of cloth is shown in the following table[1]

Year	Muslin	Woollen Cloth	Serge for Japanese Dress	Serge for Foreign Dress	Total Value (including others)
1912-14 (annual average)	58·3	1·6	8·1	—	30·7
1925	127·6	5·4	24·2	4·1	182·5
1929	165·6	9·0	28·1	19·6	210·5

[1] The figures show production in million yards, except in the last column, where they are in million yen.

Worsted spinning and top-making first became substantial industries in this period. The output of yarn rose from 21·2 million lb. in
1921 to 64·3 million lb. in 1929. Yet, in spite of this home production,
imports of yarns continued to grow up to 1928, and at the end of
the decade they were far greater than in pre-war years.[1] On the other
hand, the import of tops fell very rapidly after 1925, and by 1929
they had become insignificant.[2] Imports of woollen and worsted
tissues, which were very heavy in the early post-war years, also began
to decline steeply after 1925, though in 1929 they were still greater
than they had been before the war. The Japanese wool-using industry
thus obtained the lion's share of the great increase in home demand
for woollen and worsted goods that occurred during the twenties.
The benefit that foreign manufacturers, of both tissues and semi-
products, had received from this increased demand had been considerable in the early post-war years, but by 1929 the foreigners had
lost the market for tops and their market for tissues and yarns was
already endangered.

The branches of the industry which were concerned with tops,
yarns, muslins and certain kinds of woollens were in the hands of
large firms, many of which were vertically integrated. In these
branches progress throughout the twenties was by an enlargement of
the scale of operations rather than by the increase in the number of
producers. But in the production of serges, both for foreign and
Japanese dress, and of other kinds of worsted materials, the small
and medium mills became the typical units. It was in these branches
that development was most rapid during the twenties, as we have
seen. So, whereas in most of the textile industries, the importance of
the small technical unit was declining, in some sections of the wool-
using industry it was increasing. This tendency became pronounced,
it should be noted, in a period during which the hand-loom was
almost completely superseded by the power-loom, driven by electricity. The typical weaving shed was able greatly to enlarge its production by this change in equipment without engaging additional
workers.

In short, it could be said that between 1913 and 1929 the leading
textile industries had greatly expanded and, having thrown off the
last vestiges of primitive production methods, improved their
efficiency. In spite of the rise of other trades, textiles as a whole had
maintained their importance in the Japanese industrial system. In
1930 as in 1920 they accounted for about 25 per cent of the indus-

[1] The number of spindles rose from 316,000 in 1922 to 520,000 in 1929. In the
latter year 446,000 of these were in the worsted spinning branch and the rest in
the woollen-spinning branch.
[2] The number of combing machines rose from 244 to 605 between 1922 and
1929.

trially occupied workers of Japan. Of the total number of factory workers in 1930, excluding those in factories with fewer than five workers, half were employed in textiles. About 45 per cent of these textile workers were engaged in silk reeling or silk spinning, 7 per cent were in silk weaving, and 31 per cent in cotton spinning and weaving. Japanese factory industry was, therefore, very highly specialized, and the degree of specialization had not decreased significantly at a time when the economy as a whole was growing quickly.

The metallurgical industries expanded after 1914, but by 1929 they were still of secondary importance in Japan's economy. Although the finished steel output rose from 255,000 tons in 1913 to 547,000 tons in 1919, and to over 2 million tons in 1929, Japan continued to rely on imports for a large part of her needs. Her dependence on foreign sources of supply was, however, decreasing. Before the First World War domestic production provided only 30 per cent of her needs; in the early twenties about 45 per cent, and in the later years of the decade about 70 per cent. In the pig iron used in the steel furnaces Japan was still far from self-sufficient. The production of pig iron doubled during the twenties, and was more than four times as great in 1929 as in 1913; but imports also greatly increased, and even in 1929 she was supplying only three-fifths of her needs—about the same proportion as at the beginning of the decade. Meanwhile a considerable import of scrap had become necessary; it reached about 500,000 tons in 1929. Imports of pig and scrap together in that year amounted to 1,300,000 tons out of a domestic consumption of 2,300,000 tons. About 90 per cent of the ore needed for the blast furnaces was imported, mainly from China and Malaya. Before the First World War most of the pig iron and ingot steel was produced in the Government's works at Yawata. During the war a number of private works were established or extended; but even in 1929 the Yawata works were responsible for the larger part of the output of pig iron and ingot steel, and for a high proportion of the finished steel. The remainder was in the hands of a few great concerns associated with the *zaibatsu*.

In the coal-mining industry there was a rapid increase in output during the war, but later development was comparatively slow. Production rose from 21 million tons in 1913 to 31 million in 1919. Then a setback occurred, and even in 1929 output reached only 34 million tons. Japan was then on balance a net importer of coal, especially of coking coal required in the ironworks. The copper industry, which throughout the Meiji era had been an important exporter, made even less progress. Production was stationary over this period, and Japan in the twenties found that it paid her to import large quantities of copper from cheaper sources of supply.

In shipbuilding, Japan's post-war experiences resembled those of many other nations. During the First World War her industry became substantial, and in 1919 the gross mercantile tonnage launched from her yards was 650,000 as against a mere 85,000 tons in 1914. But Japanese costs, compared with those of other nations, were high. With the onset of the depression and with the return of foreign competition, the industry entered upon a long period of decline, during which the number of workers engaged in yards capable of building ships of 1,000 tons and over fell by nearly two-thirds. Even in 1929, which was a relatively good year, the mercantile tonnage launched was only 165,000 tons. Naval building was affected adversely by the Washington Treaties. Thus the heavy industries on the whole lagged behind the development of the Japanese economy; and even the iron and steel trade which made considerable progress had not by 1929 achieved the importance among manufacturing industries that it held in other industrial countries. Not unnaturally this led certain foreign observers to conclude that Japan's industrial future lay almost exclusively in the lighter industries, especially the textile industries, and that her deficiencies in the field of heavy industry meant that there was little likelihood of her attaining 'a position of major importance as a manufacturing nation'.[1]

Nevertheless, some branches of engineering were very progressive. The absence of competition during the war, the world demand for munitions at that time and the growth in Japan's own needs for industrial equipment provided the initial stimulus. The slump after the war ruined many of the new producers, but certain engineering trades, especially those concerned with prime movers, electrical machinery and apparatus, textile machinery and scientific instruments, continued to advance, and after the middle twenties Japan's imports of those goods declined. In the manufacture of pedal cycles, which had become a major form of local transport, she built up a substantial industry. By 1929 she was able to dispense even with imports of parts and to supply her entire needs for bicycles. Nevertheless, for machinery as a whole she was still a large importer, and her dependence upon foreign sources of supply for machine tools increased as her industrialization advanced. The same was true of motor cars, and especially of car parts and components, the imports of which grew very fast after the establishment of assembly plants in Japan by General Motors and Ford. Japan's larger engineering products were made in a comparatively few great works controlled by the *zaibatsu*; but in the lighter end of the trade (e.g. cycles and electric bulbs) numerous small establishments flourished, and many small workshops engaged in the manufacture of parts appeared in the neighbourhood of the large factories which they served.

[1] Cf. J. E. Orchard, *Japan's Economic Position*, pp. 482-3.

The only other industry which need be included in this brief survey is pottery, an ancient industry which even before the war had developed new branches engaged in a substantial export trade. This period saw the appearance in the industry of a structure characteristic of many Japanese consumption goods trades. The branch concerned with the manufacture of traditional tableware for Japanese use continued to be conducted on a very small scale, and remained associated with particular localities—fine artistic wares with Kyoto, and other high-grade specialities with Arita. Another important traditional centre, Seto, produced goods both for the home market and for export; while in Nagoya there were a few large factories turning out fine china for export and also many smaller ones which produced the lower qualities of earthenware and china. In Seto and Nagoya the small-scale section of the industry had developed an intricate organization; for the process of production was split up among numerous small body-makers and decorators, each with narrowly specialized functions. In addition to the tableware section, there grew up during the twenties a few large concerns producing heavy porcelain and electrical insulators. It was estimated that in 1931 over half the 40,000 workers in the pottery industry were in work-places employing under five workers, while at the other end of the scale there were 6,000 workers engaged in twenty factories.

Attention has necessarily been concentrated in this chapter on the manufacture of goods that enter largely into international trade. But it must not be forgotten that a large part of the goods and services produced in Japan remained peculiar to that country. Along with the development of new industries of Western style, there continued to flourish numerous small-scale trades which provided for the special wants of the Japanese purchasers. Some indication of the importance of these has been given in the description of the textile and pottery industries. But there were many others which, unlike the textiles, had been almost completely unaffected by contact with the West— the *geta*-making trade, the house-building trade, the Japanese-style dress trade, the foodstuffs industry and many others. The development of great new industries, and the appearance of large factories in the cotton-spinning, engineering, iron and steel and pottery industries, had not meant the general disappearance of older trades or of older methods of production in them. Thus, by the twenties, every observer of Japan's industrial system was impressed by the contrast between large-scale enterprise in one part of the economy and small-scale enterprise, often of an unfamiliar kind, in the rest, just as the social observer was surprised by the dichotomy, even among city dwellers, between the workaday life in factories and offices and the traditional domestic life of the people.

Many of the small-scale manufacturing industries, notably the food-producing industries, were still scarcely differentiated from retail distribution, just as there was no clear-cut occupational division between agriculture and certain branches of manufacturing industry. Hence the difficulty of interpreting Japanese occupational statistics. It is clear, however, that economic growth was accompanied by a vast extension in numbers employed in the tertiary trades as a whole. While employment in manufacturing (including building) rose from 4·7 million in 1914 to 5·9 million in 1930, the numbers employed in transport and communications, commerce, administrative, professional and personal services rose from 5·5 million to 8·5 million in the same period. In some degree this great increase was a necessary accompaniment of economic progress for, as is well known, as countries advance in wealth, an increased proportion of their man-power is absorbed in the tertiary trades. But in Japan's case it would be incorrect to regard the scale of the growth as a measure of economic prosperity. One must also observe that some part of that growth was to be explained by the fact that opportunities for employment in the new capital-intensive industries were insufficient to provide occupation for the large annual additions to the labour force. Much of the increase in this period, therefore, found its way into the small-scale industries or the service trades where productivity was low. Striking contrasts between the incomes of those employed in the modern sector of the economy and the small-scale sector appeared. In subsequent years these contrasts, and the conflicts they provoked, were to occupy a leading place among Japan's economic and social problems.

The existence of this great mass of poorly paid workers, recruited as they were by the annual flow of surplus labour from the countryside, inevitably retarded the development of organization among the workers in large-scale industry. At the same time, the composition of the labour force in the most important of those industries—the fact that in the large textile mills the majority of the workers were girls with a very short factory life—and the paternalistic system of industrial relations, were very unsympathetic to the appearance of powerful trade unions. After the First World War the comparatively liberal attitude of the Government and the influence of foreign example gave some encouragement to labour organization. It was then that a central body the Japan Federation of Labour (*Sodomei*) was founded. But leadership at the centre was in the hands of intellectuals concerned with rival political ideologies rather than with the immediate interests of their members. Except among seamen and transport workers, very few even mildly effective unions were formed. The number of trade unionists grew from 100,000 in 1923 to 370,000 in 1931, but this represented a very small proportion of Japan's labour force and only in a few trades had the right of collective bargaining been conceded. In these circumstances the determination of wages was left mainly to individual contract between employer and worker and the typical worker's earnings were made up of a complex of payments including bi-annual bonuses and payments in kind. All these constituents of wages varied from firm to firm, for standard rates were unknown.

Government intervention in labour relations and in the regulation of working conditions was narrowly limited in scope. A Factory Act passed in 1911 had among its chief provisions the abolition of night work by all females and young persons in work-places with fifteen workers and over, but it did not come into force until 1929. Other legislation dealt with the hours of underground mine-workers, factory safety, and safeguards for seamen. But the vast mass of Japanese workers at this time and for long afterwards were unaffected by official regulations and had to depend on such protection as was afforded by traditional conventions governing the relations of master and servant.

CHAPTER VIII

ECONOMIC POLICY AND THE
ZAIBATSU, 1914–32

The Japanese Government played an important part during the Meiji era in laying the foundations for rapid industrialization and also in initiating and supporting industries or services which were necessary to realize its political and economic objectives. Yet the sale of most of the State properties to private enterprise after 1880 reduced considerably the size of the public sector, and subsequently the Government's direct participation in manufacturing industry by outright ownership was limited to a very few enterprises. By 1912 only 12 per cent of 'factory' operatives were employed in Government establishments. Certain official monopolies, founded for fiscal reasons in the salt, tobacco and camphor industries, were continued; a great part of the railway system remained under Government control; and there were Government dockyards and munitions plants. Yet, in the twenties, the only major manufacturing industry in which the State had the predominant part was the iron and steel industry in its primary branches. Even though the relative importance of the Government's Yawata Works was diminishing, as late as 1931 it was still responsible for over three-quarters of the pig iron and half the ingot steel produced in Japan. In the carrying trade the Government continued to own and operate a number of steamships; for instance, it controlled a company founded in 1919 to take over tramps from shipowners who at the end of the war-time boom found themselves with a large surplus tonnage. Thus the undertakings actually owned and operated by the State were confined to those which in all countries are considered to occupy a special position (such as the railways), or were necessary for national security and unlikely in Japan to reach a substantial size under private control (such as the iron and steel industry), or were valuable for fiscal reasons (as salt and tobacco).

Apart from these State undertakings there were a number of other concerns to which the State supplied part of the capital either directly or through the medium of the special banks, particularly the Industrial Bank of Japan. Most of these concerns were in industries of strategic importance. They included enterprises on the Continent of Asia or in the Japanese colonies, and they became increasingly important in the second and third decades of the century. The chief of them was the South Manchuria Railway Company which controlled, apart from the railway itself, the most important large-scale enterprises in the railway zone.

The direction of industrial development was also influenced by other forms of State intervention. An account has already been given of the inception of the policy of subsidizing shipping, shipbuilding and private railways in the homeland, and sugar production in Formosa. This policy was continued in the post-war period, and the scope of Government subsidies was extended after the war to include certain kinds of chemical production, such as soda ash and dyestuffs, and also the exploitation of the petroleum resources of Karafuto (South Saghalien). Government help to the iron and steel industry was extended by a law of 1926, which granted producers exemption from income tax and excess profit tax and at the same time increased the rate of subsidy paid for the production of certain classes of iron and steel. The largest sums disbursed as subsidies in the post-war period were for the benefit of agriculture. The financial help given by the Government for the purposes of maintaining the prices of rice and silk in years of depression have already been referred to. The greater part of the money went, however, towards improvements in farm lands and in the rural drainage and water systems, in assisting tenants to acquire holdings, or in relieving them in times of great difficulty. Measures for farm relief became particularly prominent in the years of the world depression (1930-32), and large sums were then provided for emergency relief works. The remaining subsidies were small in amount, and consisted of grants for the encouragement of co-operative societies and of guilds of small producers and traders and for the development of certain export activities. Grants were given in connection with the Export Compensation Scheme, similar to the British Export Credits Guarantee Scheme.

Thus, except in a few fields of activity, subsidies played only a small part in the period from 1914 to 1931 in affecting the direction of Japanese economic development. In 1931 the total disbursement was only 61 million yen, of which more than two-fifths went to agriculture. This sum represented only about 3 per cent of the total budgeted expenditure of the Government under its General Account and Special Railway Account.

Tariffs, likewise, were not of outstanding importance in determining the growth of industry. It was not until the first decade of the present century that Japan found herself able to work out a tariff free from the restrictions imposed by earlier treaties. The principle adopted in framing the new tariff, which came into force in 1911, was that industrial raw materials which could not be produced easily in Japan should be admitted free or at a low rate, that low duties should be imposed on semi-manufactured goods, and that moderate duties should be imposed on finished manufactured goods. Luxury products were covered by high duties in the interest of the balance of payments. This general principle was modified in its application through agreements with certain foreign Powers, and one result was that, in practice, iron, steel, machinery and certain kinds of textiles were admitted at relatively low rates of duty. In 1914 the ratio of customs revenue to the value of dutiable imports was just under 20 per cent. This average ratio, of course, disguises the fact that clothing and certain finished consumer goods were subjected to high duties (40 to 50 per cent *ad valorem*), and that certain food-stuffs, notably sugar, were highly protected.

During the war many duties were lowered because of the scarcity of goods in Japan, and the rise of prices greatly reduced the protection offered by the specific duties. As a result, in 1919 the ratio of customs revenue to the value of dutiable imports had fallen to under 9 per cent. When the restoration of foreign sources of supply led to serious competition in the Japanese market, duties were raised on the products of the most vulnerable industries, especially chemicals and metals. The Government also forbade the import of dyestuffs save under licence, a policy which the British Government also adopted at this time. After the earthquake of 1923 *ad valorem* duties of 100 per cent were imposed on 120 luxury products in the interest of the balance of payments. Meanwhile, the conventions with foreign countries signed in 1910 had expired, and in 1926 there was a complete revision in the duties. This determined the basis of the tariff for the next decade. The most important effect of the revision was to give much greater protection to certain new industries, especially the woollen spinning and weaving, top-making and rayon trades. On balance, however, Japan still remained a country with a moderate tariff. The Minseito Government reduced duties on some semi-manufactured goods, such as cotton yarn and cement, in 1930 and 1931. With the fall of that Government a new epoch in economic policy began in which the rôle of tariffs was of little importance.

To sum up the effects of the tariff, it can be said that until 1920 it had very little influence on the economic structure of the country, for before 1911 Japan's freedom to impose protective duties was limited by treaty, and between 1914 and 1920 normal trading conditions were so disturbed as to reduce them to a position of minor significance. Even during the next decade, the effects of the tariff on foreign competition in the home market was overshadowed by exchange fluctuations, and it was never more than a secondary weapon in the armoury of economic policy. In only a few industries, as in the iron and steel, sugar, copper, dyestuffs and woollen industries, was the tariff ever of much importance.

Other aspects of economic policy deserve closer attention. Num-

I

erous forms of Government-sponsored organization were created, or fostered, during the period now under consideration to promote the development of particular industries. The Government took an active part in encouraging the expansion of the fishing industry, and the prefectural authorities were given powers to supervise methods of fishing and of sale. Further, the Government introduced into this industry a device common to Japanese economic life as a whole, namely an association of producers to assist in the supervision and guidance of those engaged in the trade. All occupied in fishing were compelled to join the *Suisan Kumiai*[1] of their neighbourhood, and one of the statutory obligations of these bodies was to inspect the produce destined for export. Government direction and control also did much to increase efficiency in the raw silk industry and to provide for the production of standardized filaments. Government grants and loans at low rates of interest were furnished for the purpose of increasing rice production both in Japan Proper and in Korea. In manufacturing industry, save in branches deemed to be of strategic importance, the Government's activities were less effective. For many years efforts were made to improve the quality of goods for export, and during the Meiji era regulations had been drawn up to provide for the inspection, by guilds of exporters, of certain classes of exports. During the First World War and the post-war period the range of goods covered was extended. The Export Guild Law and Manufacturers Guild Law of 1925 provided for the setting up of voluntary bodies with the function of maintaining standards of quality, and some of these guilds were recognized as official authorities for the compulsory inspection of goods. The policy was carried further in a consolidating measure of 1928 (the Staple Export Goods Control Regulations). This specified the goods of which the export was not permitted until they had been inspected by an authorized body. Sometimes the authority consisted of guilds of producers or traders; sometimes of Government officials. Another purpose behind the Government's decision to encourage the establishment of export guilds was the promotion of co-operation among the smaller exporters for the development of foreign markets. Much was hoped of this at the time when the law was passed, but during the twenties the results were negligible, largely because of the conflict of interest between large and small merchants in the majority of trades. As we shall see, however, these guilds came to the front in the changed trading conditions of the next decade.

The Government's efforts to promote co-operation among manufacturers were rather more successful. As early as 1884 an Act had been passed authorizing the formation of *Dogyo Kumiai* (Trade Associations) in industries producing important products, and a

[1] Fishery Guilds.

number of these were in fact formed. They carried on the usual functions of trade associations and concerned themselves, like export guilds, with the inspection of goods and with issuing certificates of quality. These *Kumiai* were composed of all kinds of firms concerned with a particular commodity, both large and small manufacturers and also dealers, and in the small-scale trades they were dominated by the merchant employers. In the early post-war period the Government became anxious to encourage co-operative effort among small manufacturers themselves, so that they might achieve some degree of independence of the merchants. So, in 1925, the manufacturers in specified export industries were authorized to form guilds with functions of inspecting products, providing joint equipment, and arranging for joint purchases and sales. The appropriate Minister could compel non-members to abide by the guild's regulations. These *Kogyo Kumiai* were the complement of the export guilds, and they received small grants from the Government for the purchase of joint equipment. By the end of 1930 111 such guilds had been formed, but it seems doubtful whether in this period they really did much to modify the existing organization of industry or to improve its efficiency. As with the export guilds, however, the *Kogyo Kumiai* later on formed a useful medium through which official control could be exercised. Among the agricultural communities encouragement was given to the *Sangyo Kumiai*, or co-operative societies, which carried out functions of co-operative purchase, sale and credit. They were given assistance—in the form of cheap credits and subsidies—by the central Government, and it seems that they played an increasingly important part in the agricultural life of Japan.

Government attempts to control and direct industrial life by edict were thus limited in scope and tentative in method. Apart from the strategic industries, in which there was active participation by the State, Government intervention seldom went beyond the encouragement of co-operation among producers and traders, and this encouragement was not always whole-hearted. The greatest measure of success seems to have been reached in agriculture (including silk-raising) and fishing, and in the industries associated with them. In raw silk the Government's participation was indispensable to the industry's prosperity. But in manufacturing industry little was achieved outside the spheres mentioned, and only the small firms were in the least affected by the legislation. Japan's industry had risen during an era of economic liberalism, and direct Governmental intervention after the initial phase seldom went beyond what was considered appropriate to such a régime. The absence of direct intervention on a large scale did not mean that the desired objectives could not be reached in other ways. Japanese statesmen had to deal with a society that was very different from Western societies, and in the pursuance of their economic objectives they had to use different means. The means that were employed, and indeed Japanese economic policy as a whole, cannot be understood without some knowledge of the enterprises that were being built up by the mighty business groups popularly known as the *zaibatsu*. References have been made to these groups in earlier chapters; but we must now consider them in some detail.

The term *zaibatsu* means literally 'money-cliques', and is used to signify certain great Japanese business houses with extremely wide-spread interests. The four major *zaibatsu* were Mitsui, Mitsubishi, Sumitomo and Yasuda. These concerns played a vital part in the economic rise of Japan, and they had come to occupy by the later twenties a position in the Japanese economy for which there was no parallel elsewhere in modern times.[1] Their importance was not limited to the economic sphere, for they had made their influence felt in politics. The Governments of the early years of Meiji had been faced with grave difficulties in executing their policy of Westerniza-tion, for there was at that time no large middle class with financial resources, with experience of modern industrial and commercial techniques, or with the habit of initiative. It was not enough to strike off the shackles of the old régime; positive measures had to be taken to ensure that the opportunities for development were seized and that the strategic interests of the country were observed in any industrial growth that occurred. The newly created bureaucracy might plan the objectives of economic policy; it could hardly concentrate in itself the detailed administration of economic resour-ces. Fortunately there were available a few business families which for decades, even centuries, had been engaged in banking and commerce on a large scale, and had served as agents of the *daimyo* in the management of their revenues. Some of these families had helped to finance the political movements that had led to the Restoration. The new Meiji Governments naturally turned to these families for financial help in tiding them over their initial difficulties, and they looked to them to carry out any financial or commercial operations, or to launch any new enterprises, which were considered necessary as part of the general policy. So these families, together with notable recruits from the ranks of the *samurai*, became agents for the execution of the Government's economic policy and this soon led to a concentration of economic power in them. A concentration of this sort is likely to occur whenever a country with a hitherto primitive economy begins a career of industrial development, especially when the initiative in this process rests with the State.

During the Meiji era close connections were established between

[1] The Fuggers of Augsburg may be compared with them in some important respects, but it would be misleading to suggest that there was a close resemblance.

particular statesmen, who had definite policies to carry out, and particular business families who could provide resources and means to assist them. In return for the financial assistance which they gave the Government, the *zaibatsu* from time to time acquired State properties at low prices and received valuable contracts. They earned large profits from underwriting Government loans. For instance, Marquis Inouye[1] worked in close association with Mitsui, and Mitsui, in return for the help it gave him, obtained possession on favourable terms of properties that had belonged to the Shogun and the clan governments. This was the origin of Mitsui's well-known Miike coalmining concern. Government purchases and sales of materials in foreign countries in early Meiji were made through Mitsui, which thus laid the foundations of its foreign trading activities. These later became the main province of the great Mitsui Bussan Kaisha. Mitsubishi, founded by a *samurai* named Iwasaki, acted as agent for the Government in carrying supplies to Formosa in the troubles of 1874, and its existing small fleet of ships was supplemented by the addition of thirty steamers bought from abroad for this purpose by the Government. This was the beginning of the great enterprise that finally emerged as the Nippon Yusen Kaisha. In 1890 Mitsubishi reluctantly purchased from the Government, then in financial straits, a tract of waste land near the Imperial Palace. This has since become one of the most valuable sites in Tokyo, for the famous Marunouchi business quarter is located there. Just as Mitsui was associated with Marquis Inouye, of the Seiyukai political party, Mitsubishi was associated in its early years with Count Okuma, who led the Kenseikai party, later known as the Minseito. The experiences of the other *zaibatsu* in Meiji times were not dissimilar. All of them played an important part in financing the foreign wars in which Japan was engaged, and in the development of the colonies. The *zaibatsu* helped to capitalize, often jointly with the Government, enterprises of strategic importance, at home and in the colonies and Manchuria, and most of the new large-scale industries were either developed by them or brought under their control. From time to time, generally in periods of financial crisis or of slump, certain older business families failed. Their properties were then usually acquired by one of the *zaibatsu*; for instance, many of the Suzuki properties passed to Mitsui after the financial crisis of 1927. We have seen in an earlier chapter how the *zaibatsu's* financial power, exercised through their banks and trust and insurance companies, increased during the twenties along with the consolidation of the banking system. Just as the First World War saw a large extension of their enterprises in the heavy industries, so the post-war decade

---

[1] A leading statesman of the Meiji era, a member of the Choshu clan, and one of the famous *Genro* (Elder Statesmen).

saw a marked growth in their commercial and financial interests.

By 1929 the *zaibatsu* had reached the zenith of their power and influence. Many rivals had been weeded out during the difficult post-war period, and the setback suffered by the militarists after 1921 greatly strengthened their own political position. Party government was making headway at this time, and the power of the Diet was increasing. The *zaibatsu*, being intimately associated with the politicians, became very important influences on policy. Thus whereas in early Meiji days they could be regarded as agents of the Government, though probably never as merely passive agents, by the later twenties they had reached a position in which they could to an increasing extent impose their wishes on the Government. The relations between the great merchants and those who were nominally the governing classes, relations of which the old chroniclers had complained in later Tokugawa times, were again appearing. But the *zaibatsu* were soon to learn that their position was by no means unassailable and, as had happened in the past, they were to receive brutal reminders that it was not for them to usurp the places and privileges of their betters.

There were, of course, other large business concerns in Japan that were independent of the great *zaibatsu*; for instance, Okura, with large interests in trade, mining and textiles; Asano in cement, mining, iron and steel and heavy engineering; Furukawa with copper mining and refining, and electrical plant. But the *zaibatsu* by 1929 occupied a special position, not merely because of the magnitude of their interests and their close and peculiar relations with the Government but also because of the very wide range of their interests. These comprised mining, metals, mechanical engineering, electrical apparatus and machinery, textiles, paper, cement, glass, chemicals, shipbuilding, shipping, foreign and domestic trade, banking and insurance. It was difficult, indeed, to find any form of large-scale economic activity in which the *zaibatsu* had not an important share. Further, the fact that they were at once predominant in finance and also in industry and commerce gave them an enormous advantage over specialist concerns. As was shown in the chapter on banking, the structure of the capital market in Japan and the habits of investors place obstacles in the way of raising capital by public issue. Enterprises in need of new capital must in general get it by selling their securities to banks or other financial institutions. Those who control these institutions can, therefore, play a dominant part in the development of industry, and an industrialist who has no bank under his control is liable to fall under the control of some great financial group, which, because of its associated enterprises, may be a rival. In the later twenties some of the *zaibatsu*, particularly Mitsui, were penetrating even into trades which were the province of small producers. These small producers were normally financed by merchants who were themselves often dependent, especially if they engaged in foreign trade, on the financial resources of the *zaibatsu*. But at this time Mitsui's trading company (Mitsui Bussan Kaisha) was competing vigorously with the merchants in their own sphere. It had extended its practice of advancing funds to small producers and of giving them technical advice, and in this way it was able to bring them under its control. Even trade in minor agricultural products was being affected by this policy. Thus the power of the *zaibatsu* did not stop short with large-scale industry and trade, but penetrated deeply into the great mass of small-scale enterprises.

The various *zaibatsu* were keen rivals with one another. Although the emphasis of each group was rather different, yet there were many spheres of industry, commerce and finance in which they competed. Their rivalries extended also to the political sphere. Nevertheless, they tended to make a common front when faced with the militarist groups, and they sometimes co-operated with each other in particular branches of enterprise. For instance, they invested in each other's trust companies, and they helped to capitalize jointly, along with the semi-official Industrial Bank, electricity-generating companies and colonial enterprises of national importance.

The internal organization of the *zaibatsu* presented some unusual features. These massive businesses, equipped with all the contrivances of modern technology and managerial science, rested on institutional foundations laid down in the feudal past. Ownership was vested in a family or group of families, and the activities of every family member was regulated, according to Japanese practice, by a council which in the case of Mitsui reached its decisions by reference to the ancient code of the house. The financial links between the constituent firms were established by a holding company usually called a *honsha*. This controlled the chief operating subsidiaries under which there was an intricate network of sub-subsidiaries and affiliated companies. Major policies and the chief appointments to the *honsha* were determined in the family councils on the advice of the leading executives. The extent to which the family members themselves exercised administrative authority varied from *zaibatsu* to *zaibatsu*. In Mitsubishi the influence of the Iwasaki family remained very strong. In Mitsui, on the other hand, control over policy had passed to *banto*, or managers, even before the Restoration. Whatever objections there may be on social and political grounds to such a concentration of economic power, there can be little doubt that it assisted in the accumulation of capital and that it contributed 'strength, efficiency and sureness of purpose' to Japan in her period of rapid economic development.[1]

[1] T. A. Bisson, *Zaibatsu Dissolution in Japan*, p. 32; see also 'The Concentration of Economic Control in Japan', by the present author, in the *Economic Journal*, June 1937.

CHAPTER IX

REFLATION AND PREPARATION FOR WAR, 1932–37

After the fall of the Minseito Government and the abandonment of the gold standard in December 1931, the key position of Finance Minister was filled for the next four years by K. Takahashi, who had on previous occasions shown his financial skill, first as long ago as the Russo-Japanese War and, more recently, during the financial crisis of 1927. The restoration of the militarists' influence over policy, which had already been demonstrated by the course of events in Manchuria and was to show itself in a steadily increasing pressure for larger armaments, meant that there was no possibility of pursuing deflation further. Even if the new path had not been marked out for him by others, it seems that Takahashi had fully realized that the strain imposed by deflation on the social and economic structure of the country was too great for it to bear. He proposed, therefore, to follow a policy of reflation which, he thought, in the course of four years or so would call the unemployed resources into use and bring economic recovery to Japan, without at the same time exposing her to the danger of cumulative inflation. His was, in fact, a 'full-employment' policy, launched four years before Keynes' *General Theory* provided him with a theoretical justification.

The new policy, which was bitterly resented by orthodox financiers and economists, involved, first of all, an increase in Governmental expenditure, financed almost entirely by borrowing, and easy credit conditions. The form of the new expenditure was determined by the demands of the military and by the new commitments in Manchuria, and the result was that the proportion of the total expenditure that was spent on the Army and Navy rose from 31 per cent in 1931-32 to 47 per cent in 1936-37. During this time the Government defrayed about one-third of its expenditure by loans, and the internal national debt was increased from 4,480 million yen at March 1931 to 8,520 million yen at March 1936. The external debt diminished slightly during this period, and was only 1,330 million yen at this latter date.[1] Takahashi refused to raise substantially the amount spent on relief measures by the Ministry of Agriculture and the Home Department, since he argued that the general rise in Governmental expenditure

---

[1] This was the amount at par of exchange; the burden had, of course, been increased by the depreciation of the yen after 1932.

would diffuse benefits throughout the economy. At the same time he refused to increase taxation except by a modest excess profits tax, because he thought that any increase would discourage business revival. Thus, while he aimed at raising national expenditure by the amount required to restore 'full employment' he was determined not to press Government expenditure beyond the point at which inflationary tendencies would begin to appear.

He pursued his policy successfully up to the time of his assassination by the military in the revolt of February 1936, and by then the economic recovery at which he had aimed had been largely achieved. For this he has deservedly won praise, whereas Inouye, his predecessor, has been sternly criticized. Yet the balance of justice cannot be struck so easily. If Inouye, with his 'orthodox' financial policy, is to be condemned because he did not realize that deflation would provoke unendurable social distress and an inevitable political upheaval, he at least brought to bear pressures which led to sharp reductions in Japan's industrial costs. To this extent he prepared the way for the subsequent recovery. Without the discipline of the depression years, Japan's advance after 1932 might have been far less triumphant. On the other hand, Takahashi, for all his merits, can also be charged with a lack of political realism and foresight. He had cheerfully acquiesced for four years in a financial policy which made it possible for the militarists to pursue their ambitions. He knew that in them he was dealing with a group which did not easily recognize economic limitations on strategic designs, and that their appetite would grow with any effort to satisfy it. Consequently when the time came to call a halt on economic grounds, it was to be expected that the militarists would refuse to comply and that they would deal with Takahashi as they had dealt with Inouye. Judged solely from the standpoint of what we should now call a 'full employment' policy, Takahashi was amply justified in introducing measures for raising the public expenditure. But since the additional expenditure was of such a nature as to promote the strategic plans of the militarists, and since in the last resort policy was determined by them and not by the requirements of sound finance, the outcome was necessarily disastrous.

Before examining the effects on industry and trade of reflation up to 1936, we must glance at the cheap money policy that was followed during this time and also at the repercussions of the policy as a whole on the financial system. The discount rate of the Bank of Japan on commercial bills, which stood at 6·5 per cent in November 1931, was lowered by stages to 3·65 per cent in July 1933, and, what is more important, the interest rate of the Treasury Deposits Bureau was cut down during 1932 from 4·2 per cent to 3 per cent. At the same time the maximum fiduciary issue of the central bank was raised from 120 million yen to 1,000 million yen, and the note issue rose steadily from 1,330 million yen at the end of 1931 to 1,870 million yen five years later. Meanwhile, the exchange value of the yen was allowed to slide down from par in December 1931 (49·85 dollars=100 yen) to 20·70 in December 1932. After the revaluation of the dollar in the spring of 1933, the rate rose and reached 30·25 in December of that year. From this time it remained stable for the next five years, and became linked with sterling at 1s 2d.

Wholesale prices which averaged 70 in 1931 (1929=100) began to rise during 1932; but it was not until the end of 1936 that they recovered virtually to the 1929 level. Retail prices which had fallen from 91 in 1929 to 68 in 1931 (1926=100) rose steadily after that year and reached 80 in 1936. The course taken by wages is particularly interesting. The Bank of Japan's index of wage rates fell sharply, during the period of the depression, and its index of actual earnings declined even more. After 1932 the latter rose only slightly, while the former continued to fall.

BANK OF JAPAN'S INDICES OF WAGE-RATES, EARNINGS AND RETAIL PRICES [1]

(1926 = 100)

Year	Wage Rates A	Actual Earnings B	Retail Prices C	Real Earnings B/C
1929	98·6	103·9	91	114
1931	91·3	90·7	68	137
1932	88·1	88·1	69	128
1936	80·7	91·8	80	115

It is a matter for comment that average money wages fell steeply during the period of reflation, and that in 1936, after a period in which production and employment rose very substantially, the real earnings of the workers were no higher than they had been in 1929. These general indices do not reveal, however, the diversity in wage movements experienced by different industries. In all the heavy industries (engineering, shipbuilding, metal manufacture) which grew rapidly, the workers, especially skilled workers, improved their position, and their real wages were much higher in 1936 than they

[1] The Bank of Japan's indices of wage-rates and actual earnings cover only factories employing more than fifty (or in some cases forty) workers. For the method of compilation, see Uyeda, *The Small Industries of Japan*, pp. 298 *et seq.* Since these indices do not cover wages paid in small workplaces, they are not wholly representative of conditions in Japanese industry and tend to give too favourable a view of them. The wage index of the Ministry of Commerce and Industry fell by 24 per cent between 1926 and 1932; this index covers the earnings, including allowances, of workers in large and small establishments.

had been in 1929. On the other hand, the real wages of men in the light industries and of women, especially those engaged in textiles, deteriorated. In cotton spinning and silk reeling, for instance, real wages in 1936 were scarcely 70 per cent of those of 1929. Professor Uyeda, in commenting on the trend disclosed by statistics of real wages, reached the conclusion that observations of actual facts bore out the truth of the statistical evidence and that after 1931 'earnings did not increase sufficiently to compensate for the rising cost of living, and real wages were, therefore, on the average definitely falling'.[1]

A full explanation of what occurred requires an examination of first the changes in industrial production, secondly the trends in agriculture, and thirdly the movement of foreign trade. The index of industrial production rose steeply after reflation was introduced. Between 1931 and 1936 the index (1931-33=100) rose from 91 to 149.[2] But the rise was much steeper for producers' goods than for consumers' goods; in 1936 the index stood at 172 for the former but only 125 for the latter. Thus the greater part of the increased industrial production was not in the form of goods available for consumption, but consisted of munitions and capital equipment for industry at home and in Manchuria. In the second place, the boom did not communicate itself to agriculture. The price of rice did not recover to the 1929 level until 1935, while the price of raw silk, and so cocoon prices, remained low throughout the period. Even in 1936, after a slight improvement had set in, raw silk prices were still only a little above the 1932 level, and were not much more than half those of 1929. So a very large part of the economy remained depressed in spite of the boom in manufacturing industry. This has a direct bearing on the movements of wage rates. The members of agricultural families were driven by the depression to offer themselves in increasing numbers for industrial employment in the towns. The girls who had previously found jobs in the silk-reeling mills in rural areas now competed for jobs in other textile factories, especially the cotton mills. Yet, as technical improvements had reduced the number of workers required for a given output in the cotton industry, the demand for workers in that trade did not rise to an extent corresponding to the increase in output. Thus the persistent agricultural depression impelled a large-scale transference of workers from

---

[1] T. Uyeda, *The Small Industries of Japan*, p. 306. Professor Uyeda also states (p. 303) that in 1936 'the position [of the standard of living of the industrial workers] is not as good as that in 1924'. There are some difficulties in interpreting the statistics quoted above, but in spite of all the qualifications that have to be made, the general conclusion seems well established. For these qualifications, see Uyeda, *op. cit.*, p. 300.

[2] *Oriental Economist's* Index.

agriculture to industry and from rural to urban trades, and it exercised a powerful influence in keeping down industrial wages.

Thirdly, although the fall in the yen helped to raise the exports of manufactured goods, and although exports as a whole increased during this period, the terms of trade moved strongly against Japan. The following table demonstrates this. In interpreting it, one must remember that as Japan's industrial efficiency was rising at this time, the fact that she had to offer more export goods for a given quantity of imports does not necessarily mean that she had to devote a *correspondingly* greater amount of her resources to the production of those export goods.

TERMS OF TRADE

Year	Index of Import Prices	Index of Export Prices	Terms of Trade
1928	100	100	100
1932	65	57	88
1936	98	68	69
1937	126	76	60

Finally, in the course of the period from 1929 to 1937 the population rose from 63 to 71 million, and part of the increase in consumer goods was, therefore, required to meet the needs of the additional population, and was not available to raise consumption per head.

One may conclude that reflation and the depreciation of the yen enabled Japan to create a condition of virtually full employment, to redistribute her resources by transference from agriculture to industry, and to enlarge her production and foreign trade. It was because her resources were not fully employed at the beginning of this process, and because of the chronic depression in agriculture, that the increased loan-financed Governmental expenditure did not produce symptoms of inflation. At the same time it was because the increased production took the form of munitions, new capital equipment for home industry, and investment goods for Manchuria and, to a lesser extent, because of the worsened terms of trade and of the benefit bestowed by rising prices on the profit earner, that this increased employment of resources did not lead to any improvement in the workers' general standard of life.

This process of development and adaptation was affected by the rise in the efficiency of Japanese industry during the thirties. The point will be discussed in the next chapter; but it must be mentioned here because, clearly, the reduction in costs so caused contributed to the increase in output and exports that occurred during this time. Had costs not been reduced by technical improvements, it is probable that equilibrium in the balance of payments could have been achieved only by a further depreciation of the yen, and that either the development of Manchuria and rearmament would have progressed more slowly, or the standard of life would have been forced down far lower.

The behaviour of the banking system in response to the Government's deflationary policy throws considerable light on the relations between the ordinary banks and the Governmental financial institutions. In the first place, it is observed that the bulk of the Government bonds issued between 1931 and 1936 were taken up by institutional lenders, namely the ordinary banks, savings banks, the special banks and the Bank of Japan. The ordinary and savings banks together absorbed about two-thirds of the amount issued, and they held by the end of February 1936 some 43 per cent of the Government bonds outstanding, while the Treasury Deposits Bureau held well over 20 per cent. By the end of 1936 the proportion of Government bonds to total deposits was about 23 per cent in the case of the ordinary banks and 55 per cent in the case of the savings banks. That the Government had to rely on the banks to take up its issues could not be regarded as ominous, as it would in some other countries in peacetime. It was a necessary consequence of the structure of the capital market in Japan and of the disposition of ordinary investors. As we have already seen, the latter are accustomed to entrust their savings to the banks, trust companies or post office savings system, which then invest these resources, and the increasingly large holdings of these bonds did not in the least disturb the confidence of the bank depositors.

It might have been expected that the ordinary banks would have followed the lead of the Government and the central bank in extending credit on a larger scale to their clients, and that this would have set going an inflationary movement. But no such movement occurred, and it appears that the ordinary banks, instead of following the lead given by the Government, rather pursued a credit policy appropriate to a deflationary period. The central bank's influence over the credit policy of the other banks was still weak, and during this time the latter remained adherents of Inouye's financial principles and were sceptical of Takahashi's policy. They weeded out their less sound debtors and were cautious in making advances. The volume of their loans outstanding even declined substantially between 1931 and 1936. The cautious policy of the banks was not, however, the only factor that produced this result. The high industrial profits earned in the years of rising prices and stationary or declining wages, enabled manufacturers not merely to finance extensions to their businesses out of their own resources, but also to repay their outstanding loans to the banks.

Reflation in Japan thus has some peculiar features. The Government was able to spend heavily on armaments out of loans without bringing about competition with itself for the necessary resources, largely because the ordinary banks refrained from creating private credit to match that of the Government and of the official financial institutions. Consequently, it was able to carry through the redistribution of the country's labour and capital in order to build up a 'quasi-war-economy' without provoking a steep rise in prices and without imposing vexatious administrative controls over the disposition of resources.

By 1936 recovery had been achieved, and the time had come, in Mr Takahashi's opinion, to call a halt to the process of reflation. The Army, however, far from being prepared to accept any limitation on its war-preparation expenditure, asked for further increases. The ensuing conflict was a contributory cause of the outbreak of February 1936, when Takahashi was murdered. His successor was more amenable to military pressure, and accepted the proposition that no halt could be called in loan-financed expenditure. In the first few months of office, he carried through extensive conversion operations by which a great number of 5 per cent bonds were exchanged for 3·5 per cent bonds; while the Bank of Japan's discount rate was further lowered and the deposit rates of the ordinary and savings banks were brought down sharply. The budget for the financial year 1937-38, as originally drawn up and passed, provided for large increases in expenditure which were to be met mainly by expanding the deficit bond issues, although some new taxes were imposed.

Subsequent events showed that Takahashi was right in thinking that, on economic grounds, the time had come in 1936 to modify the reflation policy; for, by the end of 1936, symptoms of financial strain began to appear. There was a sharp upward movement in wholesale prices; the rate of export expansion began to slow down; and the yen showed signs of weakness. A fall in the exchange, however, would have endangered the policy of creating a 'quasi-war-time economy' which was now being pursued more vigorously than ever; for a lower yen would have raised the price of imports of strategic materials which were now being acquired in large quantities. So, early in 1937, control over exchange dealings, which had previously been of little account, was tightened. Traders now had to secure official permission before they could obtain exchange in payment for imports for an amount in excess of 30,000 yen a month, and just before the Lukouchiao incident in July, the limit was reduced to 1,000 yen a month. Between March and July large exports of gold also became necessary and these amounted during that period to 380 million yen (at the valuation of 1930). In July the outbreak of war with China brought a new era in economic policy, and from then on Japan began to adopt the devices for creating a war-time economy with which most countries of the world were later to become familiar. There was an immense increase in Government expenditure financed partly by higher taxation, but mainly by bond issues; there was a large-scale transference of resources from peace-time to war-time industries; and there was a wide extension of control over economic processes.

An examination of Japan's economic war-time policy lies beyond the scope of this chapter,[1] but one fact of outstanding importance must be emphasized. The economic circumstances of Japan on entering the war of 1937 were very different from those attending the inception of the Manchurian campaign of 1931 and the subsequent rearmament. In 1931 a large section of Japan's resources were unemployed or under-employed. It was possible for her to rearm and to develop her strategic industries at home and on the Continent by drawing on those idle resources and without making it necessary for her to call a halt to the expansion of her civilian industries or to her exports. By 1937, however, her resources were virtually fully employed,[2] and any further growth in the armament industries was inevitably at the expense of civilian production and of the normal export trade. So, from the very beginning of the war, drastic controls to effect the necessary transferences had to be imposed, and even some of the leading exporting industries (e.g. cotton) had to be contracted. Indeed, this point appears to have been reached early in 1937, when the financial and exchange controls were instituted in order to complete preparations for the war.

---

[1] For this, see J. B. Cohen, *Japan's Economy in War and Reconstruction*; also, for the period before the Pearl Harbour attack, see E. B. Schumpeter (ed.), *The Industrialisation of Japan and Manchukuo, 1930-40*, especially pp. 789-854, and G. C. Allen, *Japanese Industry: Its Recent Development and Present Condition*.

[2] 'Fully employed' at least to the extent that bottlenecks in the supply of certain factors (e.g. skilled labour) were being encountered.

CHAPTER X

INDUSTRIAL DEVELOPMENTS AFTER THE WORLD DEPRESSION, 1932-37

In the previous chapter it was shown that a great expansion took place in industrial production and in the volume of manufactured exports during the years preceding the outbreak of the Sino-Japanese War in 1937. The changes in the relative importance of the different industries and in the composition of the export trade were equally significant. For several decades before 1929 the trend in industrial development had altered very little, and the export trade was becoming increasingly specialized to textiles. Although the scope of Japan's industrial activity was constantly extending, it did not then seem likely that her main industrial interests would alter profoundly for many years to come. Yet when the country began to emerge from the depression it was soon seen that a new course had been set. This is clearly brought out by contrasting the composition of Japan's industry and export trade in 1937 with that of 1929. Some indication of the nature of the change has already been given, since it has been shown that the expansion of industrial output between 1931 and 1937 occurred mainly in the capital goods industries. But a more detailed consideration of the changes is needed for a complete understanding of the industrial history of the period.

We cannot precisely measure the changes in the relative importance of the various industries between 1929 and 1937, because the statistics of production and employment are incomplete. For instance, the Factory Statistics do not cover workplaces with less than five operatives, which were responsible for a high proportion of employment in many trades. But the information is sufficient to show the broad extent of the movements; these are set out in the table on page 145 and in Tables VI and XII in Appendix B.

The outstanding changes were the steep *relative* decline in textiles and the rise in the metal, engineering and chemical groups. These increased their proportion of a larger industrial labour force from just over a quarter in 1930 to well over two-fifths by the end of 1937. Such figures of the volume of output as are available for these trades support these conclusions. The output of pig iron nearly doubled between 1929 and 1936, while the raw steel production rose from $2\frac{1}{4}$ million tons to $5\frac{1}{2}$ million tons, and the range of finished steel products turned out was widely extended. In the chemical industry there was a very substantial growth in the output of explosives, sulphuric acid, soda ash, caustic soda, calcium carbide, dyestuffs, and paints and most other products. In the machinery and instrument trades the rise in output is difficult to measure. Both the Factory Statistics and the Bank of Japan's index of industrial employment show, however, that the number of workers engaged in these indus-

PERCENTAGES OF TOTAL FACTORY EMPLOYMENT IN VARIOUS MANUFACTURING INDUSTRIES, 1929-37

	1929	1936	1937
Textiles	50·4	37·9	35·2
Metals	6·2	9·7	10·6
Machinery, Vehicles, Instruments, etc.	13·8	18·3	20·5
Chemicals	6·4	11·1	11·0
Others	23·2	23·0	22·7
Total	100	100	100
Total Factory Employment (*in thousands*)	1,825	2,593	2,937

tries grew very fast, and the testimony of foreign technical observers suggests that not merely was the quantity of output greatly increased but quality was improved and the range of the production extended. By 1937 Japan was able to produce most kinds of machinery required by her industries, such as textile machinery, many kinds of machine tools, scientific instruments and electrical apparatus, and she was by then well able to meet her own needs for complete power-station plants. A substantial export to Manchuria had also been worked up, and if she was still importing machinery in large quantities, this could be attributed mainly to the fact that she was trying to build up her equipment rapidly in preparation for war. Shipbuilding also took an upward turn after 1931 partly because of the recovery in international trade and partly because of the introduction of a 'scrap and build' plan to which reference will later be made. The number of workers in the chief shipbuilding yards rose from 34,000 in December 1931 to 51,000 in January 1936, and the tonnage of merchant ships (motor and steam) launched rose from 54,000 gross tons in 1932, the lowest point reached, to 446,000 gross tons in 1937. This was far greater than any figure of launchings since 1919. The industry also benefited by the revival of naval building. By June 1937 Japan possessed a

K

merchant marine of 4,500,000 gross tons,[1] the third largest mercantile fleet in the world. Much of this was composed of new
ships.

Progress was by no means limited to the capital goods industries.
Even in the textile group which, taken as a whole, became relatively
less important, there was no significant fall in total employment. The
cotton industry continued to advance at a time when Japan's main
competitor in international trade was still losing ground, and there
was a strong tendency for that industry to move from a concentration
on cheap bulk lines towards the production of higher quality goods.
This led to important relative changes in the different sections of the
cotton industry. The section which concerned itself with fancy goods
and which was made up of medium-sized specialist weaving sheds
grew much faster than that composed of the large sheds which formed
part of the great spinning-weaving mills, were equipped with automatic looms and produced cheap shirtings and sheetings for export.
The result was to reverse the tendency, which had been characteristic
of the twenty years before 1929, towards an increasing concentration of cotton manufacture in the combined spinning-weaving
concerns.

The woollen and worsted industry also greatly expanded during
these years. The annual average imports of raw wool rose from
774,000 piculs in the period 1926-29 to 1,665,000 piculs in the period
1933-36; yarn output doubled; and imports both of yarns and tops
dwindled to insignificance. The several branches of the weaving
industry were very differently affected. Whereas the output of muslin
for Japanese dress, which previously formed an overwhelmingly
large proportion of the total output of fabrics, remained stationary,
there was a large growth in the manufacture both of serge for foreign
dress and of woollen cloth. On the basis of this rising production, a
substantial export trade was built up in the thirties. Japan thus
completed the process which had been taking place in the later years
of the previous decade. She freed herself from dependence on foreign
supplies of tops and yarns, and she built up into substantial trades
the new branches of the industry which first began to develop in the
early twenties.

An even more rapid advance occurred in the rayon industry which,
though merely in its initial stages in 1929, became by 1937 the largest
in the world. In that year Japan produced 326 million lb. of rayon
compared with 27 million lb. in 1929. After 1934 the output of staple
fibre began to grow quickly, and it reached 167 million lb. in 1937.
This manufacture was encouraged for strategic reasons, since it

---

[1] Ships of 100 gross tons and over, including registrations in the Japanese
Colonies.

provided Japan with a supply of textile materials which could be used as substitutes for imported cotton and wool in the event of war. Several other branches of the textile trade, for example, hosiery, also expanded during this time. If, in spite of the absolute growth in all these industries, the importance of the textile group as a whole declined, this was partly because of the continued depression in raw silk. The production of raw silk did not diminish greatly in quantity between 1929 and 1936, but the value of the output fell from 857 million yen in 1929 to 398 million yen in 1934 (when the depression in this trade reached its lowest point), and even in 1936 it was only 517 million yen. The labour force attached to the industry declined from 525,000 to 321,000 during this period. The relation of this depression to the fall in raw silk exports will be considered presently. Here it is sufficient to point out that the period saw a rise in the proportion of the output consumed at home (from 19 per cent to 29 per cent), and, indeed, a substantial increase in the absolute amount of raw silk sold in the home market. The silk weavers therefore did not suffer in company with the reelers, and as those weavers were at the same time developing a large trade in rayon fabrics, their industry expanded considerably.

The relative decline in textile employment cannot be wholly attributed to the depression in the raw silk trade. Another cause was the technical improvements effected during these years, for these economized labour. Technical progress was especially marked in the cotton industry. Among the spinners there was a considerable rise in the scale of operations. In 1929 only 8 per cent of the spindles were in mills with more than 100,000 spindles; by 1935 this proportion had increased to 24 per cent. In 1929 half the capacity was in mills with under 50,000 spindles; in 1935 the proportion had fallen to one-third. This decline in the importance of the small *mill* was accompanied by a tendency for the small spinning *firm* also to disappear. Firms with more than 100,000 spindles increased their proportion of the total spindleage from 70 per cent in 1929 to 86 per cent in 1935. At the same time the improvements in mill equipment which had begun in 1927 were carried much further. The period between 1927 and 1933 saw the almost complete replacement of ordinary rings by high-draft rings throughout the industry, and the change made possible the elimination of many processes between carding and spinning and so brought about economies in labour. Other improvements were effected, such as the substitution of overhead carriers for rail conveyors, better methods of temperature- and humidity-control and the improved layout of the mills. The extent of these economies in labour is shown by the fact that whereas the output of yarn increased from 1,012 million lb. in 1927 to 1,204 million lb. in 1933, the number of operatives engaged on the ring spinning machines was unchanged and the number engaged on the preliminary and intermediate processes, from mixing to roving, fell from 45,000 to 31,000. The result over the whole period in which economies were being effected was a rise in output per operative in the spinning mills from 5,700 lb. in 1926 to 7,000 lb. in 1929, and to 9,300 lb. in 1935. The average number of spindles in operation rose from 5,800,000 in 1929 to 8,200,000 in 1935.

In the weaving branches there were changes of equal importance. The period saw the general adoption of automatic looms by the weaving section of the combined spinning-weaving mills, and this was the main cause of the rise in output per operative in that part of the cotton-weaving industry from 22,300 yards in 1926 to 36,000 yards in 1929 and 49,000 in 1935.[1] Among the specialist weavers, whose output grew very fast after the world depression, there were marked changes in scale and equipment. Between 1929 and 1936 the proportion of the looms which were in sheds with fifty looms and over grew from 38 per cent to 48 per cent. While the number of hand-looms was halved and the number of narrow power-looms fell by one-third, the number of wide power-looms increased about $2\frac{1}{2}$ times. According to Professor Uyeda's estimates, the number of looms per worker in mills with fifty looms and over increased by more than 60 per cent between 1926 and 1935 and in mills with from ten to forty-nine looms by 40 per cent. It can be inferred that the growth of scale and the improvements in equipment were accompanied by considerable savings in costs.

During the twenties generalizations about the Japanese cotton industry had been usually based on observation of conditions in the combined spinning-weaving mills. During the next decade, in which the cloth output of those mills increased far less rapidly than that of the specialist weavers, these conditions became less typical of the weaving industry as a whole. By 1935-36 the specialists were consuming 70 per cent of the cotton yarn used in Japanese weaving sheds; and they had by then become responsible for 58 per cent of the piece goods exports (in value). It should be explained that the use of automatic looms was confined to the combined spinning-weaving mills, which concentrated on the manufacture of a narrow range of standardized goods; for the ordinary loom was still preferred for the types of fabric which were turned out by the specialist weaving industry. To describe the Japanese cotton industry during the thirties in terms of the combined spinning-weaving mills and of automatic looms is, therefore, to give an incomplete picture. In 1936, out of

---

[1] In the *Report of the Cotton Mission* (p. 27), the proportion of automatic looms to the total number in the sheds owned by the spinning-weaving firms was estimated to be one-fifth. This was in 1930. During the next five years the substitution of automatics for ordinary looms was completed.

266,000 wide power-looms in the whole of the Japanese cotton-weaving industry, only about one-third were automatic. If the output of the section that used automatics was still growing, it was from the ordinary looms used by the specialist weavers that the greater part of the increased production of piece-goods came.

In the wool-using trades, also, there was an advance in efficiency. Rings instead of mules came to be used to a greater extent for low counts in the worsted spinning section, and the growth of the weaving sections led to the establishment of many new sheds which, though not large, were well-equipped and highly specialized. In one of the chief new centres of the industry (Aichi Prefecture) it was calculated that the cloth output per operative increased threefold in quantity between 1926 and 1933.[1]

Depression in the raw silk industry led to the introduction of many economies. A better co-ordination of the activities of silk-raisers and reelers brought about the cheapening of cocoons and improvements in their quality. The reelers made greater use of multiple-reeling machines by which an operative could reel twenty filaments at once compared with five on the older type of machine, and this brought about a steep fall in labour costs. In silk weaving the replacement of the hand-loom by the power-loom, which had already occurred in other textiles, went forward rapidly in the early thirties, and there was a considerable growth in the number of wide power-looms for the production of both silk and rayon piece goods for export. In rayon yarn production there were far reaching changes both in the quality of the filament and the cost of manufacture. The price of 100 lb. of 120 denier yarn, which ranged between 253 and 130 yen in 1929, was down to between 88 and 53 yen in 1936.

In the chemical industry there were marked improvements. There was an enlargement of the scale of plants in the ammonium sulphate and other chemical trades, and costs were reduced substantially. The same is true of the paper industry. Here costs were brought down partly by rationalization, which permitted greater mill specialization, and partly by reducing waste. One example may be given. In 1928 94 lb. of coal were used for every 100 lb. of paper produced; this fell in 1936 to 57 lb. Other economies were effected in the consumption of electric power.[2]

In the pottery industry, especially in the large factories, there was a revolution in methods after 1930. The chief producers installed mechanically operated conveyors in the body-making and decorating departments, and in this way production was speeded up. Coal was superseded by gas and electricity in firing, and tunnel kilns were

[1] Nagoya College of Commerce, *The Present Status of the Woollen Industry in Japan*, p. 41.
[2] Information provided by the *Oriental Economist* in 1936.

introduced with the result that in the decade before 1936 unit-costs were halved in the large factories. Even in the workshop section of the trade efficiency was improved, chiefly through changes in organiz- ation which enabled the small producers to specialize to a greater extent than formerly.

In the iron and steel industry, also, there was an improvement in technique. The average capacity of the blast furnaces doubled between 1929 and 1936 because of the installation of a number of large modern furnaces. In steel-making the size of the typical open- hearth furnace increased, and on the eve of the Sino-Japanese War it was estimated that in the previous nine years the amount of fuel needed to produce a ton of open-hearth steel had fallen by 40 per cent. There was a striking increase in the production of electrically smelted steel—an indication of Japan's newly found ability to produce high-grade steel. At the same time she was enlarging her capacity for producing the different kinds of finished steel. In spite of a large growth in her consumption of finished steel, imports fell, and in 1936 her exports (in tonnage) exceeded imports. For the metal- lurgical trades as a whole a Japanese writer has estimated that output per man-hour rose by 25 per cent between 1930 and 1936, and this estimate seems to be reasonable.[1]

Advances in engineering are much more difficult to measure. We have seen that Japan greatly enlarged the quantity, improved the quality and extended the range of her engineering output at this time, and a few additional examples may be given. Before 1929 nearly all turbines above 10,000 kilowatt capacity were imported; by 1937 most of the greatly increased demand was being satisfied from home sources. At the beginning of this period Japan had to import nearly all her boiler tubes; at the end of it she was making tubes of good quality to satisfy her needs. Foundry technique also advanced. Large steel castings of satisfactory quality could not be produced by Japanese foundries before 1932; by 1936 engineers could obtain them from local sources of supply without difficulty. Foreign technicians in Japan who a few years before were loud in their complaints about the deficiencies of Japanese engineering labour testified to the marked improvements that occurred during the thirties, both among the workers in the shops and among technicians. During the twenties these foreign observers frequently commented on the over-staffing of Japanese plants, when judged from European or American standards. This over-staffing was a necessary consequence of the employers' practice of retaining workers in their employment even in years of depression, as well as of the cheapness of labour at that time. The depression of trade in 1930-32 was so serious as to enforce economies in labour, while the subsequent buoyancy of trade

[1] I. Asahi, *The Economic Strength of Japan*, pp. 91-2.

took up the slack that remained. The result was that over-staffing was far less noticeable in 1936 than previously. Improvements in organization and technical skill, moreover, greatly reduced the proportion of technicians and supervisory staff to the total numbers employed, especially in metallurgical, machinery and chemical plants.[1] Even in mining, which had been stagnating during the twenties, costs were reduced, chiefly during the years of depression when mineowners were forced to seek new methods. In coal-mining output per man-shift (underground workers only) rose from 0·7 metric tons in 1928 to 1·2 metric tons in 1931, mainly because of the greater use of mechanical conveyors.[2]

Japanese industry thus made a notable advance in efficiency in the decade preceding the outbreak of the war with China in July 1937. The advance was associated with a rise in skill among her workers and technicians, especially in the metal and engineering trades, and with an improvement in the equipment and organization of her plants. In some industries there was a rise in the scale of operations, and in others, where the small workplace remained typical, the producers became increasingly specialized. The main improvements in manufacturing methods (especially in the textile trades) were effected during the years of depression; but the period of expansion after 1932 made it possible for further economies to be realized both through a rise in the scale of operations and also through the 'full running' of the various plants.

The advances in industrial efficiency resulted mainly from the responses of entrepreneurs to the pressures exerted on them during the years of depression. Industry in this way prepared itself to take full advantage of the opportunities of the succeeding period. The Government also played a part. Its financial and rearmament policy had, of course, an important influence on the direction of the industrial development after 1932. But, in addition, it concerned itself more intimately than in the past with industrial organization. This intervention probably had only a mild effect on efficiency, but its political and social consequences deserve close attention. During the years of intense depression, 1930 and 1931, the Government was drawn into a policy of intervention either with the object of implementing the deflationary policy of the time or to prevent the collapse of particular trades. Its most ambitious project was the establishment of the Industrial Rationalization Bureau, as part of the Ministry of Commerce and Industry. The practical function of this Bureau was to devise and to introduce means for the co-ordination of policy within the various trades and for the increase of efficiency. Com-

[1] Cf. I. Asahi, *op. cit.*, p. 93.
[2] Most of the information about technical improvements has been derived from special investigations made by the *Oriental Economist* in 1936 and 1937.

mittees were set up to promote standardization and simplification and to encourage co-operative selling among manufacturers. One of the Bureau's duties was to supervise the administration of the Major Industries Control Law, passed at this time with the object of creating for every large-scale industry a cartel for the control of production, sales and price policies. The Government was given power under this law, and under subsequent amendments to it, both to compel non-members of the cartels to abide by the cartel regulations and also to prevent any abuse of monopolistic power. It is doubtful if this law had any important effect on the structure of Japanese industry. Although many cartels were formed at this time, it was the depression rather than the law which was responsible for their appearance. The Government used its coercive powers very cautiously, in part, no doubt, because it was not prepared to antagonize the business groups concerned, but mainly because the purpose of the law was ambiguous. It was not by any means clear whether the main object of the legislation was the reduction of manufacturing costs, or whether it was the improvement of the market position of the producers through the creation of monopolistic organizations among them. It is significant, however, that the use that was made of these powers by the Governments of the thirties changed with the political forces in control. A report of the Industrial Rationalization Bureau in October 1935 stated 'Along with improvements in market conditions in 1933 and 1934 the administration of the law was altered so that from being chiefly concerned with strengthening the control exercised by cartels, the executive authority directed its attention to the protection of the public interest.'[1] The meaning of this statement is not difficult to understand. In 1930-31 the Government was in the hands of business groups and was chiefly concerned with rescuing industry from the effects of the depression. By 1935 not merely had the depression lifted, but political power had shifted largely to the military and naval groups which were desirous of subjecting private enterprise to regulation in such a way as to promote the strategic interests of the State.

Thus measures that had been conceived for the purpose of rationalizing industry came to be used, first, to support cartels, and later to impose national control over the policy of industrialists. It seems that as neither of the main contending political groups had during this period established complete supremacy over the other, the application of the law was at no time very vigorous. The change of emphasis which has been noted was common to other fields of economic policy. For instance, the laws governing the Manufacturers' Guilds

[1] Bureau of Industrial Rationalization, *The Principle and Administrative Policy of the Major Industries Control Law*, October 1935.

(*Kogyo Kumiai*) and the Export Guilds (*Yushutsu Kumiai*) were revised in 1931 with the object of encouraging co-operation among small manufacturers and traders so as to reduce their costs. With the subsequent political and economic changes, the functions and status of the guilds were also changed. The *Kogyo Kumiai* came to be regarded as organs for freeing small producers from the control of the great merchants and financiers and for supporting those social groups which made common cause with the military in their antagonism to the *zaibatsu*. The Export Guilds after 1933 became less concerned with the promotion of greater efficiency in the export field than with controlling and diverting foreign trade so as to meet restrictions imposed by foreign nations on Japanese exports.

The policy towards rural communities throws further light on the political trends of the period. Financial encouragement was given to the peasants' co-operative societies. Co-operative storehouses, fertilizer factories and filatures were set up with Government help, and the co-operatives displaced merchants from several lines of rural trade. Attempts were also made to divert industry to remote rural prefectures, and munitions contracts were distributed with this end in view. When the great depression struck the raw silk industry the Government at first followed the practice of earlier years and provided funds for valorization. As the depression became intensified, it passed laws designed to increase efficiency. Then, in 1935, it introduced a redundancy scheme for removing excessive capacity both from the silk-raising and the reeling branches, and it controlled by licence the establishment of filatures and silk merchanting businesses. Help was also given towards the setting up of co-operative reeling mills by the silk-raisers so that they might escape from the financial control of the large reelers.

The policy of extending national control over industry partly for strategic reasons and partly for the promotion of the interests of particular social groups came to a head in the controversy over the electricity-generating industry. The nationalization of this industry, which the military and certain sections of the bureaucracy advocated, was desired partly because it would make possible the sale of electricity at cheaper rates to small users at the expense of the large users. But the business interests were sufficiently powerful to thwart this policy up to the outbreak of war in 1937. They could not defeat similar attempts in other trades. For instance, in 1934 legislation provided for the establishment of the Japan Iron and Steel Company by the amalgamation of six large private concerns with the State's Yawata works. The result was to place nearly all the pig iron capacity and more than half the steel capacity in the hands of a company whose capital was held mainly by the State. Again, firms (including foreign firms) engaged in the distribution of oil were obliged to store oil equivalent to their sales in a six months' period, and the production, refining and distribution of oil were brought under close Government control. Duties on imported oil were raised so as to provide funds for the subsidizing of home production and for the development of hydrogenation. The shipping and shipbuilding industries were also the object of intervention. During the depression years the Government adopted a 'scrap and build' plan to support these industries, and as a result the merchant marine became equipped with a high proportion of new fast ships. In 1936 the Government assumed large powers of supervision over the activities of shipping companies.

There were other examples of this trend towards Government control within Japan itself; but the policy received its most unambiguous expression on the continent, especially in Manchukuo. There the influence of the Army was paramount; and the kinds of industries that were fostered after 1932, no less than the methods employed to foster them, indicate that the policy which in Japan itself was only gradually and tentatively adopted was there unchallenged. The industries that were introduced into Manchukuo, or were extended after the establishment of that State, were chiefly branches of the metallurgical and chemical industries—the war industries—and all forms of industrial investment in that country were strictly controlled and were supplied up to 1937 by or through the South Manchuria Railway Company or companies in which the Manchukuo and Japanese Governments held a large part of the capital. The most striking developments occurred after the outbreak of war against China and are, therefore, not within the scope of this chapter. But the foundations of the great expansion that later occurred were laid in the years from 1931 to 1937. During that period the output of iron ore and pig iron in Manchukuo more than doubled (the latter reached 762,000 metric tons in 1937); and steel production, which hardly existed before 1935, reached 430,000 tons two years later. There were considerable advances, too, in coal production (which amounted to 12,500,000 metric tons in 1937), and in the output of cement, chemicals, gold and many other minerals and manufactured goods. Japanese investment in Manchuria rose very fast. At the time of the Manchurian campaign in 1931 total Japanese investment in that country stood at 1,600 million yen; by the end of 1937 it was well over 3,000 million yen. The resources of Korea were also extensively developed after 1931, especially her mining industry and the industries that depended on minerals.

The expansion of Japanese enterprise on the continent, together with the political changes in Japan, had important effects on the position of the *zaibatsu*. It has been shown that the depression discredited the Minseito Government, and also the great business groups associated with it. Particularly strong opposition was encountered from the military, who disliked the policy of that Government in the fields of foreign relations and armaments, and from the peasantry and small producers who had suffered most bitterly from the economic collapse. Violent attacks were made on the *zaibatsu* on the ground that, in promoting their own financial prosperity, they had jeopardized the interests of the State and had done great hurt to the peasants and the small producers and traders. These attacks came to a head in May 1932 in the assassination of Baron Dan, the chief executive of Mitsui, at the hands of a 'young officer' group. The *zaibatsu* retreated. They tried to disarm popular resentment by relegating to obscurity officials who had been responsible for their previous business policy. Mitsui, which was the main target of criticism, withdrew from trade in minor agricultural products and sold to the public large holdings of shares in some of its leading companies. It made a donation of 3 million yen for the relief of distress, and it established in 1933 a fund of 30 million yen for the promotion of social services. After the mutiny of February 1936 (the 'February Incident'), which was in part the outcome of 'anti-capitalist' feeling, the members of the Mitsui family announced their intention of withdrawing from directorates and from active participation in the business. The *zaibatsu* attempted to show their devotion to the national interests by establishing, or investing in, new enterprises of strategic importance, such as synthetic oil production; and they provided most of the capital for a new bank intended to finance those small traders and industrialists who were members of Manufacturers' or Export Guilds.

Their opponents found it hard to believe that the *zaibatsu* were 'sincere' in their new policy, which was referred to as a 'camouflage policy'. The critics may well have been right. Powerful groups in the Army were advocating at this time the creation of a 'quasi-war-time economy' (*Junsenji Keizai*). By this they meant the destruction of the liberal and capitalistic influences in society and the direction of the country's resources along lines determined wholly by strategic needs. This process proceeded slowly between 1932 and the 'February Incident' of 1936, since it encountered opposition from the older bureaucrats and statesmen as well as from the threatened business groups. After 1936 the pace was quickened; but it cannot be believed that the *zaibatsu*, though they could no longer resist openly, were enthusiastic supporters of the policy.

It is true that the creation of a *Junsenji Keizai* brought certain compensating advantages to the *zaibatsu*, since if it damaged their political, commercial and financial interests, it stimulated the development of the heavy industries in which they had many important enterprises. But the compensation was hardly adequate;

for much of the new industrial development, especially in Manchukuo, was in the hands of business groups other than the *zaibatsu*. The military could not dispense with the help of big business in the development of the strategic industries and the resources of Manchukuo; but since they were hostile to the *zaibatsu*, they had to look elsewhere for the capital and business experience that were needed. Among the new business groups that grew in strength in consequence of this policy, the most important was the Nippon Sangyo Kaisha (Nissan), controlled by Y. Aikawa. This concern commended itself for two reasons. Its capital structure was very different from that of the *zaibatsu* undertakings; for its shares were fairly widely distributed, instead of being concentrated in a few families. In the second place, Nissan's fortunes were wholly bound up with the promotion of a *Junsenji Keizai*, and it was likely to be amenable to militarist influences. When the development of Manchukuo was accelerated after the outbreak of the Sino-Japanese War in 1937, the industrial undertakings which had hitherto been conducted by the South Manchuria Railway Company were transferred to a new concern, the Manchukuo Heavy Industries Development Company, in which Nissan held half the capital and the Manchukuo Government the rest. Nissan also obtained financial support from the special banks. Whether Nissan was as independent of the *zaibatsu* in reality as in appearance may be doubted. At all events the *shinko-zaibatsu* did not survive the collapse of Japanese imperialism.[1]

The changes in the volume, composition and destination of Japanese exports in the period from the world depression until the outbreak of war with China reflect faithfully the financial and industrial developments that have been described. The total value of Japan's exports to foreign countries fell from 2,149 million yen in 1929 to 1,147 in 1933; but recovery was rapid after the fall of the yen, and in 1936 it reached 2,693 million yen. The course of the import trade was similar; 2,216 million yen in 1929, 1,236 million yen in 1931 and 2,764 million in 1936. In the first six months of 1937 there was a sharp upturn in the foreign trade, particularly in imports; for Japan was then buying heavily from abroad in preparation for the coming war.

In volume exports were probably some two-thirds greater in 1936 than in 1929, and this increase, it must be remembered, took place at a time when international trade as a whole was stagnating. The structure of the export trade altered profoundly. There was no significant change in exports of raw materials and foodstuffs, which were comparatively small in both years. The proportion of finished manufactures in the total, however, rose from 44 per cent in 1929 to

[1] *Shinko-zaibatsu* (or New *zaibatsu*) is a term commonly used to describe these new capital groups.

59 per cent in 1936; while there was a steep decline in exports of semi-manufactured articles—from 43 per cent to 27 per cent. The cause of the declining importance of the last class of goods is, of course, to be found in the persistent depression in the raw silk trade; in 1929 raw silk accounted for 37 per cent of the exports, in 1936 for only 15 per cent. In the cotton trade, although there was a great expansion in the quantity of piece-goods—from 1,791 million square yards in 1929 to 2,710 million square yards in 1936—yarn and piece-goods together barely maintained their importance in the export trade as a whole. It was about one-fifth of the total in each of these years. Exports of other textiles expanded considerably, notably rayon yarn and piece-goods, woollen and worsted piece-goods and knitted goods, and the proportion of textiles other than cotton and raw silk in the total trade rose from 13 per cent to 18 per cent. Even so, textiles as a whole formed a less important part of Japan's exports in 1936 than in 1929; the proportion having fallen from 69·4 per cent to 52·6 per cent. It was mainly to the rise in exports of metals, metal manufactures, machinery and instruments that this fall can be attributed. The share of these products in the total exports rose from 4 per cent in 1929 to over 14 per cent in 1936. There had also been a remarkable increase in the exports of numerous miscellaneous industries—toys, lamps, pottery, glass, and many others. Many of these goods were the products of small-scale trades which had expanded after the fall of the yen; and the result was that by the end of the period Japan's export trade was far more highly diversified than it had been in 1929.

The destination of the exports had also altered. The United States, which had taken 43 per cent of the exports in 1929, took only 22 per cent in 1936; this was because of the fall in raw silk exports to that market. China, including Kwantung, Manchuria and Hong Kong, took 25 per cent in 1929 and 27 per cent in 1936; for the steep rise in exports to Manchuria, in consequence of the heavy investments in that country, more than offset the fall in exports to China Proper. Exports to other Asiatic markets—British India, the Dutch East and Straits Settlements—also rose considerably, and so did exports to Africa, South America, Europe and Australasia. As a broad generalization, it may be said that in 1936 Japan's export trade consisted of raw silk, together with certain other products like canned fish, tea and pottery, supplied to the United States; machinery and other capital goods supplied to Manchukuo and North China; and textiles and cheap miscellaneous consumption goods supplied to many countries, particularly to continental Asia and the South Seas.

The lessened specialization both in markets and commodities which occurred over this period may suggest that Japan's trade had become less vulnerable than formerly to changes in demand; but this conclusion cannot be accepted without important qualifications. The rise in exports of metals and machinery, which did much to affect the trade, was in some degree the result of Japan's strategic plans and of the measures necessary to carry them out. Some part of the diversification, moreover, can be attributed to Japan's being compelled to find alternative markets and export goods in consequence of restrictions placed on traditional exports to her former chief markets or because of the steep fall in the value of her raw silk trade.

The outcry that greeted the expansion of Japan's exports during the thirties seems, at first sight, difficult to understand, since she accounted for only 3·65 per cent of world exports in 1935 and for 3·59 per cent in 1936. It is true that there had been an increase after 1929, when the proportion was 2·94 per cent; but Japan's share in world exports was still small and, further, her imports had risen correspondingly. The explanation is not far to seek. In 1929 a large proportion of Japan's exports was not competitive with those of other leading industrial countries. During the thirties, however, she replaced raw silk by finished manufactured goods in her export trade, and while some of these finished manufactured goods, because of their low prices, went to meet demands hitherto unsatisfied, others (especially cotton piece-goods) displaced the exports of foreign industries which were for other reasons already depressed. For example, the British cotton industry in the inter-war years declined continuously chiefly because former customer-countries, especially India, became able to supply the bulk of their own needs. In these circumstances of dwindling international trade the growth in the export of Japanese cotton piece-goods was a particularly severe blow at the British industry.

Changes in the import trade reflected the same tendencies. There was a steep rise in imports of raw materials (especially textile raw materials) and of semi-manufactured materials (such as pig iron and scrap, non-ferrous metals and pulp), whereas there was a fall in the importance of finished manufactured goods, with the exception of certain kinds of machinery and automobiles and parts. This was symptomatic of Japan's increasing industrialization. There was also a change in the sources of imports. Australia became a larger supplier, because of Japan's increasing demand for wool. The United States became more important, since Japan increased her purchases of American machinery, automobiles and raw cotton. The necessity for balancing her trade with particular countries because of import restrictions on her goods led to a growth in imports from Africa and South America.

Finally, the Japanese colonies grew in importance both as markets and as sources of imports. For this the autarkical tendencies in world

trade as a whole, as well as Japan's own policy of colonial development, were largely responsible. Whereas in 1929 the colonies supplied
Japan Proper with 20 per cent of her total imports and took about
18 per cent of her total exports, in 1936 the corresponding figures
were 24 per cent and 25 per cent. It was not until after the outbreak
of the war with China, however, that there occurred that fundamental
change in the direction of Japanese trade that was associated with the
development of the 'yen bloc'.

On balance, it can be said that Japan had adjusted her foreign
trade very successfully to the catastrophic world changes of the early
and middle thirties. She had found new customers and alternative
commodities as compensation for the decline that occurred in some
of her chief markets and major lines of trade. Her industrial expansion had made her a leading market for some of the chief raw material
producing areas, notably the cotton-belt of the United States and the
wool-growing areas of Australasia. She had become increasingly
self-sufficient in finished manufactured products, even for machinery
and other capital goods for which her demand had grown very
rapidly both for her own use and for the development of Manchuria.
Yet she had not escaped the effects of the trade restrictions of the
time. Her trade had been diverted by those measures. She was
obliged to accept limits to the expansion of her exports to certain
markets, and this led her to conclude a number of bilateral agreements which were intended to balance her trade with particular
countries. These restrictions certainly accounted in part for the
worsening of her terms of trade during the middle thirties; while their
political influence was extremely unfortunate. Japan, with her rapidly
growing population and her increasing dependence on foreign trade
for the maintenance and improvement of her standard of life, was
in a position similar to that of Great Britain in the middle of the
nineteenth century. Her economy possessed the same resilience and
flexibility. Her economic interest favoured liberal international
trading arrangements which would enable her to exchange on good
terms her manufactured goods for the raw materials she needed in
increasing quantities. But these conditions were disappearing from
international trade. Her main competitors had rigid economies which
could not adapt themselves to her competition. The world trend was
towards restrictionism—towards the parcelling out of markets among
the established suppliers. Thus conditions were unfavourable for the
success of an expansionist economic policy which her own interest
so urgently required. The political groups who sought not economic
welfare but territorial expansion, and who wished to establish
Japan's ascendancy in Eastern Asia so that she might enjoy monopolistic advantages, were consequently strengthened. Apologists for
Japan's aggression in China were at one time inclined to argue that

her policy was wholly, or mainly, the result of her reaction to the barriers that were being erected against her commercial expansion. This is greatly to overstate the case. The root of Japanese imperialism is certainly not to be found in economic causes. But the circumstances just described no doubt contributed in some measure to the success of the extremists in gaining support for their policies.

CHAPTER XI

SUMMARY AND CONCLUSIONS

In 1867, when this story of economic development begins, Japan's economy was given over predominantly to small-scale agriculture and to household industry. She then lacked modern communications and modern educational, administrative and financial systems. Factories driven by mechanical power and industrial equipment of the kind with which the leading Western countries had been familiar for the best part of a century were novelties. She had only slight experience of foreign trade and of the operation of an ocean-going mercantile marine. It is true that at that time even in parts of the Western world modern industrialism and modern transport systems were comparatively recent innovations, and that the influence of the great technical discoveries of the eighteenth and early nineteenth centuries had still not completely shattered the old economic forms. Yet the contrast between Japan and the West lay not so much in the fact that Japan was a late starter in the development of the new economy, but rather that the conditions precedent to such a development did not seem to be present in her society. There had been no expansion of overseas commerce such as preceded the industrial age in Great Britain. The minds of her people had not been subjected, as in Europe, to the philosophic influences which had weakened the forces of custom and tradition, had made them receptive to the discoveries of science, and had brought about the great liberation of individual human energies that had occurred at the end of the eighteenth century. There had been no accumulation of scientific knowledge and no widespread appreciation of the scientific method as applied to the processes of production. Japanese society in the later years of the Tokugawa era had certainly not been stagnant and, as we have seen in the first chapter, the older forms of social and political organization were then disintegrating. The changes were, however, very different from those that brought to an end the *ancien régime* in Europe and led to the emergence of liberalism in both the economic and political spheres. Thus in 1867 the Japanese economy was not merely backward when compared with that of the chief Western nations but the foundations for a new era of expansion seemed, at any rate to casual observers, to be ill prepared.

In the space of some sixty years Japan had been transformed into a modern industrial State, equipped with all the resources of applied

L

science and technology, and capable of producing efficiently most types of manufactured products. She had established adequate systems of finance and communications. Her mercantile marine was the third greatest in the world. Her overseas trade was large and was still growing rapidly; in its composition it was in most respects typical of that of a modern industrial State. In the nineteen-thirties Japan was conducting with success large-scale undertakings beyond her shores, and she was becoming an important investor in overseas enterprise. She possessed an efficient bureaucracy and a skilful and experienced class of entrepreneurs, technicians and managers. Her workers rivalled in skill those of far older industrial countries. Since the beginning of the Meiji era her population had doubled itself and the standard of life of her people had risen. Political changes had accompanied this economic expansion. Japan had made herself into a great military and naval Power, and since 1894 she had pursued with success a policy of imperialist expansion on the continent of Asia.

These achievements did not depend on great natural resources. Although she possessed ample supplies of water power and fair supplies of coal and copper, she was not well endowed with the raw materials of industry, and like Great Britain she had to import most of them from overseas. Yet she had become eminent as a producer not merely of the older textiles, to which new countries usually turn in the early stages of their industrialization, but also of the more recently introduced man-made fibres and, in the last decade, of the typical manufactures of the most advanced industrial nations, metal and engineering goods and chemicals. Nor, in the inter-war years, could she be regarded as a sedulous imitator of the West. Her economy and her civilization could no longer be described as a 'traduction mal faite'. She herself was making contributions to science and to technology, and she had evolved forms of social and economic organization which were peculiar to her.

To record the course of this development is one thing; to explain how it came out as it did is another and more hazardous task. No explanation that would be accepted by all inquirers into the Japanese problem can be found, and dogmatism would be out of place. Moreover, he who would bring to light the springs of action cannot confine himself to economics. Why certain individuals or groups were brought to act at certain moments as they did; why their actions had such far-reaching effects on national life; and how the succession or accumulation of small events gave rise to significant trends; these things cannot be fully disclosed by research into the facts of economic development alone. Yet among the many factors that contributed to the rise of Japan, there are some that would probably be accepted by all investigators as significant. At these we may now glance.

Japan entered the modern era far better equipped for economic expansion than contemporaries realized or than a superficial assessment of her assets would suggest. At the time of the Restoration, in spite of internal dissensions, the people of Japan possessed an underlying sense of national unity which was the product of her geographical position, of linguistic uniformity and of her long history. There was a way of life and a scale of values which were widely accepted by the people and were brought into high relief when the Japanese came to confront the Western nations whose cultural background was entirely different. Secondly, Japan, in spite of the autonomy enjoyed by the feudal magnates in Tokugawa times, possessed a central administration which had managed to impose its will upon the country with a fair measure of success for more than two centuries. There also lingered memories of a still more highly centralized form of government. She had in the Emperor an institution that could be used as a focus for the sentiment of absolute loyalty to a superior, which was the most honoured virtue of the race. This institution had its roots deep in the past, and round it clustered the myths and traditions of the people. When the need came, the Emperor could be transformed into a ruler with divine attributes, who claimed not merely respect and obedience, but also fanatical devotion. Yet if Japanese society was moved by these ancient traditions, in the middle of the nineteenth century it was in a condition which made it receptive of stimulus from the West. Moreover, if it was constituted so as to be capable of providing the country with a ruling class that possessed prestige and self-confidence, that class was not rigidly demarcated from the rest of the population, nor was it conservative in its outlook. Men of talent found opportunities to enter it, and many of its members were themselves avid for change in the ordering of their country's affairs. The mass of the people were docile in the presence of acknowledged authority, and in every class there was a capacity for co-operation and organized effort which was in part the product of a long experience of group action in the family, the clan and the guild. This society, while it often threw up men of strong personality and will, usually contrived to ensure that their activities were subordinated to the interests of the group or the nation as a whole.

Nor was Japan's economic and technical inheritance to be despised. Indeed, in the decades before the Restoration there had been a remarkable convergence of influences and events congenial to change and growth. These were discussed in earlier chapters and require only brief comment at this point. The creation or enlargement of a surplus of agricultural income, above what is necessary to maintain the farming population at a conventional standard of life, is generally considered to be a condition of capital accumulation and construction in the early days of industrial development. In Japan the surplus had been increased by the rise in agricultural productivity during the centuries preceding the Meiji era. In feudal times the surplus was directed chiefly to the maintenance of the *samurai* who had become to a large extent economically functionless. After the abolition of feudalism much of this surplus was diverted into the coffers of the central Government by taxation, and became available for investment in new industries and in the apparatus of the new society. Here was a source of already mobilized capital. The disposition of the peasantry towards modern economic processes and practices is invariably an important factor in deploying resources for what is now called the 'take-off'. The Japanese peasants in the early nineteenth century not only possessed traditional skill in agriculture and in many crafts associated with it but they had also been prepared for commercial activities and industrial wage employments by changes in technique and organization within the rural communities. The most outstanding of these changes were the development, within the fiefs, of commercial farming and the expansion in the villages of industrial by-employments organized on a 'putting out' system. In the towns during Tokugawa times there flourished a small but highly skilled class of craftsmen engaged in producing fine textiles, metal goods, pottery and lacquer wares, that is to say the *meibutsu* trades which for centuries had served the *daimyo* and the rich merchants. Then, in addition to the actual plants of modern design inherited from the *daimyo* and the *Shogun*, the New Japan had at its command a commercial and financial organization of some sophistication and a number of business houses experienced in large-scale operations. Japan provides a good example of how quickly large new industries may be built up on the basis of a nucleus of organizing capacity and craftsmanship and of a mass of docile, unskilled workers.

In the period of transition from the old to the new economy, Japan was favoured by fortune. It happened, as we have seen, that in the earliest years of New Japan a large foreign demand arose for the very commodity which she was eminently fitted to supply, raw silk. And in the middle period (indeed, right down to 1929), the great expansion of the American market enabled her to build up a substantial foreign trade, chiefly on the basis of this product. Thus before her new manufacturing industries had attained a degree of efficiency that would enable them to export on a large scale, she was able to draw on foreign supplies of equipment and materials in exchange for this product of a peasant industry. Here certainly was an important factor in accelerating her development as an industrial nation. Added to this was the fact that her agriculture and fisheries were able to raise the production of food for the growing population to a sufficient level to render her almost independent of food imports except from her colonies.

The forms assumed by Japan's economy and the direction of her development can be explained partly by the condition of her economic system at the time of the Restoration, and partly by the political objectives which she set herself. Japan's first problem was to take over as quickly as possible the technical apparatus of the West. Because of her own backwardness, and since entrepreneurs capable of initiating and organizing Western-style industrial and commercial undertakings were few, she could not hope to achieve this purpose merely by throwing open the country to Western economic influence. The *laisser-faire* prescription was not for her. Moreover, she feared for her security, and her leaders could not neglect the strategic aspect of economic development. Hence the active part played by the State in the early and middle years of Meiji in the founding of new industries; hence the continued concern of the Government and of the business families through which it worked with enterprises that touched on national power. Yet the vitalizing influence of the new-found freedom in the country's economic life must not be under-estimated. The impact of international trade, because of the provisions of the 'unequal treaties', could not be cushioned by import duties designed to protect established industries. Resources had to be transferred quickly to trades where Japan enjoyed the greatest relative advantages. There could be no question of her being seduced by the meretricious charms of a 'balanced economy'. She was compelled to choose specialization, particularly in her export trade. And the presence of many alert individuals eager to seize new opportunities brought a ready response to those pressures and carried Japan into new fields of endeavour, many of them related closely to traditional activities.

If much was changed, there still remained in Japan many vestiges of the ancient order. This was demonstrated in the organization and conduct even of the large-scale businesses. It was seen in the mutual relations of the Government and entrepreneurs, of workers and employers, landlords and tenants. In the Japanese version of 'welfare capitalism', as practised by the great concerns, there was reproduced in a different medium the pattern of relationships found in the old workshops, where the *detchi* (apprentices) lived with their master and were subjected in both working and leisure time to his discipline. Again, the relations of the *zaibatsu* with the State were in some ways akin to those that formerly existed between the *daimyo* and Shogun on the one hand and the rich *chonin* who financed them on the other. In a sense, both the modern *zaibatsu* and the old *chonin* were merely agents of national or feudal policy, but from time to time they could influence or perhaps determine what that policy should be. Even the older social conflicts were reflected on the unquiet sea of modern economic life. With the contempt and envy felt by the *samurai* when confronted by the growing wealth of the *chonin*, we may compare the bitterness and at times the ungovernable fury aroused among the military by the steady growth of *zaibatsu* wealth and influence during the inter-war period. The internal organization itself of these great business houses is infused with a spirit peculiar to Japan; for it shows marked traces of both the Japanese family system, with its widely ramifying claims and loyalties, and also the emotional dispositions associated with the lords and their retainers under the old régime.

If the broad policy of the Japanese Government in the Meiji era, and subsequently, was directed primarily towards raising the power of the State and towards inducing the economic expansion necessary to sustain that power, particular measures were usually intended to serve more immediate and restricted purposes. Despite the initiative and drive supplied by the Government, Japan could at no time be considered to possess a 'planned economy' in the modern sense. Nor were the authorities ever inspired by any general principle of economic development, such as the maintenance of a steady rate of growth. On the contrary, throughout the modern period Japan's development has been attended by frequent and severe fluctuations, and it is arguable that her progress was made possible, in part, by her vigorous pursuit of an expansionist policy, and at the same time by her readiness to apply checks ruthlessly whenever that policy provoked, as it frequently did, a crisis in her balance of payments. The recessions which the checks from time to time produced were accompanied by a scaling-down of costs which prepared the way for the ensuing period of growth. The policy was not followed consistently. There were periods when the economy was rescued from grave disequilibrium by fortuitous external events, such as the outbreak of the First World War, or when, as in the early nineteen-twenties, the Government hesitated to take the drastic steps to correct a succession of balance of payments deficits. But in the main Japan showed resolution in applying the checks as well as boldness in organizing expansion. Two outstanding examples have been given in the course of this history. First, the inflationary boom of the later seventies followed by the Matsukata deflation of the early eighties, and secondly the deflation of 1927-31 which was succeeded by the reflationary period of Takahashi.

The effectiveness of these policies is a tribute to the resilience of the economy. It was a remarkable fact that, as Dr Ohkawa has stated, '. . . even in the 1930 period of depression the growth rate of the Japanese economy did not show a serious decrease',[1] and the achievement demands an explanation. How is it that the deflationary pressures at that (as at other times) succeeded not only in compelling Japanese industrialists to use resources more economically but also

[1] K. Ohkawa, *op. cit.*, p. 22.

in maintaining high investment in re-equipment which contributed to the expansion of the middle and later thirties. Some part of the explanation is to be found in the plasticity of Japanese wages, for the steep wage reductions of the recession period permitted firms that survived to earn profits from which the new investment could be financed. The plasticity of wages is in turn to be explained partly by the nature of the wage system itself (notably the close correlation between the earnings of particular workers and their employers' prosperity), but mainly by the structure of the economy. The rapid and constant growth in the number of persons of working age produced an intense competition for industrial jobs, particularly on the part of recruits from the over-populated countryside. Whenever agriculture or agricultural by-employments became depressed, the competition became fiercer. In these conditions there could be little resistance to economic pressures exerted on wages. If this was true of factory employment, in the small and medium-scale sector wages could obviously be compressed without meeting with any serious resistance in times of depression. In the absence of this wage plasticity, the policy of 'boom and bust' might have payed less handsome dividends in economic progress. And if this was one of the chief reasons for the resilience of the Japanese economy, as well as for the high rate of capital accumulation, it must be remembered that it had its dark side. For wage plasticity was the product of the desperate search for employment on the part of the surplus rural population.

If, throughout the modern period, Japan gave a ready welcome to Western novelties in technique and organization, there was no desire, at any rate on the part of the ruling classes, to assimilate Western civilization in the sense of substituting a Western scale of values for its own. Dr Hu Shih has pointed a contrast between Japanese and Chinese experience in this respect.[1] In China, he says, there occurred a 'gradual penetration and assimilation of ideas and practices'; and in the absence of centralized control, fundamental cultural changes took place through a process of free contact and slow diffusion. The result was that the foundations of Chinese society were affected before the superstructure had been much altered. In Japan, on the other hand, rapid changes in the technical equipment and the economic organization of society were achieved as the result of the deliberate policy of the ruling class, and these changes were imposed on a people whose values remained those of their native civilization. Indeed, care was taken to protect their cultural heritage from the corrosive influences of the West, and in this process the ancient system of values was given a clearer definition than it

[1] In an address on 'The Modernization of China and Japan' to the American Historical Association at Washington on December 29, 1939.

formerly possessed, and the claims of the Japanese way of life were more vigorously asserted. Japanese society, however, could not escape completely from the political and cultural concomitants of Western industrialism and applied science; but where liberalism and rational humanitarianism appeared they were often greeted with bitter opposition, and at no time penetrated deeply into many Japanese minds.[1] During the twenties, it is true, it seemed reasonable to expect that the material transformation would sooner or later lead to fundamental changes in social and political ideas, and that, in politics, Japan might gradually proceed by way of a senatorial parliamentary system to democracy and representative government. But the times were unfavourable. At a critical point in her history she was overwhelmed by the 'great depression', and she was caught up in the fascist trend of the thirties. Knowing little of the inner meaning of Western civilization, she applied a purely pragmatic test in her judgment of its outward manifestations, its forms of government, social organization and economic systems. The successful alone was impressive. Hence her great material achievements came to be wrecked on the rocks of national ambition.

In the thirties she directed all her newly found technical skill to the creation of what she herself called a *Junsenji-Keizai* (a quasi-war-time economy). Discarding the policy of 'sound finance', which had proved so disastrous for all countries which had continued to practise it, she rescued herself from depression. But her new policy, even if it satisfied in its technical aspects the canons of what is now called a 'full employment' policy, became increasingly associated, as in Germany, with large-scale rearmament and military aggression. Economic affairs passed under the control of the militarists, and were moulded by the needs of war preparation. In a sense the very forces which had supplied the impulse to economic expansion during the Meiji era, and the very conditions which made the development of Japan so great and so rapid, were responsible for the catastrophe in which she became involved. It was not from the decay of vigour, nor from administrative inefficiency and corruption, nor from internal social conflict, that disaster proceeded. It was rather from patriotism corrupted into immoderate ambition, from a strong national spirit degenerating into fanaticism unrestrained at the last either by morality or the calculations of expediency, and from confidence in material success turned to excessive pride in achievement.

Japan might well have been expected to render great services to mankind. She was the first and only Asiatic nation to show marked practical capacity in spheres in which Western nations had led the way. By her geographical and her cultural affinities she was well fitted

[1] This statement applies, of course, to the period before the Second World War.

to introduce applied science and industrialism to the peoples of Asia and to supply the organizing ability and the advanced technique which those peoples needed so that the burden of their grinding poverty might be lifted. She had already made available to them new kinds of consumption goods at prices which they could afford, and she might have played a leading part in raising further their standard of life. She possessed a resilient economy lacking the rigidities that had appeared in the Western world. An immense field of industrial expansion lay before her; but she turned aside from it to pursue other ends.

ECONOMIC RECOVERY AND EXPANSION, 1945–60

1. *The Phases of Recovery*

During the half-century before 1937 Japan's economic expansion was unquestionably influenced by her success in war. The Sino-Japanese War of 1894-5, the Russo-Japanese War of 1904-5, the First World War and the campaigns against China in the early and middle thirties all led to the enlargement of territory under her control and opened up opportunities for investment and trade in areas where she enjoyed special advantages. This is not to deny, of course, that the real costs of preparing for, and of fighting, these wars had outweighed their economic benefits, nor that the diversion of so much of Japan's energy and resources to imperialist expansion had been at the expense of economic welfare. However this may be, defeat in the Second World War stripped her of all she had gained from previous military successes. She lost her colonies and her spheres of influence on the continent of Asia; her great foreign investments, notably those in Manchuria and China Proper, were wrested from her; and her commercial dominance in the Far East was overthrown. What is more, in 1945 the economy of Japan Proper itself lay in ruins. Most of the cities had been devastated by air attack which had destroyed about a quarter of the housing accommodation of the country together with a high proportion of industrial buildings and plants. The amount of physical destruction, it is estimated, was equivalent to about twice the national income of the fiscal year 1948-9.[1] At the same time the economy had become structurally defective when viewed from the standpoint of peace-time needs. From July 1937, when the war with China began, the mobilization of the country's resources for war had been pressed forward vigorously, and after the outbreak of the Pacific War in December 1941 the economic order was transformed. Firms that had served the civilian market or the export trade were required to use their resources for war production or go out of business, and the capital equipment of the transport and other basic service industries was run down. The heavy manufactures greatly expanded, but the end of the war found many war plants without any useful function. Production and distribution had become disorganized and in 1945 a violent inflation was in progress. Raw materials were then very

[1] J. B. Cohen, *op. cit.*, pp. 406-8.

scarce and the townspeople were short of food and other necessaries of life. Most serious of all, morale had sunk very low. The people had lost faith in their leaders and the spirit of enterprise seemed to have abandoned them. The Occupation Authority (SCAP)[1] was not merely concerning itself with day-to-day administration but was ambitious to achieve fundamental institutional reforms.

Fifteen years later the country was independent, prosperous and progressive. The apparatus of social and economic life had been restored and much enlarged. Industrial production was probably three and a half times that of the middle thirties and, with the appearance of many new branches of manufacture, the whole structure of industry had been reshaped. Agriculture had participated in the economic advance, and the export trade, after a long hesitation, was rising fast. The institutional reforms set going by SCAP had been assimilated or modified, and economic organization had regained its former efficiency. Despite a growth in population of about 25 per cent between 1940 and 1960 and a very high ratio of annual investment to the gross national product, the standard of life had risen, in town and country, well above the pre-war level.

This remarkable achievement, matched only by that of Germany in the post-war world, must be explained in detail. But since the causes are numerous and complex, the explanation will be deferred until the main features of the recovery have been described. Between August 1945 and the end of 1960 several distinct phases of economic development may be distinguished. The first lasted until February 1949. This was a period of economic confusion. The Government and the banking system poured out funds lavishly for the reconstruction of the basic industries at a time when savings were negligible and resources scarce.[2] These operations set going a violent inflation which raised the index of wholesale prices from 15 in April 1946 to 197 in March 1949 (1934-6=1).[3] Industry which was in complete collapse in 1945 recovered slowly and in 1948 industrial production was little more than two-fifths of that of 1937. Even in agriculture, the only branch of the economy in which there had been a substantial revival, output in 1948 was well below the pre-war level.[4] An export trade hardly existed. The war-time destruction of the mercantile marine

[1] Supreme Commander of the Allied Powers, a term used to designate both a person and the Occupation Administration in general.

[2] A new institution, the Reconstruction Finance Bank, was founded in 1947 for this purpose. Its funds were obtained mainly by selling its debentures to the Bank of Japan.

[3] S. Tsuru, 'Business Cycles in Post-War Japan' in International Economic Association, *The Business Cycle in the Post-War World*, pp. 178 *et seq.*

[4] The statistical data on which the general statements are based were obtained from Economic Planning Agency, *Japanese Economic Statistics* and *Economic Survey of Japan* (various years).

together with the loss of foreign assets left Japan without any source of earnings from invisible exports. Even the modest recovery that ôccurred during these years depended on lavish aid granted by the United States.

The efforts of the Japanese themselves to organize recovery were frustrated by doubts about the political future. Japan was faced with a heavy bill for reparations from the countries she had devastated and with uncertainties about when it would be presented. Her freedom to reconstruct industries conceived to be of strategic value was narrowly restricted. The Occupation Authority was zealous for social and political reform, and its purpose was not merely to prevent the re-creation of a war potential but also to democratize the country by encouraging a wider diffusion of wealth and political and economic power. Business executives who had taken an active part in administering the war economy, as well as political and military leaders, were 'purged'. The great aggregates of economic power, the *zaibatsu*, were dissolved, and an anti-trust law designed to prevent consolidations or cartels in the future was promulgated. A policy of land reform was introduced with the object of destroying the rural landlord class and transforming tenants into peasant proprietors. A series of labour laws and social reform measures aimed at increasing the power and well-being of the workers was passed by the Diet on the instructions of the Occupation Authority. These reforms, whatever their merits from the social and political standpoint, made no immediate contribution to economic recovery.

The period was brought to an abrupt end by an important change in American policy, the result of the deterioration in relations with Russia and the advance of the Communists in China. An impoverished and enfeebled Japan, it was realized, would not serve America's strategic interests, and as long as trade and industry faltered, the burden on the American tax-payer in providing 'aid' could not be relieved. The reformist temper was, therefore, moderated, and the energies of SCAP were henceforward directed primarily to economic recovery. As a first step towards that goal inflation had to be checked, and a programme of monetary stabilization drawn up in the early months of 1949 provided for a balanced budget and credit restrictions. The success of these measures prepared the way for industrial recovery, and by the beginning of the next year manufacturing production, though still less than before the war, was rising quickly. Meanwhile agricultural output had regained its pre-war level.

The period of stabilization came to an end with the outbreak of the Korean War in June 1950. Large orders for Japanese goods were at once received on account of the United Nations forces, and in 1951 industrial production exceeded the pre-war volume for the first time since 1944. Despite a rise in general wholesale prices of more than 50 per cent during the twelve months after the beginning of the Korean War, the balance of payments became very favourable, for the boom had been produced entirely by the great expansion in foreign demand. The war also affected Japan's political relations with the West. It was now clear that she constituted a necessary base for the deployment of American power in the Pacific, and this consideration influenced the terms of the Peace Treaty and the Security Treaty which in the spring of 1952 restored sovereignty to the Japanese Government, while permitting the Allied Powers to maintain bases and troops in the country.

An important economic consequence was that even after the end of the fighting Japan, whose own military expenditure remained very small, continued to benefit by United States' procurement payments made chiefly in connection with American military establishments. The expectation that 'procurement' would prove to be a precarious source of foreign income was not fulfilled. Between 1952 and 1956 the payments amounted to 3,381 million dollars, equivalent in value to more than a quarter of Japan's commodity imports during that period. Even though there was a tendency to decline in subsequent years, procurement expenditure in 1958-9 was sufficient to pay for about 14 per cent of the imports.[1] It is true that to the extent that these exceptional demands diverted scarce resources from other uses, they affected Japan's competitive capacity in foreign markets. But since in the early and middle fifties the price elasticity of demand for Japan's exports was probably low, it seems reasonable to conclude that the net effect was to provide the country with a large and fairly steady foreign income which she would not otherwise have been able to earn. If this is so, then procurement expenditure contributed powerfully to industrial re-equipment and to the restoration of the pre-war level of consumption.

Even after the collapse of the war boom Japan's industrial output continued to expand. By 1953 it was probably more than 50 per cent greater than in the middle thirties, and the real national income some 30 per cent greater. Income per head had just about regained its pre-war level. During the war-boom, however, Japanese prices had moved out of line with world prices, and the country found itself with a stagnating export trade which produced difficulties with its balance of payments. As was to happen on subsequent occasions, the Government by imposing sharp monetary and fiscal correctives succeeded in restoring equilibrium at the expense of a short recession which had a salutary effect on industrial costs. In 1955 economic expansion was resumed at a faster rate than ever and by 1957 it could be said that Japan's recovery was complete. Most of her industries had been re-equipped and reorganized. Industrial production was probably

[1] See Table XXIII in Appendix B.

over two and a half times the pre-war volume, gross national product in real terms about 50 per cent higher and national income per head perhaps 10 per cent higher. Even the export trade, which had long been hesitant, went ahead very fast during this period. In 1954 it had amounted in volume to under half that of the middle thirties; by 1957 the proportion had risen to about nine-tenths.

Despite the export expansion, rapid economic development again led to difficulties with the balance of payments, and when in the later months of 1957 the growth in exports was checked, the country's reserves of gold and foreign currency began to run down. Again the Government applied corrective measures. Soon prices fell and the rise in industrial production was halted. Yet, as before, the recession was short. Costs proved to be sensitive to deflationary pressure and the way was prepared for a recovery which began towards the end of 1958. During the next two years the economic advance was faster than ever. In 1960 industrial production was well over twice that of 1955. The export trade (in volume) had risen above, though not far above, the 1937 level, and Japan was earning a substantial surplus in her current transactions with the outside world. During the period from 1953 to 1959 the average rate of increase in gross national product is estimated to have reached 7 per cent per annum, which is far above that attained by any other country except Western Germany during the post-war period. It was also far higher than the rate achieved by Japan before the war; between 1925 and 1939 the annual rate of increase averaged 4·6 per cent.[1] The rapid industrial growth was associated with a high rate of capital formation, and during the nineteen-fifties the proportion of the gross national product invested is believed to have been of the order of 30 per cent. The standard of personal consumption also rose considerably during the later years of the nineteen-fifties. Real wages advanced though more slowly than productivity.

In the past the rural population had participated to only a limited extent in the material benefits conferred by economic development, but in the post-war period those benefits were more widely distributed. Agriculture had suffered less than industry from the upheavals of war and defeat, and the high food prices of the years immediately after 1945 together with the land reforms and the inflation (which wiped out farm debts) brought about a redistribution of income in favour of the farmers. During the nineteen-fifties rural standards of living continued to improve, though scarcely at the rate of those of townspeople. A contributory factor in this further advance was the growth in agricultural productivity. During the period of industrial disorganization just after the war people crowded into agriculture and there was a large absolute increase in the size of the farming

[1] *Fuji Bank Bulletin*, June 1960, p. 1.

population for the first time for many decades. This trend was reversed as recovery proceeded, but the volume of agricultural output continued to rise as a result of improvements in agricultural methods, especially the application of greater quantities of chemical fertilizers and insecticides and the increased use of power machinery. The effect on the rice supply was indeed remarkable. Whereas before the war Japan had depended on Korea and Formosa for about a quarter of her rice consumption, during the later fifties the domestic rice output increased sufficiently to supply almost the whole of the population's needs, even though numbers were 25 per cent greater.[1] It is true that rice has lost some of its former importance in the Japanese diet, for more bread and other foods are now eaten.[2] But this does not detract from the agricultural achievement, for besides producing more rice the farmer also enlarged his output of other products. During the nineteen-fifties the production of livestock, dairy products, fruit and vegetables was far greater than before the war.

2. *Structural Changes in Industry*

Japan's achievements depended on her success in effecting massive structural changes, and these must now be described. First of all, it is clear that the progress has been mainly associated with the growth of secondary industry, for after the troubles of the immediate post-war years were surmounted, it was the manufacturing sector that went ahead most rapidly. Despite all the improvements in agriculture, that branch of the economy since 1950 has been responsible for a steadily diminishing proportion of the gross national product, and its share of the occupied population had also been falling. Mining, too, has made comparatively little progress, and the tertiary industries, though very large and rapidly growing, include many trades where incomes are very low and under-employment common. The manufacturing sector has contributed most to Japan's economic advance, but within that sector the most rapid growth has occurred in industries other than those which a generation ago were regarded as Japan's special field of activity. This is in continuance of a pre-war trend. During the thirties, despite the still overwhelming predominance of textiles, industrial development was becoming increasingly dependent on the expansion of the metal, chemical and engineering industries. The war, as in other belligerent countries, accelerated the structural change. Textile manufacturers suffered particularly from the transference of resources to the heavy industries. Much of their capacity was scrapped to provide metal for munitions production,

---

[1] In the period 1955-59 rice imports amounted to only 6 per cent of rice production.

[2] Consumption of rice per head has fallen by about 15 per cent since the war.

and in 1945 the cotton industry found itself with under 2 million spindles compared with 12 million in 1937. In the raw silk industry the whole basis of the raw material supply was drastically contracted through the substitution of food crops for mulberry trees in the former silk-raising areas.

During the early years of reconstruction, efforts were directed towards restoring capacity in these war-contracted trades. Yet in 1951 the volume of textile production was only half that of 1937, and it was not until 1959 that pre-war production was exceeded. Within the textile group itself important changes took place. In the late nineteen-fifties the annual production of cotton yarn and fabrics had still not completely recovered and the output of raw silk was under half the pre-war amount. The production of silk fabrics was also much lower. On the other hand, the output of wool yarn and fabrics had been well maintained, and the rayon industry, especially the section concerned with spun yarn and fabrics, was far larger than ever before. After 1950 Japan built up a synthetic fibre production which expanded very fast towards the end of the decade. The old-established textiles based on natural fibres, either imported or produced by the native peasantry, had to a considerable extent given place to textiles composed of man-made fibres produced in large plants from native raw materials.

In all the other major industrial groups, apart from mining, output in the late fifties was considerably greater than before the war, but the outstanding development took place in the metal, chemical and engineering groups. In 1960 the output of steel (in tons) was about four times greater than in 1937, and the range of the finished steel output had been extended and its quality improved. The volume of output of machinery and chemicals had grown even more than that of steel. Within each of these groups certain trades grew especially fast. By the late fifties Japan had become the world's leading ship-builder, a very large supplier of electrical apparatus and electronic equipment and an important manufacturer of motor vehicles. Several industries which were of little significance to her economy before the war had grown into substantial industries; examples are to be found in the manufacture of scientific instruments, cameras and sewing machines. The chemical industry had added a variety of products, including derivatives of the oil-refining process now undertaken on a large scale. There was hardly any modern industry in which Japan did not possess some representative plants.

The net result of these changes was that whereas in 1936 the textile trades as a whole were responsible for about 29 per cent of the gross value of factory production and for about 38 per cent of factory employment, in the late fifties the proportions had fallen to 13 per cent and 20 per cent respectively. The metal, chemical and engineering groups, which together turned out about a third of the total value of factory production in 1930 and for rather more than a half in 1936, had raised its share to well over three-fifths by 1959. Thus Japan's industry by the end of this period had assumed a structure characteristic of that of other leading industrial countries, and it was constantly being extended in scope.

A reliable index of Japan's industrial advance is given by her power consumption. During most of the post-war period her coal output was well below that of the nineteen-thirties and even in 1959-1960 it was only slightly greater, with the result that she had to rely increasingly on imports. As in other countries, however, oil became a major source of power during the fifties. In 1958-9 her imports of petroleum and petroleum products were four times those of the middle thirties. The amount of electric power generated rose from 30 million kWh in 1937 to 73 million in 1956 and 99 million in 1959. Of the total energy supplied in that year coal accounted for 38 per cent, water power for 28 per cent and oil for 30 per cent.

3. *Foreign Trade*

In the past Japan's industrial growth had been closely bound up with the development of her foreign trade. During the post-war period, while the structural changes already described were clearly reflected in the composition of the exports, the relationship between the quantity of industrial output and the volume of exports was less obvious than formerly. It has already been shown that exports were very slow to recover and that even in 1960 their growth compared very unfavourably with that in production. The reasons for this disparity must be examined. In the nineteen-thirties Japan depended on two great regions both as markets and as sources of supply, namely East Asia and the United States. South East Asia followed at some considerable distance. The pattern of commodity trade between Japan and these regions was clearly marked. The United States bought from her raw silk, canned fish, tea and pottery, and supplied raw cotton, mineral oil, wheat, steel scrap and engineering goods. East Asia and South East Asia bought textiles and miscellaneous goods and, in addition, North China and Manchuria were important customers for machinery and other capital goods in consequence of Japan's investment in those countries. Imports from Asia consisted of raw materials and semi-products (cotton, rubber, vegetable oil, mineral oil, ores and metals) and also food (especially rice from Formosa and Korea, sugar from Formosa and soya beans from Manchuria). In China, Manchuria and the Japanese colonies, which all formed part of the 'yen bloc', the Japanese traded on privileged terms.

The basis of this great export was destroyed by war and by

M

subsequent territorial changes. The complex fabric of trade between Japan Proper, her colonies and Manchuria was torn apart by the postwar political settlement. Japan's privileges in those markets disappeared, and with the appearance of New China and the dismemberment of Korea, those regions ceased to count as valuable markets or sources of supply. The raw silk trade to the United States suffered a steep and permanent decline through the coming of nylon. At the same time conditions became unfavourable for the revival of exports of cotton textiles to other Asian countries where domestic textile industries greatly expanded during and after the war. So Japan, in rebuilding her trade from its foundations, had to seek new markets and new sources of supply. She was assisted by the general buoyancy of international trade and, for a time, by the inability of her chief competitors to deliver certain classes of manufactures quickly. Even so she could hardly expect any rapid recovery in her exports.

When at length the trade was restored to its pre-war volume, it presented a sharp contrast to that of the thirties in regard to both markets and types of goods. Although textiles still occupied a larger place in Japan's trade than in that of other great industrial countries, their relative importance in the late fifties was much less than in pre-war times. Their composition had also altered profoundly; rayon, synthetic fibre and woollen and worsted goods now ranked with cotton among the chief textile exports. The main successes, however, were in other directions. Japan created a large and widely distributed export of both light and heavy engineering goods (machinery, railway materials, ships, electrical equipment, sewing machines) and of highly finished instruments, such as cameras and binoculars. She supplied large quantities of steel to foreign buyers at a time when the Western steel makers lacked capacity to meet the urgent world demand. She much enlarged her exports of chemicals, both heavy chemicals (including fertilizers) and pharmaceuticals. Before the war, except in textiles and certain artistic products, Japan tended to serve the lower end of the various trades. Today she exports a wide variety of finished goods of high quality. The structure of the import trade also changed. Textile materials diminished in importance, and imports of fuel, especially of oil, greatly increased.[1] For the first ten or twelve years after the war food imports made up a larger part of the total trade than formerly, but in very recent years, despite the growth in the population, they have tended to decline because of the growth in domestic food production.

[1] The shift to oil as a source of energy has greatly increased Japan's reliance on overseas supplies of fuel. In 1934-36 about 19 per cent of the country's energy needs were supplied by imports. In 1962 the proportion is expected to be 33 per cent. The percentage of fuel imports to total imports was 5 in 1934-36 and 16 in 1959.

Equally important changes took place in the geographical distribution of Japan's commerce. Her trade with North East Asia became insignificant after the war. South East Asia, on the other hand, rose in importance and the United States moved into the position of chief customer and supplier. In general, Japan's trade became more widely distributed than formerly, although the growth of some markets was frustrated by restrictions. For example, the United Kingdom and certain other countries have still not accorded her the benefits associated with full membership of GATT, and Japan's traders have been obliged to limit their sales, even in the United States, for fear that their low-priced competition would provoke the American Government to introduce import quotas. Japan has been on weak ground in pressing for a more liberal policy on the part of governments, because she herself long maintained various types of import restriction as well as controls that had the equivalent effect of export subsidies. These controls have lately tended to become milder, and one may expect that in future Japan's influence will be thrown on the side of free, multilateral trade, since her continued progress must in part depend on easy access to foreign markets and sources of supply. The outstanding fact about her post-war trading position up to 1960, however, was that industrial development was able to proceed so far despite the modest recovery in the export trade. In other words, the ratio of the value of exports (and imports) to the gross national product, which used to be high, is now low compared with that of most other countries. This raises a question which will be considered when the causes of Japan's economic recovery are being analysed towards the end of this chapter.

4. *Economic Policy and the Zaibatsu*

From this review of the course of production and trade we now turn to consider Government policy which has profoundly influenced the post-war organization of industry and agriculture and the *modus operandi* of the economy as a whole. Any account of Government policy in this period must begin with the revolutionary changes introduced by SCAP in the early years of the Occupation. Those changes may be considered under three heads, first, the dissolution of the *zaibatsu* and the attempt to decentralize economic control, secondly, the land reforms, and, thirdly, the labour laws. We shall briefly describe each of the policies in turn and analyse its effects on economic organization.

During the course of the Second World War concentration of control within the economy had greatly increased. The *zaibatsu*, both the older groups and the *shin-zaibatsu*, were closely associated with the Government in running the war economy; the heavy sector of industry which had always been in their hands was the sector that expanded; and the war-time concentration of the banking system raised the already dominant importance of the *zaibatsu* banks. The Occupation Authorities in 1945 were determined to destroy what they believed to be the main obstacle to the development of democratic institutions and a liberal economy, and although their zeal diminished in later years, the policy of dissolving the *zaibatsu* was pursued until the Occupation ended. The methods employed to achieve the aim have been described in detail elsewhere.[1] Here it is sufficient to say that they were intended to destroy the power and wealth of the *zaibatsu* families and to dissolve each group into numerous independent enterprises. The dissolution applied not only to the main holding companies, in which power was centred, but also to many of the major subsidiaries, such as the trading companies of Mitsui and Mitsubishi which were broken up into a very large number of separate undertakings. Nor was the dissolution confined to the *zaibatsu*. It was extended to the 'National Policy' companies, that is to say, the semi-official concerns which had been founded during the nineteen-thirties for the purpose of strengthening the Government's control over the economy. Two of the best known of these companies were the Japan Iron and Steel Company and the Japan Electricity Generation and Transmission Company. An anti-monopoly law passed in 1947 was intended to extend further the area of competition and to prevent the re-emergence of great concerns.

By the end of the Occupation the *zaibatsu* empires were in fragments and initiative in the nation's economic affairs had passed from the *banto*, or managers, to Government officials. Concentration of control had thus been increased rather than destroyed by the American policy. After 1952, however, the concerns of the former *zaibatsu* began to draw together again, and by the late nineteen-fifties the three major *zaibatsu*, Mitsui, Mitsubishi and Sumitomo, were again in control of a mass of industrial and financial undertakings of many kinds. The great trading companies of Mitsui and Mitsubishi had gradually been re-formed by the assembly of the parts into which they had been dissolved, and the *zaibatsu* banks which had escaped dissolution had become the pivot of each empire.[2] On the other hand, the lesser *zaibatsu*, whose enterprises had also been affected by the policy, and the *shin-zaibatsu*, many of whose enterprises had been lost when Manchuria passed out of Japanese control, found

---

[1] See especially T. A. Bisson, *Zaibatsu Dissolution in Japan;* also G. C. Allen, *Japan's Economic Recovery*, Chap. IX.

[2] Yasuda, the fourth *zaibatsu* in order of size, did not emerge in its old form or under its old name. The Fuji Bank, the successor of the Yasuda Bank, has become the largest of the city banks, but no re-grouping of the former Yasuda industrial concerns has taken place. See G. C. Allen, *op. cit.*, pp. 138-44.

difficulty in re-grouping their undertakings. Some of these, however, later developed into large businesses in their own right.

Although the *zaibatsu* by 1960 again occupied a position of great power in the Japanese economy, they were hardly as dominant as in their heyday. They had owed their position partly to their function as agents of Government policy but mainly to the scarcity of modern entrepreneurial skill and of capital in a society intent upon rapid development. Managerial and technical skill and knowledge capable of handling the problems of a modern economy were now more widely diffused in Japan. The sources of investment capital had become more numerous and many great industrial undertakings with diverse interests were able to develop without being linked by common ownership and control with banks and other financial institutions. It remains true, however, that control over the large-scale sector of the economy is still highly concentrated and that the three great *zaibatsu* are again at the centre of the scene. With the further development of the science-based industries, which demand very large capital resources and often technical co-operation with great foreign concerns, their rôle is unlikely to lose its importance.

In the emergence of the present industrial organization, the Government also has played a leading part. In the early post-war years economic control was strongly centred in the State. Later, as the result of the transference of the 'national policy' companies to private enterprise and the revival of the *zaibatsu*, direct control by the Government diminished. Indeed, the public sector in the nineteen-fifties was a good deal smaller than before the war and certainly smaller than in many Western countries. This, however, should not lead to an underestimate of the influence of the Government in directing the economy. As in the past, Government and industry have been closely associated in working out national economic policy. From such association the plans regarding the future size and shape of the Japanese economy proceed.[1] These plans are not merely estimates of the future, for the Government is able through various fiscal devices and through the operations of its financial institutions, such as the Japan Development Bank, to encourage or to compel growth along the approved lines. Where the main economic power resides—in Government or in great business—is difficult to determine today, as it was in the past. The war may have made less difference in this respect than at one time seemed likely.

An identity between past and present conditions can also be seen in the dichotomy between the large-scale sector of industry where

---

[1] The latest plan, which provides for the doubling of the national income between 1961 and 1970, was prepared by the Economic Planning Agency. The previous plan covered the years 1958 to 1962. See references in Bibliography, pp. 231, 232.

control is strongly concentrated, and the sector composed of a vast concourse of small and medium-sized, highly competitive firms. This contrast, clearly marked before the war, was not destroyed by the growth of Japanese industry nor by its structural transformation after 1945. It is difficult to find comparable figures for pre-war and post-war periods, but such statistics as are available support the conclusion that as yet no profound change has occurred in the distribution of employment among small and large workplaces. In the early post-war years it is even probable that the importance of the small and medium firms increased, for at that time large-scale industry had not yet been rehabilitated. During the early fifties the large firms again went ahead, while the recession of 1953-4, like that of 1949, drove many small undertakings out of business. On the other hand, they appear to have stood up well to the recession of 1958.[1] This contrast in experience is significant, and a glance at its causes suggests that the identity between pre-war and post-war times may be less complete than at first appears. For an increasing number of the small firms during the last decade consisted of sub-contractors in the newer industries (especially in the newer branches of engineering) which maintained production well during the 1958 recession. Many of these sub-contractors have been equipped by the larger producers whom they serve. Independent small firms in the textile and consumer-goods industries suffered more seriously, despite their efforts to save themselves by turning to new lines of products.

On the whole, it seems that the smaller units are better equipped than a generation ago and that their efficiency has improved. Some of them, notably in such industries as the motor components trade, have grown out of their class with the development of the industry they serve. Yet although prosperity has lapped over from the large-scale to the small-scale sector during recent years, the dichotomy persists. Productivity is still much higher in the larger firms and the wage disparities remain. In 1959 average monthly wages in establishments with from ten to ninety-nine workers came to only 57 per cent of those paid in establishments with 1,000 workers and over. The removal of this distinction between the two economic worlds of Japan is recognized as one of the major tasks of economic policy for the next decade.[2] When it is achieved, it will inevitably lead to a profound change in the way the Japanese economy works, a point to be considered in the last section of this chapter.

5. *The Reconstruction of the Banking System*

The post-war history of the banking system also illustrates the strong

---

[1] Economic Planning Agency, *Economic Survey of Japan, 1958-59*, p. 141.
[2] Economic Planning Agency, *New Long-Range Economic Plan of Japan (1961-70)*, pp. 98 *et seq.*

thread of continuity that runs through Japan's institutions, even though they may be subjected from time to time to disruptive influences, or compelled to adapt themselves to considerable changes in their environment. During the war highly centralized control over the banking system was imposed, mainly through the agency of the central bank. To facilitate effective control the Government enforced amalgamation among the commercial banks, with the result that by the end of the war their number had been reduced to sixty-one. The functions of many other banks changed. For instance, the Industrial Bank of Japan in the early years of the war became the Government's instrument for financing the war industries under official guarantees.

The reconstruction of the system after the war was at first closely affected by the policy of SCAP. That authority, as we have seen, was anxious not merely to break up private concentrations of economic power but also to loosen the State's control over processes and institutions. Therefore, besides separating the *zaibatsu* banks from other undertakings in the same group so as to destroy the integration between finance and industry offensive alike to liberal opinion and to the principles of good banking practice, SCAP also ordered that the special banks, which it regarded as instruments of Japans' imperialist policy, should be closed or transformed into ordinary commercial banks. This put an end to the colonial banks and the Yokohama Specie Bank, while the Hypothec Bank and the Hokkaido Development Bank became commercial banks. Since most of the specialist savings banks and trust companies ceased to exist as separate institutions during or shortly after the war, the former variegated pattern of Japanese banking, composed of institutions with distinct functions, disappeared.

Gradually, in the course of the next decade, a structure in many though not all respects similar to that of the pre-war period was re-established. In 1952 a special category of long-term credit bank, with the privilege of raising funds by debenture issues, again came into existence; one of them was the former Industrial Bank of Japan which in effect resumed its previous rôle though it was now independent of Government control. About the same time several new financial institutions, owned or directly controlled by the Government, were set up, including the Export-Import Bank, for making loans in connection with the export, the Japan Development Bank, for long-term lending to the basic industries. Various other banks, partly financed by the Government, were founded for particular purposes, for example, to finance small businesses, and to provide for long-term investment in agriculture, forestry and fisheries. Finally, by a law of 1954, a specialized foreign exchange bank was re-established, namely the Bank of Tokyo. Thus, by the middle fifties, the 'reverse course' in finance seems to have been completed.[1]

Other identities with the pre-war situation can also be found, namely the part played by the Trust Fund Bureau[2] (which receives the postal savings of the people) in financing the Government and its special financial agencies, the dependence of industry on bank loans rather than on the securities market for investment resources, and the generally undeveloped state of the money market which has always presented special problems of credit control to the Bank of Japan and the Government. But the resemblances with the past should not be over-stressed. Concentration has been carried much further than before the war among the ordinary banks. Twelve city banks (apart from the Bank of Tokyo) and sixty-four local banks, each with numerous branches, now make up this sector of the banking system which twenty years ago was composed of some hundreds of separate institutions. With the rise in incomes, Japanese investors are beginning to enter the securities market instead of putting their savings into fixed deposits in the banks. The Bank of Japan is beginning to make use of modern techniques of credit control and the bank rate has become a more effective instrument than formerly. In finance, as in other branches of the economy, Japan faces special problems and prefers her own solution of them, but she is eclectic and adaptable, ready to experiment with novel devices and to change her methods when circumstances require it.

6. *The Rise of Labour Organizations*

The work of the Occupation Authorities in the sphere of industrial organization failed to survive the restoration of sovereignty to the Japanese Government, but other reforms endured, notably those affecting industrial relations and agriculture. These will be treated briefly in turn. In pre-war Japan trade unions existed precariously. Apart from political and social factors unfavourable to workers' organization and the development of collective bargaining, the underlying conditions were hostile; for example, the constant flow of new recruits into urban employments from the over-populated countryside, the vast number of small firms and work places, the high proportion of females (whose industrial life was short) among the factory workers. Only the seamen and the transport workers possessed effective organizations, and the right of collective bargaining had been conceded only in a few cases. In the political climate of the thirties, the disabilities suffered by the unions tended to increase, and their membership declined. In July 1940 the Government dissolved all independent labour organizations.

[1] The process of modifying or getting rid of the institutional reforms of the Occupation period is known as '*Gyaku-kosu*', or 'Reverse course'.
[2] Formerly called the Treasury Deposits Bureau.

The Occupation Authorities thus had little to build on, when as part of their task of democratizing Japan, they set out to create a trade union movement and to introduce legislation designed to improve working conditions. Yet their measures were effective and comprehensive. By a series of laws, the Trade Union Act and the Labour Relations Act of 1946, and the Labour Standards Act of 1947, the workers were given the right to organize, to bargain collectively and to take strike action, while employers were penalized for failure to afford recognition to the unions. Machinery was set up for conciliation and arbitration in industrial disputes; and improved labour standards, which applied *inter alia* to hours and conditions of work were laid down. Welfare provisions, such as industrial health insurance and workmen's compensation for accidents, were also introduced.

The result was startling. The number of trade unionists rose from none at the end of the war to nearly $6\frac{3}{4}$ million in 1948, and the unions quickly launched themselves on a career of militant activity which SCAP soon had to restrain in the interests of economic efficiency. After the introduction of the first deflationary plan in 1949 management regained much of its former power and the trade union movement suffered a set-back. Subsequently, the favourable legal conditions were modified and in the fifties the path of the trade unions became rougher. But they remained well-established institutions, even though their organization and methods of bargaining differed markedly from those of their Western counterparts. The typical union and real locus of power in the movement became the 'enterprise union', that is to say, a union whose members were drawn from persons employed by a particular firm, and the national bodies to which these unions became affiliated were in most cases merely co-ordinating bodies concerned primarily with political objectives. The 'enterprise union' may be regarded as the result of the impact of the new labour legislation on the existing form of industrial organization and the traditional system of industrial relations. It has considerable positive advantages for an economy where there are wide variations in scale of operations and technique among firms in the same industry.

If Japan's essay in trade unionism led to the emergence of some novel types of organization, the increase in the power of the workers and the changes in the industrial system left largely intact the methods of wage payment long familiar to Japanese industry. There is still no 'rate for the job'. Apart from a basic wage dependent upon the work performed the monthly earnings of a typical worker are made up, as in the past, of numerous constituents which include allowances for age, education, length of service, family responsibilities, housing, transport and cost of living. In addition, workers receive bi-annual bonuses which vary with the prosperity of the firm and are sometimes the equivalent of several months' wages, and they are entitled to allowances on dismissal or retirement. All this applies to the permanent or established workers for whom the employer accepts responsibility. The temporary workers who make up a substantial fringe in many trades enjoy less security and receive less consideration from the employer. The growth of trade unions and the new laws do not seem to have disturbed this system. Its relation to the functioning of the Japanese economy as a whole and in particular to certain critical phases of the post-war recovery will be discussed later.

7. Land Reform

The intervention of SCAP in Japanese agriculture had the most far-reaching consequences of all the economic policies of the Occupation period. It was based on the view that the rural landlord constituted the backbone of Japan's militant nationalism and that popular support for the 'Fascist' movements of the thirties was derived largely from the peasants' poverty and discontent. The Occupation Authorities, therefore, decided to destroy the landlord class and to convert the tenants into peasant proprietors. This process was set going by the Owner-Farmer Establishment Law of 1946 which, in broad terms, provided that landlords should be dispossessed by the Government of all land in excess of a small-holding and that this land should be sold by the Government to the former tenants. The vast transaction was practically completed by the end of 1949, and by then the ratio of tenanted land to the cultivated area had been reduced from 46 per cent to 8 per cent. The money compensation due to the landlords under the scheme proved in practice to be insignificant because of the inflation which coincided with the land reform. The inflation also wiped out other forms of rural indebtedness. Thus the landlords were in fact expropriated and rural Japan became predominantly a land of peasant proprietors.

This redistribution of incomes naturally led to a rise in the farmers' standard of living. In the early post-war years high food prices and, later, increased opportunities for other than agricultural employments that arose through the spread of industry into country areas and through improved communications, also favoured them. At first these benefits were partially offset by the increase in the size of the agricultural population and, in certain areas, by the loss of income from raw silk. But in the later fifties industrial expansion was accompanied by an active demand for labour from rural areas,[1] while

[1] One effect of this was considerably to increase the proportion of what are classified as 'part-time farm households' to total farm households.

agricultural productivity rose through the increased use of chemical fertilizers and methods of pest control and through mechanization and diversification. Japanese agriculture which before the war was highly specialized to rice and other cereals became increasingly concerned with livestock, fruit and vegetables, Formerly the farmer made little use of power machinery. After the war, despite the inherent difficulties of introducing certain types of agricultural machinery into very small farms, mechanization advanced rapidly. Over much of the countryside the former sharp contrast with city ways of life became less sharp than a generation ago.

8. *The Causes of the Recovery: An Analysis*

The sweeping economic successes of Japan in the last decade are not in question. There is general agreement about the broad features of the recovery and the advance. But an analysis of causes must raise controversy. It is not to be expected that any explanation of the reasons for Japan's outstanding accomplishments would be generally acceptable. Nevertheless, this chapter would be incomplete if none was offered.

In the first place the American contribution to Japan's rehabilitation is difficult to exaggerate. It may be that in the first years of SCAP preoccupation with reform impeded recovery. Yet without the 'aid' furnished so lavishly by the Americans at that time Japan might have plunged further into ruin, and the foundations of recovery could certainly not have been laid. Similarly, in the period after 1952 the heavy procurement expenditure supplied Japan with dollars which enabled her to re-equip her industries at a time when the export trade was still very small. Even the reforms themselves cannot be lightly dismissed as a means to economic progress. Some of them were out of tune with Japan's purposes and did not long survive. But others, of which the land reform was the outstanding example, endured and contributed not merely to social stability but also to economic efficiency.

In the second place, Japan was favoured by fortune at critical moments in her post-war career. In particular, the Korean War, which came at a time when 'aid' was drying up, was the origin of the procurement expenditure which sustained the economy for several years. Again, the world investment boom of the middle fifties helped to rescue Japan from her balance of payments difficulties by leading to an exceptionally large foreign demand for Japanese goods, especially ships. Up to that time Japanese economists and businessmen had been pessimistic about their country's future, insisting that Japan was a 'marginal supplier', would be the first to suffer from a recession in world demand, and was heavily dependent upon precarious sources of income such as procurement. In fact, Japan was more successful than most countries in keeping her costs down during the fifties, and her temporary sources of income turned out to be remarkably long-lived.

Some of the pessimism resulted from the laggardliness of the export revival. So we are led to consider how it was that Japan, despite her very modest export performance, was able to finance the volume of imports required for her great industrial expansion; American procurement by no means provides the complete answer. First, although the volume of imports recovered far more rapidly than exports after the war, in 1953-4 it was still only about three-quarters of the pre-war level and not until 1956 did it rise above that level. The volume of industrial production and the real gross national product were by then far higher than pre-war. Even the great surge forward in production after 1958 was accomplished with a relatively small increase in imports; in 1959-60 their volume was only 8 per cent greater than in 1956-7, although industrial production was up by more than 50 per cent. How did Japan succeed in economizing in imports without retarding recovery? Part of the explanation is to be found in the change in the country's industrial structure— the transference from textiles, which, apart from raw silk, used to depend heavily on overseas raw materials, to types of product the import-content of which is relatively small. Further, within particular industrial groups, a notable substitution of home-produced for imported materials has taken place. In textiles, for instance, it is not merely that cotton has been replaced to a large extent by rayon and synthetic fibres, but also that, in the manufacture of rayon, domestic pulp has taken the place of foreign pulp. In the production of nitrogenous fertilizers the former import of soya bean cake from Manchuria has given way to ammonium sulphate produced synthetically, and in the pig iron trade technical changes have made it possible for domestic supplies of iron sand and sulphuric acid dross to be used to a far greater extent than formerly. Finally, in the later fifties, dependence upon overseas supplies of food declined with the expansion of domestic food production. These changes were only in part the concomitant of technical advances in Japan. To some extent they were the result of a deliberate policy of trade diversion. Under the Government's economic plans for the next ten years it is proposed to carry these tendencies much further, but this may be difficult to accomplish if commercial policy becomes more liberal. Another factor that helped Japan to finance her imports was the reconstruction of her mercantile marine. This enabled her to avoid the large deficit on shipping services which she had to meet in the early post-war years.

So far we have taken a synoptic view of her post-war career. There were, however, several periods in which rapid industrial expansion and heavy investment brought about serious disequilibria in the balance of payments, and it must be emphasized that by no means the least important factor in Japan's progress was her skill in coping with that problem. In 1953-4 and in 1957-8, when rapid expansion threatened to disrupt her cost structure and to deplete her foreign exchange reserves, the Government ruthlessly applied monetary and fiscal measures which were effective in checking the rise in costs and in quickly restoring equilibrium. On both occasions the check was administered so as to prepare the way for the advance that soon followed the short-lived recession.

The analogy with the period from 1927 to 1937 is close but not exact. The disciplinary effects of the deflation of 1927-31 certainly led to a sharp reduction in industrial costs and in some measure laid the foundations for the advance in output and exports during the next six years. But that advance was accompanied by a steep decline in the exchange value of the yen and by heavy investment in the strategic industries at home and on the Continent. The result was a fall in the terms of trade (although because of the increasing efficiency of Japanese industry the fall was much greater in the barter than in the factoral terms of trade), and there was a decline in real earnings over a large part of the economy. The recovery of the nineteen-fifties, on the other hand, was achieved without any deterioration in the terms of trade—indeed they improved considerably in the later fifties—while real wages in manufacturing industry and agricultural incomes increased.[1] It is not without importance that Japan's military expenditure in this period was so small; for the first time in modern history she was able to devote her resources almost exclusively to economic development.[2]

We are still left with the question of why the deflationary measures were so successful. How was it that the inflationary trends inseparable from rapid industrial expansion were so quickly stamped out without checking for more than very brief periods the upward movement in investment and production? The explanation is to be found in certain well-known features of the economy, especially the large, highly competitive small-scale sector of industry and the peculiar wage system already described. Despite all the changes of the post-war years the former has retained its vitality and the latter its distinctive character. In consequence, Japan's costs, including wage costs,

[1] But not nearly as fast as productivity. Between 1955 and 1960 wages are estimated to have risen by 22 per cent, productivity in manufacturing industry by 55 per cent.

[2] In recent years only about one-tenth of the central Government's expenditure has been on defence, compared with well over two-fifths in the middle thirties. Defence expenditure in the late nineteen-fifties was under 2 per cent of the national income.

have responded very readily to deflationary pressure. Even in large businesses the system of wage payment has created intimate links between the profits of the firm and the wages of the employees, with the result that output could be well-maintained even in times of falling prices. But the main effect was to be seen among the small and medium firms among whom competition has always been keen and wages exceedingly sensitive to changes in economic conditions. In these circumstances the authorities found it comparatively easy to eliminate inflationary tendencies by monetary and fiscal measures, and it has been possible for the Japanese economy to grow very fast without giving rise to troubles with her balance of payments that were resistant to remedial measures. This responsiveness to deflationary pressure has been almost as important to Japan's economic success as the investment of a high proportion of her national income.[1]

There are, however, signs of change. Cost and wage plasticity and the vitality of the small-scale sector have depended on the constant flow of labour from the countryside into urban employments. This ample supply of fresh recruits for industry has indeed lain at the root of Japan's capacity to maintain a high rate of industrial expansion. But agricultural prosperity has lately raised the supply price of industrial labour and the small-scale sector has begun to enjoy more completely the benefits of the industrial advance. There are some indications that the disparities in wages between large and small firms, though still wide, are tending to diminish. If these tendencies persist, the plasticity of industrial wages and costs are likely to be reduced. The economy may then become less resilient than in the past and Japan may face problems of the same order as those that perplex the older industrial nations of the West.

In seeking to analyse the causes of Japan's post-war successes we have necessarily focused attention upon a few of the major economic influences. But the explanation so far given is by no means complete. The causes of her recovery as of her progress in the Meiji era must also be sought in certain features of her social and political organization, her comprehensive educational system, her admirable methods of technical training and her competent Civil Service. It is remarkable that the cohesion of Japanese society should have been preserved throughout the years of defeat and ruin; otherwise economic recovery would have been impossible. The older forms of economic organization and leadership survived the policies of the Occupation and again played their part in promoting progress. At the same time Japan showed a capacity for assimilating reforms thrust upon her from

[1] Prices have been remarkably stable over the whole period since 1952, despite fairly considerable short-term fluctuations. Average wholesale prices for 1958-60 were just about at the 1952 level; retail prices were up by only 4 per cent.

outside when she judged them to be in accord with her own purposes, and some of these exerted a stimulating effect on the economy. This does not apply merely to such economic measures as the land reforms. The release of fresh energies by the post-war political reforms may be compared with the effects of the revolutionary political changes at the time of the Restoration. The new freedom kindled many fires.

GLOSSARY

Japanese Term	English Equivalent
Bakufu	The feudal government as carried on by the Shogunate
Chonin	The merchants
Chosen	Korea
Daimyo	Feudal lord before the Restoration
Detchi	Apprentice
Dogyo Kumiai	Trade association or guild
Genro	Elder Statesman
Geta	Wooden footwear
Goyokin	Money for government use; may be compared with the Tudor benevolences
Gyaku-Kosu	Reverse course; the process of disentanglement from the Occupation reforms
Habutae	A silk fabric
Han	A fief or clan ruled by a *daimyo*
Hibachi	A brazier of pottery, wood or metal, used for warming Japanese houses
Joka-machi	Castle towns
Junsenji Keisai	Quasi-war-time economy
Kabu	Share, or membership privilege, as applied to the former guild system
Karafuto	Japanese Saghalien
Kawase-gumi	Exchange company
Kogyo Kumiai	Manufacturers' association or guild
O-bon	Festival of the Dead, held annually in mid-July. The ancestral spirits are supposed to visit the living members of their families
Meibutsu	Speciality products
Rangaku	Dutch learning
Sakē	Alcoholic drink distilled from rice
Samurai	A member of the military class in feudal Japan
Sangyo Kumiai	Co-operative society
Sankin Kotai	Alternate attendance, referring to the obligation imposed on *daimyo* of residing for part of each year in Yedo
Shogun	Military governor of the State during period when the Emperor held aloof from the administration
Shokunin	Journeyman
Taiwan	Formosa
Tonya, or Toiya	Wholesale dealer or commission merchant

Yedo	The name for Tokyo before the Meiji era
Yushutsu Kumiai	Export guild
Zaibatsu	Money groups or plutocracy

Tokugawa Era	1603-1868; the House of Tokugawa ruled Japan during this period as *Shogun*
Meiji Restoration	The Restoration in 1868 of the Emperor to his former position as *de facto* head of the State
Meiji Era	Reign of the Emperor Meiji, 1868-1912
Taisho Era	Reign of the Emperor Taisho, 1912-26
Showa Era	The present reign, 1926 to date

WEIGHTS AND MEASURES

Cho = 10 tan = 2·45 acres
Koku = 4·96 bushels
Kwan = 8·27 lb.
Picul = 100 kin = 132·3 lb.
Yen = 100 sen = 2s ·058d at pre-war gold parity; stabilized at 1s 2 from 1934 to 1939. 1950 to 1961 : 360 yen = one u.s. dollar

N

STATISTICAL TABLES[1]

TABLE I

POPULATION, 1873-1960
(in thousands)

Year	Population	Year	Population
1873	35,200	1935	69,300
1903	46,100	1940	73,100
1920	56,000	1950	83,200
1925	59,700	1955	89,300
1930	64,500	1960	93,400

Source: *Statistical Year-Book of the Empire of Japan* for period before the Second World War; Economic Planning Agency, *Japanese Economic Statistics*, Part III (monthly) for post-war years. The figures for 1873 and 1903 are estimates based on local records of family registrations and corrected in the light of subsequent Census returns. The figures for 1920 and later years are based on the Census returns.

TABLE II

DISTRIBUTION OF POPULATION ACCORDING TO SIZE OF TOWNSHIPS
(as percentages of total population)

Size of Unit	1893	1903	1913	1920	1930	1935
Under 10,000 persons	84	79	72	68	59	54
10,000-49,999	10	10	14	16	16	15
50,000-99,999	—	2	3	4	7	6
100,000 and over	6	9	11	12	18	25
	100	100	100	100	100	100

Source: *Statistical Year-Book of the Empire of Japan*

[1] These tables refer to Japan Proper only, except when otherwise stated. Before 1945 Japan Proper consisted of the four main islands of Honshu, Kyushu, Shikoku and Hokkaido, together with the Kuriles, the Luchus and other small outlying islands. A few of the tables, notably those showing the foreign trade, also cover Karafuto (Southern Saghalien) up to the Second World War. After that war Karafuto and the Kuriles were transferred to Russia.

TABLE III

THE INDUSTRIAL DISTRIBUTION OF THE OCCUPIED POPULATION, 1872-1957

(in thousands)

Industry	1872	1895	1913	1920	1930	1940	1957
Agriculture and Forestry	14,100	16,912	15,527	14,287	14,131	13,842	16,530
Fishing	395	473	535	561	590	559	660
Mining	6	96	364	448	315	597	600
Manufacturing	705	2,392	3,957	4,357	4,891	7,160	8,110
Construction	122	385	637	758	963	955	2,010
Transport and Communication	118	288	772	952	1,159	1,364	2,150
Commerce	947	1,916	2,831	3,662	4,906	4,881	7,450
Government and Professional Services	502	952	1,305	1,517	1,791	2,194	} 6,120
Miscellaneous	179	355	494	721	873	926	
Total	17,074	23,769	26,422	27,263	29,619	32,478	43,630

Sources: K. Okkawa, *The Growth Rate of the Japanese Economy since 1878*, pp. 245-6; and (for 1957) Statistics Bureau of Prime Ministers' Office. For 1957 the classification is according to main occupations and the figures cover persons above 14 years of age.

Table IV

THE INDUSTRIAL DISTRIBUTION OF THE OCCUPIED POPULATION, 1920-1955

(as percentages of total)

Industry	1920	1930	1940	1947	1955
Agriculture	50·9	46·8	41·5	49·9	37·9
Forestry	·7	·6	·9	1·4	1·3
Fishing	2·0	1·9	1·7	2·1	1·8
Mining	1·6	1·1	1·8	2·0	1·4
Construction	2·7	3·3	3·0	4·0	4·6
Manufacturing	16·5	16·0	21·2	16·3	17·8
Distribution (Wholesale and Retail)	9·8	14·0	12·7	6·3	13·8
Transport and Communications	4·2	4·4	4·7	5·1	5·2
Public and Other Services	9·8	11·6	11·8	11·5	16·2
Others	1·9	·2	·7	1·3	—
	100·0	100·0	100·0	100·0	100·0
Total (*in thousands*)	26,970	29,340	32,230	33,330	39,150

Source: I. B. Taeuber, *The Population of Japan*, p. 87. In the construction of this table, an attempt has been made to reclassify the population to accord with the classification of the 1950 Census. Adjustments were also made to take account of small changes in the area covered. The table is, therefore, not comparable with Table III, but the trends shown by them are identical for the period from 1920 to 1940. Any discrepancies, in this and other tables, between the totals and the sum of the individual items are due to rounding off.

TABLE V

NUMBER OF FACTORY OPERATIVES, 1900-1937
(*in thousands*)

Year	Males	Females	Total
1900	165	257	422
1904	208	318	526
1909	307	494	801
1914	384	564	948
1919	741	871	1,612
1925	852	956	1,808
1929	855	970	1,825
1933	968	933	1,901
1936	1,458	1,135	2,593
1937	1,727	1,210	2,937

Source: Department of Commerce and Industry, *Factory Statistics*. The figures for 1900 and 1904 are of factories employing ten persons or more. The figures for the years from 1909 to 1925 are of factories employing five or more persons. The figures for the remaining years are of factories equipped to employ five or more persons.

TABLE VI

DISTRIBUTION OF FACTORY EMPLOYMENT AMONG CHIEF INDUSTRIAL GROUPS
(*Employment in each Group as Percentage of Total Employment*)

	1923	1929	1933	1936	1959
Textiles	52·2	50·4	43·4	37·9	17·7
Metals	5·2	6·2	7·4	9·7	14·3
Machinery, Vehicles, Tools, etc.	13·0	13·8	15·9	18·3	29·8
Ceramics	3·8	3·5	3·4	3·9	5·0
Chemicals	5·5	6·4	8·0	11·1	14·2
Wood-working	2·8	3·0	4·3	3·7	4·2
Printing, Book-binding, etc.	2·3	2·9	3·3	2·4	3·8
Fook and Drink	9·6	8·7	6·8	6·7	7·3
Others	4·7	5·1	7·4	6·3	3·7
	100·0	100·0	100·0	100·0	100·0

Source: Pre-war figures from the Department of Commerce and Industry, *Factory Statistics*; the figures do not cover small factories with less than five workers, nor employment in Government factories. Post-war figures from Ministry of International Trade and Industry. The two series are not precisely comparable. Chemicals include rubber and paper.

TABLE VII

A

DISTRIBUTION OF EMPLOYMENT ACCORDING TO SIZE OF ESTABLISHMENT IN MANUFACTURING INDUSTRIES IN 1930

Size Group	Number in Thousands	Per cent of Total Employment
Under 5 persons	2,345	53
5-9 persons	271	6
10-49 persons	497	11
50 persons and over	1,330	30
Total	4,443	100

Source: T. Uyeda, *The Growth of Population and Occupational Changes in Japan, 1920-1936* (I.P.R.), p. 8. The table does not cover employment in building and certain other trades; hence the discrepancy between the total figure and those given in Tables III and IV

B

DISTRIBUTION OF EMPLOYMENT IN MANUFACTURING INDUSTRY ACCORDING TO SIZE OF ESTABLISHMENT IN 1955

Size Group	Percentage of Total Employment in Manufacturing
1-9 persons	19·9
10-49 persons	31·2
50-99 persons	9·6
100-199 persons	8·2
200-499 persons	10·3
500-999 persons	6·2
1,000 persons and over	14·6
	100·0

Source: *Census of Manufacturers for 1955*, quoted in T. Yamanaka (Ed.), *Small Business in Japan*, p. 151.

TABLE VIII

GROWTH OF RAW MATERIAL PRODUCTION,
1873-1934

(Annual Average of Volume of Production in 1921-25=100)

Year	Agricultural (71)	Livestock (6)	Fishery (8)	Forestry (4)	Minerals (11)	All Raw Materials (100)[1]
1873	28·6	—	—⌐	—	—	15·7
1880	37·2	3·9	—	—	3·7	23·4
1890	50·1	11·3	—⌐	—	11·2	36·7
1900	65·3	34·4	16·8	26·6	28·2	52·1
1910	76·4	56·0	33·9	72·9	61·3	68·4
1913	84·6	58·0	45·4	77·6	81·3	78·1
1920	104·1	77·5	82·9	95·7	105·5	100·3
1921	96·4	89·2	79·6	104·6	91·4	94·2
1922	100·7	94·9	88·4	96·1	94·9	98·5
1923	96·0	98·6	102·2	104·1	100·6	97·5
1924	98·9	105·9	104·0	[97·8	102·9	100·1
1925	106·8	109·9	115·7	96·0	108·8	107·4
1926	102·0	110·7	120·2	97·0	111·4	104·7
1927	109·5	115·2	125·8	98·9	117·8	111·5
1928	108·5	128·3	118·9	105·2	121·5	111·7
1929	108·8	138·5	126·5	107·0	124·8	113·4
1930	117·9	135·0	123·9	101·1	120·6	118·9
1931	104·2	149·9	133·1	104·9	113·5	109·7
1932	108·4	172·0	132·1	110·1	113·8	113·9
1933	125·7	168·2	155·6	117·7	128·0	130·1
1934	101·0	171·5	151·4	129·0	141·2	112·9

Source: Y. Koide, *Physical Volume of Raw Material Production in Japan*

[1] Figures in brackets give weights.

TABLE IX

INDICES OF AGRICULTURAL AND FISHERY
PRODUCTION,[1] 1933-1960
(1933-5=100)

Agriculture

Year	General	Rice	Vegetables	Livestock	Fruit	Cocoons	Fisheries
1936	105	112	109	81	96	92	111
1937	111	111	113	107	107	95	105
1938	107	110	108	113	109	84	105
1945	60	65	89	24	63	25	83
1949	93	104	124	87	92	18	86
1950	99	107	131	119	109	24	109
1951	99	100	136	133	93	28	132
1952	111	110	139	154	176	31	171
1953	97	96	123	162	139	28	171
1954	107	101	123	181	173	30	171
1955	130	131	148	222	175	34	186
1956	121	115	150	240	210	32	179
1957	126	120	156	255	275	36	202
1958	131	126	155	292	286	35	205
1959	135	132	162	303	306	33	215
1960	139	135	181	327	340	33	226

Source: *Statistical Abstracts* of Ministry of Agriculture and Forestry.

[1] In this as in some of the other production tables, two official index numbers
have been linked. Figures for 1960 are provisional.

TABLE X

RICE PRODUCTION AND CONSUMPTION, 1880-1937
(annual averages)

Period	Production (in million koku)	Yield per Cho (in koku)	Net Import (+) or Net Export (—) (in million koku)	Consumption per Head (in koku)
1880-84	29·96	11·59	— 0·18	0·80
1885-89	36·58	13·78	— 0·74	0·93
1890-94	40·36	14·64	+ 0·37	1·01
1895-99	39·27	14·00	+ 1·15	0·95
1900-04	44·64	15·64	+ 2·74	1·05
1905-09	47·58	16·34	+ 3·18	1·07
1910-14	51·17	17·06	+ 2·96	1·07
1915-19	56·89	18·46	+ 4·18	1·13
1920-24	56·34	18·59	+ 5·91	1·10
1925-29	59·45	18·71	+ 10·01	1·14
1930-34	62·23	18·95	+ 10·80	1·08
1935-37	63·71	19·50	+ 12·46	1·06

Sources: Statistical Section, Department of Agriculture and Forestry, *Statistics of Rice*, quoted in Ishii, *op. cit.*, p. 165; and E. F. Penrose, in Schumpeter (ed.), *op. cit.*, pp. 151-3. The total area under rice increased only from 2,685,000 cho in 1888 to 3,127,000 cho in 1920 and to 3,217,000 cho in 1937. The figures in the fourth column include trade between Japan Proper and her Colonies. During the nineteen-fifties the production of rice rose well above the pre-war average. In 1950-4 the annual average production was 64 million koku and in 1955-9 76 million koku. During the period 1955-9 imports declined steeply and amounted to only 6 per cent of the domestic production. Consumption per head fell to ·9 koku.

In this and other tables all production figures for the Meiji era should be regarded as approximate.

TABLE XI

RELATIVE IMPORTANCE OF THE PRINCIPAL AGRICULTURAL PRODUCTS

(*in percentages of total value of output for Japan Proper*)

	1926	1931	1936	1957
Rice	49	46	53	51
Cocoons	17	14	11	3
Wheat, Barley, Oats	8	8	9	6
Vegetables	7	8	7	7
Beans, Potatoes and Other Cereals	6	6	6	8
Industrial Crops	3	4	3	7
Meat	2	3	3	}18
Eggs	2	4	3	
All Others	6	7	6	
	100	100	100	100

Source: E. F. Penrose, in *The Industrialization of Japan and Manchukuo* (Ed. Schumpeter), p. 131; for 1957, *Statistical Year book of Ministry of Agriculture.*

All Others include, Fruit, Poultry, Milk, Tea and Green Manures.

TABLE XII

A

GROWTH OF PHYSICAL VOLUME OF MANUFACTURING PRODUCTION, 1895-1938[1]

ANNUAL AVERAGE

(1910-14=100)

	1895-99	1905-09	1925-29	1930-34	1935-38
Textiles	41	70	270	352	416
Metals and Machinery	25	61	255	410	920
Chemicals and Ceramics	—	53	453	643	1,255
Wood Products	—	91	570	601	1,018
Food Products	80	85	193	186	190
Electricity and Gas	—	27	653	1,002	1,517
All Manufactures	(37)	69	313	377	600

[1] Based on indices of Bureau of Industrial Research, Nagoya Commercial College; quoted in W. W. Lockwood, *The Economic Development of Japan,* p. 115.

B

INDICES OF INDUSTRIAL PRODUCTION, 1937-1960
(1934-6=100

Year		Year	
1937	130	1954	167
1940	149	1955	181
1946	31	1956	221
1948	55	1957	262
1950	84	1958	263
1951	114	1959	325
1952	126	1960	410
1953	155		

Source: Ministry of International Trade and Industry. See note to Table IX.

C

INDICES OF PRODUCTION OF CERTAIN MANUFACTURED GOODS 1937-1960
(1934-6=100)

	1937	1945	1950	1955	1958	1960
Food and Tobacco	117	37	84	207	241	265
Textiles	114	12	41	86	101	139
Metals	131	55	97	219	271	484
Machinery	148	147	126	250	540	1,110
Chemicals	144	29	103	318	467	623
Printing	115	26	45	125	—	—
Ceramics	120	30	98	175	236	354

Source: Ministry of International Trade and Industry, and Economic Planning Agency.

TABLE XIII

DISTRIBUTION OF OUTPUT AMONG CHIEF INDUSTRIAL GROUPS BY VALUE ADDED

(output of each group as percentage of total)

	1930	1955	1957	1959
Textiles	36·5	17·5	14·8	10·3
Metals	8·5	17·0	21·2	16·4
Machinery, Vehicles, Tools, etc.	11·6	14·6	23·6	31·2
Ceramics	2·7	3·4	3·4	4·8
Chemicals	15·2	19·1	19·6	21·0
Wood-working	2·7	5·1	2·2	2·3
Printing, Book-binding, etc.	3·2	3·3	2·7	4·4
Food and Drink	16·0	17·9	11·0	7·3
Others	3·6	2·1	1·4	2·3
	100·0	100·0	100·0	100·0

Source: See note to Table VI. Because of a difference in classification, the 1959 figures are not precisely comparable with those for earlier years.

TABLE XIV

STATISTICS OF THE COTTON INDUSTRY

A

IMPORT OF RAW COTTON [1]

(in thousand piculs)

1875-79	20	1915-19	7,490
1880-84	30	1920-24	8,460
1885-89	100	1925-29	11,190
1890-94	710	1930-34	11,900
1895-99	2,230	1935-37	13,750
1900-04	2,740	1951-55	7,760
1905-09	3,610	1956-59	11,150
1910-14	5,610		

[1] Annual Averages.

B

YARN OUTPUT [1]
(*in million lb.*)

1894-98	177	1935-37	1,485
1909-13	492	1950	518
1919-23	796	1955	827
1925-29	1,026	1959	1,010
1930-34	1,158	1960	1,199

C

EXPORTS OF COTTON GOODS

	Piece-Goods [2]		Yarn
Year	*in million square yards*	*(in million yen*	*(in million lb.)*
1896	45	2·2	17
1900	113	5·7	83
1903	94	6·9	123
1907	182	16·3	91
1913	235	43·0	187
1918	1,006	268·6	169
1921	689	204·7	117
1925	1,298	432·9	124
1929	1,791	412·7	27
1931	1,414	198·7	13
1934	2,577	492·4	26
1936	2,710	483·6	44
1937	2,644	573·1	52
1950	1,103	—	25
1955	1,139	—	26
1959	1,263	—	24
1960	1,424	—	87

[1] Annual Averages.
[2] The value figures include types of goods additional to those covered in th first column.

D

EQUIPMENT OF COTTON-SPINNING INDUSTRY

Year ending	Number of Cotton Spindles in place (in thousands) [1]	Number of Power-Looms Owned by Spinning Companies (in thousands)	Number of Power-Looms Owned by Specialist Weavers (in thousands)
1877	8	—	—
1887	77	—	—
1893	382	—	—
1897	971	—	—
1903	1,381	5	—
1907	1,540	9	—
1913	2,415	24	—
1920	3,814	51	—
1925	5,186	68	—
1929	6,650	74	199
1933	8,525	84	220
1935	10,330	90	237
1937	12,297	108	255
1945	2,064	25	112
1950	4,340	52	178
1955	8,168	81	294
1959	7,713	68	293
1960	7,781	66	307

E

TOTAL NUMBER OF LOOMS IN COTTON INDUSTRY
(in thousands)

Type of Loom	1922	1926	1929	1936
Hand-looms	165	105	86	51
Narrow Power-looms	122	116	106	76
Wide Power-looms	96	146	171	266

Sources: Department of Commerce and Industry, *Statistics of Commerce and Industry*; Japan Cotton Spinners' Association, *Cotton Statistics of Japan*; Oriental Economist, *Foreign Trade of Japan: A Statistical Survey*; Toyo Spinning Company, Institute for Economic Research, Statistical Digest of Japanese Textile Industry.

[1] Mainly ring spindles, the number of mules being very small.

TABLE XV

STATISTICS OF THE WOOLLEN AND WORSTED INDUSTRY
(*in million lb.*)

A

RAW WOOL AND YARN

Annual Averages	Raw Wool Imports (Greasy)	Yarn		
		Imports	Exports	Output
1896-1900	5·5	1·2	—	—
1901-05	8·7	2·6	—	—
1906-10	9·9	3·7	—	—
1911-14	11·4	5·8	0·2	—
1915-19	47·1	0·4	0·6	—
1920-24	57·2	13·9	0·2	33·0[1]
1925-29	93·2	13·1	0·3	52·8
1930-34	186·5	4·7	2·4	85·4
1935-37	239·2	·8	7·4	145·2
1955-59	278·2	·9	8·4	226·6

B

TISSUES

Output

Year	Output (*million yards*)			Total Value (including other kinds) (*in million yen*)	Imports (all kinds) (*million yen*)	Exports (all kinds) (*million yen*)
	Muslin	Serge	Woollen Cloth			
1900	5·1	0·4	0·8	—	17·8	—
1907	23·8	1·3	2·6	19·9	12·2	0·2
1913	69·6	9·8	1·8	23·3	12·4	0·5
1922	89·3	24·5	6·7	136·5	50·0	1·8
1925	127·6	28·3	5·4	182·5	57·2	3·7
1929	165·6	47·6	9·0	210·5	19·9	4·3
1934	132·9	90·5	16·9	264·0	5·2	29·8
1936	—	—	—	340·0	1·0	46·0

[1] 1921-24.

C

Tissues — All Kinds

(in million square yards)

Year	Output	Exports
1934-36 (annual average)	314·9	39·5
1955-59 (annual average)	248·6	25·2
1960	384·6	39·2

Sources: Oriental Economist, *The Foreign Trade of Japan: A Statistical Survey*; Department of Commerce and Industry, *Statistics of Commerce and Industry*; Economic Planning Agency, *Japanese Economic Statistics*.

Table XVI

PRODUCTION AND EXPORT OF RAW SILK, 1868-1960

Year or Annual Average	Production (in thousand kwan)	Exports (in thousand kwan)	(in million yen)
1868-72	(1868) 278	175	6
1889-93	1,110	662	27
1899-1903	1,924	1,110	69
1909-13	3,375	2,563	144
1919-23	6,317	4,224	531
1924-28	9,085	7,358	753
1929	*11,292*	*9,140*	*781*
1930-34	11,489	8,126	366
1935-36	11,465	8,424	390
1945-49	1,910	900	—
1950-54	3,580	1,200	—
1955-59	5,010	1,190	—
1960	4,810	1,420	—

Sources: Oriental Economist, *Foreign Trade of Japan: A Statistical Survey; Japan Silk Year-Book;* and Toyo Spinning Company, Institute for Statistical Research, *Statistical Digest of Japanese Textile Industry,* May 1960.

TABLE XVII

IRON AND STEEL PRODUCTION
(*in thousand metric tons*)

Year	Pig Iron	Finished Steel
1896	26	1
1906	145	69
1913	243	255
1920	521	533
1925	685	1,043
1929	1,087	2,034
1931	917	1,663
1936	2,008	4,539
1937	—	5,800
1949	1,549	3,100
1955	5,136	9,407
1959	9,446	16,629
1960	11,896	22,141

Source: Department of Commerce and Industry, *References for Steel Works*, and (post-1945) Ministry of International Trade and Industry, *Monthly Statistics*. The figures for steel production for 1937 onwards are for steel ingots and castings.

TABLE XVIII

COAL PRODUCTION
(*in million metric tons*)

1875	0·6	1931	28·0
1885	1·2	1936	41·8
1895	5·0	1937	45·2
1905	13·0	1945	23·0
1913	21·3	1950	38·5
1919	31·3	1955	42·4
1921	26·2	1959	47·3
1925	31·5	1960	51·1
1929	34·3		

Source: Department of Commerce and Industry, Mines Bureau, *General Conditions of Mining in Japan*, and (post-1945) Ministry of International Trade and Industry, *Monthly Statistics*.

O

TABLE XIX

A

ELECTRICITY GENERATING CAPACITY
IN OPERATION
(*in thousand kilowatts*)

1913	504
1920	1,214
1925	2,768
1930	4,399
1936	6,777
1937	7,276

Source: Economic Statistics of Japan.

B

ELECTRIC POWER GENERATED
(*in thousand million kWh*)

1937	30
1945	22
1950	45
1955	64
1959	85
1960	99

Source: Ministry of International Trade and Industry, *Monthly Statistics.*

TABLE XX

SHIPBUILDING

(*annual averages*)

Period		Steamships and Motor Ships Launched (*in thousand gross tons*)	
1899-1903		23	
1904-08		41	
1909-13		52	
1914-18		267	
1919-23		294	
	1919		646
	1922		71
1924-28		66	
1929-33		106	
	1929		165
	1932		54
1934-37		259	
	1937		446
1950-54		472	
	1952		608
1955-59		1,758	
	1957		2,432

Sources: Department of Communications, *Record of Ships and Shipbuilding; Statistical Year-Book of League of Nations*; and United Nations, *Monthly Bulletin of Statistics.*

TABLE XXI

TRANSPORT

Year	Mileage of Railway Track (*in units*)	Year	Steamships and Motor Ships (*in thousand gross tons*)
1872	18	1873	26
1883	240	1880	42
1887	640	1890	143
1894	2,100	1896	363
1904	4,700	1903	657
1914	7,100	1913	1,514
1924	10,400	1925	3,496
1930	13,400	1929	3,802
1934	14,500	1931	3,918
1960	17,500	1934	3,812
		1939	5,729
		1945	1,344
		1955	3,303
		1959	5,913

MOTOR VEHICLES IN USE
(*in thousands*)

Fiscal Year ending March	Commercial Vehicles and Buses	Passenger Vehicles
1936	123	70
1946	122	29
1950	298	56
1955	728	208
1959	1,224	386
1960	1,379	490

Sources: *Statistical Year-Book of Empire of Japan* (for pre-war shipping figures which cover registrations of ships of 20 gross tons and over in Japan Proper); *Economic Survey of Japan* (Annual) for post-war figures which cover ships of 100 gross tons and over. In August 1945, it is estimated, only 557,000 gross tons were operable. The figures for motor vehicles are also from *Economic Survey of Japan*; the figures for passenger vehices exclude scooters and certain other light vehicles.

TABLE XXII

FOREIGN TRADE OF JAPAN PROPER, 1868-1937

(Excluding trade between Japan Proper and her Colonies)
(in million yen)

Period	Imports	Exports
1868-72 (annual average)	23	16
1873-77 (annual average)	27	22
1878-82 (annual average)	33	30
1883-87 (annual average)	33	42
1888-93 (annual average)	73	77
1894-98 (annual average)	223	139
1899-1903 (annual average)	270	244
1904-08 (annual average)	442	377
1909-13 (annual average)	544	496
1914-20 (annual average)	1,300	1,434

Year	Imports	Exports	Year	Imports	Exports
1919	2,173	2,099	1929	2,216	2,149
1920	2,336	1,948	1930	1,546	1,470
1921	1,614	1,253	1931	1,236	1,147
1922	1,890	1,638	1932	1,432	1,410
1923	1,982	1,448	1933	1,917	1,861
1924	2,453	1,807	1934	2,283	2,172
1925	2,573	2,306	1935	2,472	2,499
1926	2,377	2,045	1936	2,764	2,693
1927	2,179	1,992	1937	3,783	3,175
1928	2,196	1,972			

Source: Oriental Economist, *The Foreign Trade of Japan: A Statistical Survey* (mainly). The tables dealing with foreign trade apply to Japan Proper and Southern Saghalien. The exports include a small amount of re-exports.

TABLE XXIII

VALUE OF FOREIGN TRADE, AMERICAN AID AND SPECIAL PROCUREMENT, 1945-1960

(*in million U.S. dollars*)

	Exports (f.o.b.)	Imports (c.i.f.)	Aid	Procurement
Sept. 1945—Dec. 1946	103	306	193	—
1947	174	526	404	—
1948	258	684	461	—
1949	510	905	535	—
1950	820	974	361	149
1951	1,355	1,995	164	592
1952	1,273	2,028	—	824
1953	1,275	2,410	—	809
1954	1,629	2,399	—	596
1955	2,011	2,471	—	557
1956	2,501	3,230	—	595
1957	2,858	4,284	—	549
1958	2,876	3,033	—	482
1959	3,456	3,599	—	458
1960	4,055	4,491	—	549

Source: Ministry of Finance and Economic Planning Agency. Procurement includes Allied military expenditure in dollars and pounds, yen purchases for Joint Defence Account, expenditure of Allied soldiers and civilian officials in Japan, and payments in respect of certain off-shore procurement contracts.

TABLE XXIV

THE STRUCTURE OF THE EXPORT TRADE

A   1868-1936

(*the value of each group shown as percentage of total exports*)

Period	Food and Drink	Raw Materials	Semi-Manufactured Goods	Finished Goods	Others
1868-72	25·4	23·1	40·8	1·9	8·8
1878-82	37·1	11·6	40·4	7·2	3·7
1893-97	16·8	10·3	43·3	26·2	3·4
1903-07	11·9	9·1	45·3	31·1	2·6
1908-12	11·1	9·2	48·1	30·5	1·1
1918-22	7·6	5·8	42·4	42·6	1·6
1923-27	6·7	6·5	45·9	39·8	1·1
1928-32	8·3	4·2	39·0	46·8	1·7
1933-36	8·0	4·4	26·4	58·4	2·8

Source: K. Taniguchi, Strukturwandlungen des japanischen Aussen-handels im Laufe des Industrialisierungsprozesses, in *Weltwirtschaftliches Archiv*, July 1937. The table does not cover trade between Japan Proper and her Colonies.

B   1934—1959

(*in percentages of total value*)

	1934-36	1955	1959
Textiles and Products	52·0	37·3	29·8
Raw Silk	*11·1*	*2·5*	*1·3*
Cotton Fabrics	*16·5*	*11·4*	*8·4*
Clothing	—	*5·3*	*6·0*
Metals and Metal Products	8·2	19·2	11·6
Machinery and Vehicles	7·2	12·3	23·4
Textile Machinery	*0·4*	*1·3*	*1·0*
Sewing Machines	—	*1·7*	*1·5*
Ships	—	*3·9*	*10·6*
Food and Drink	9·5	6·8	7·6
Chemicals	4·3	4·7	4·8
Ceramics	2·9	4·2	1·7
Toys	0·9	2·1	2·2
Other Goods	15·0	13·4	18·9
	100·0	100·0	100·0

Source: Ministry of International Trade and Industry; Economic Planning Agency, *Economic Survey of Japan*. Covers trade with colonies in 1934-36.

TABLE XXV

THE STRUCTURE OF THE IMPORT TRADE
1868—1936

A

(*the value of each group shown as percentage of total imports*)

Period	Food and Drink	Raw Materials	Semi-Manufactured Goods	Finished Goods	Others
1868-72	29·0	4·1	20·2	44·5	2·2
1878-82	14·8	3·5	29·9	48·6	3·2
1893-97	20·8	22·7	19·1	35·1	2·3
1903-07	23·5	33·0	16·7	25·5	1·3
1908-12	12·0	44·3	18·9	24·1	0·7
1918-22	12·9	49·2	22·2	15·0	0·7
1923-27	14·3	53·5	16·1	15·5	0·6
1928-32	12·7	55·3	15·5	15·7	0·8
1933-36	8·2	61·8	17·8	11·3	0·9

Source: See note to Table XXIV, *A*.

B

1934-1959

(*in percentages of total value*)

	1934-36	1955	1959
Food	23·3	25·3	13·8
Textile Materials	31·8	24·4	18·2
Petroleum and Coal	4·9	11·7	15·5
Iron Ore and Steel Scrap	3·2	5·9	13·8
Machinery	4·7	5·4	9·8
Others	32·1	27·3	28·9
	100·0	100·0	100·0

Source: See note to Table XXIV *B*.

TABLE XXVI

A

CHANGES IN EXPORT MARKETS
(*in percentages of total exports*)

	1934-36	1955	1959
United States	17	22	30
China (mainland)	18	1	0
Korea and Formosa	21	5	4
South East Asia	19	28	22
Europe (including U.S.S.R.)	8	10	11
Other countries	17	34	33
	100	100	100

B

CHANGES IN SOURCES OF IMPORTS

	1934-36	1955	1959
United States	25	31	31
China (mainland)	10	3	1
Korea and Formosa	24	4	2
South East Asia	16	22	16
Europe (including U.S.S.R.)	10	7	10
Other countries	15	33	40
	100	100	100

Source: Mitsubishi Economic Research Institute, *Monthly Circular*, January 1957; Economic Planning Agency, *Economic Survey of Japan, 1959-60*, p. 323.

TABLE XXVII

A

THE VOLUME OF FOREIGN TRADE, 1873-1937
(1913=100)

Year	Exports	Imports	Terms of Trade
1873	5·3	6·3	103·7
1880	7·8	11·2	129·4
1885	11·4	10·1	130·8
1890	15·0	23·8	125·9
1895	27·2	29·2	130·4
1900	31·9	48·4	124·4
1905	48·7	81·6	132·4
1910	76·8	73·6	108·7
1913	100·0	100·0	100·0
1918	146·5	105·2	81·9
1920	108·0	123·9	97·4
1922	123·6	162·1	128·7
1925	158·8	174·2	104·4
1929	204·8	199·2	102·3
1930	188·9	175·1	95·4
1931	194·9	194·3	100·2
1932	230·2	191·8	89·0
1933	254·4	198·8	82·2
1934	300·9	212·2	72·7
1935	341·3	222·2	71·4
1936	373·0	244·1	69·2
1937	388·1	259·5	60·8

Source: K. Kojima, Japan's Foreign Trade and Economic Growth, in *Annals of the Hitotsubashi Academy*, April 1958, pp. 166-7. Terms of trade: export price index as percentage of import price index (as on p. 140 supra). Trade with colonies excluded.

B

POST-WAR VOLUME OF TRADE
(1934-36=100)

Year	Exports	Imports	Year	Exports	Imports
1948	8	18	1954	55	86
1949	16	28	1955	72	90
1950	30	33	1956	86	114
1951	31	48	1957	95	143
1952	38	61	1958	99	117
1953	41	83	1959	117	148

TABLE XXVIII

SPECIE HOLDINGS OF BANK OF JAPAN AND GOVERNMENT

1903-1936

(in million yen)

Year ending	At Home	Abroad	Total
1903	120	19	139
1905	37	442	479
1910	135	337	472
1913	130	246	376
1919	702	1,343	2,045
1920	1,116	1,062	2,178
1926	1,127	230	1,357
1929[1]	1,087	91	1,178
1931[1]	—	—	470
1936[1]	—	—	548

Source: Ministry of Finance, *Financial Statistics.*

TABLE XXIX

FOREIGN EXCHANGE RESERVES

(in millions of U.S. dollars)

1951	930	1956	941
1952	913	1957	524
1953	637	1958	831
1954	738	1959	1,322
1955	839	1960	1,824

Source: Ministry of Finance. The figures for 1951 to 1955 are for the end of the fiscal year and for 1956 to 1960 for the end of the calendar year. The figures are based on a new method of calculation introduced in April 1958 and therefore differ from estimates published before that date.

[1] The figure for 1929 is for March, shortly before the decision to return to the gold standard was announced. For the period 1929-36 there is no information about total holdings, Government holdings or foreign holdings. But as both holdings abroad and Government holdings had become very small by 1929, it may be assumed that the figures for 1931 and 1936 cover substantially all the holdings. It should be noted, however, that they were not revalued after the fall of the yen during this period.

TABLE XXX

A   WHOLESALE PRICE INDEX, 1900-1936
(*October* 1900=100)

Average for Year		Average for Year		Average for Year	
1900	100	1913	132	1925	267
1901	96	1914	126	1926	237
1902	97	1915	128	1927	225
1903	103	1916	155	1928	226
1904	108	1917	195	1929	220
1905	116	1918	255	1930	181
1906	120	1919	312	1931	153
1907	129	1920	343	1932	161
1908	125	1921	265	1933	180
1909	119	1922	259	1934	178
1910	120	1923	264	1935	186
1911	125	1924	273	1936	198
1912	132				

Bank of Japan's index of wholesale prices of 56 commodities in Tokyo; an unweighted index.

B   TOKYO COST OF LIVING INDEX, 1914-33
(1914=100)

Average for Year		Average for Year		Average for Year	
1915	93	1922 {	223	1928	199
1916	101	{	215	1929	193
1917	124	1923	205	1930	175
1918	174	1924	208	1931	156
1919	217	1925	214	1932	157
1920	235	1926	208	1933	161
1921	208	1927	204		

Source: T. Uyeda, *The Small Industries of Japan*, p. 298. The break at 1922 is explained by Uyeda's use of two incomplete series.

C   WHOLESALE PRICE INDEX, 1946-60
(1934-36=1)

Average for Year		Average for Year		Average for Year	
1946	16	1951	343	1956	358
1947	48	1952	349	1957	368
1948	128	1953	352	1958	344
1949	209	1954	349	1959	347
1950	247	1955	343	1960	354

Source: Bank of Japan.

TABLE XXXI

INDICES OF WAGE MOVEMENTS, 1918-36
(TOKYO)
(1914=100)

A

Average for Year	Actual Earnings (a)	Cost of Living (b)	Real Wage Index
1918	164	174	94
1921	297	208	143
1924	356	208	171
1926	348	208	168
1929	331	193	171
1931	296	156	190
1933	290	161	180

(1926=100)

B

Average for Year	Wage Rates (c)	Actual Earnings (d)	Cost of Living (e)	Real Wage Index
1929	99	104	91	114
1930	96	99	78	127
1931	91	91	68	137
1932	88	88	69	128
1933	85	89	73	122
1934	83	91	75	121
1935	81	91	76	120
1936	81	92	80	115

(a) Ministry of Commerce and Industry's Index.
(b) Uyeda's Index.
(c), (d) and (e) Bank of Japan's Indices.

TABLE XXXII

INDEX OF REAL WAGES IN MANUFACTURING INDUSTRY
(1934-36=100)

Year	Index	Year	Index
1947	30	1956	126
1950	85	1957	127
1952	102	1958	130
1953	107	1959	139
1954	108	1960	146
1955	115		

Source: Labour Ministry. The Index includes allowances and covers 'productive' workers in establishments with 30 or more employees.

TABLE XXXIII

A

NUMBER OF BANKS (HEAD OFFICES), 1893-1937

Year	Special Banks	Savings Banks	Ordinary Banks	Total
1893	—	—	—	703
1901	—	—	—	2,359
1913	53	648	1,457	2,158
1922	34	145	1,794	1,973
1928	32	123	1,417	1,572
1929	33	94	874	1,001
1934	32	78	481	581
1937	32	72	377	481

Source: *Financial and Economic Annual of Japan.*

B

BANKS AND OTHER FINANCIAL INSTITUTIONS IN 1960

Type of Bank	Number (Head Offices)	Loans as Percentage of Total
City Banks	13	31·3
Local Banks	64	15·1
Trust Banks	7	1·7
Long-term Credit Banks	3	6·2
Official Banks	6	8·8
Trust Fund Bureau	1	10·1
Savings Banks	72	6·3
Other Financial Institutions	—	20·5
		100·0

Source: Bank of Japan, *Money and Banking in Japan*, March 1961, p. 51. Other Financial Institutions include co-operative credit societies and their central institutions; there were about 13,000 agricultural and fishery co-operatives in 1960. The Official Banks were the Export-Import Bank, the Japan Development Bank, the Agriculture, Forestry and Fisheries Finance Corporation, the Peoples Finance Corporation, the Small Business Finance Corporation and the Housing Loan Corporation.

TABLE XXXIV

NATIONAL DEBT, 1872-1937

(in million yen)

Year	Internal	External	Total
1872	23	10	33
1877	213	27	240
1885	223	16	239
1894	230	4	234
1903	441	98	539
1907	1,078	1,166	2,244
1914	1,036	1,525	2,561
1919	1,995	1,331	3,326
1926	3,685	1,478	5,163
1929	4,459	1,447	5,906
1931	4,477	1,479	5,956
1936	8,522	1,332	9,854
1937	9,258	1,317	10,575

Source: Department of Finance, *Statistical Annual of National Debt*; and *Financial and Economic Annual of Japan*.
The year covered is the calendar year, except for 1931, 1936 and 1937

when the figures are for March 31st. Certain temporary borrowings (Rice Purchase Notes and Treasury Bills) are excluded; but the figures for the internal debt include the funded Iron Foundry Debt and the State Railway Debt. The latter rose from 27 million yen in 1894 to 729 million yen in 1914 and to 1,757 million yen in 1934.

TABLE XXXV

REAL NATIONAL INCOME PRODUCED

(*in million yen at 1928-32 prices*)

Year	Total	Primary Industry	Secondary Industry	Tertiary Industry
1878	1,117	691	95	331
1890	2,308	1,429	224	655
1900	3,640	1,671	818	1,151
1914	5,665	2,127	1,354	2,184
1920	6,316	2,147	1,686	2,483
1925	9,268	2,779	2,216	4,273
1929	10,962	2,740	2,911	5,311
1930	12,715	2,477	3,550	6,688
1931	13,726	2,372	3,716	7,638
1932	13,843	2,594	3,987	7,262
1936	16,133	3,149	5,096	7,888

Source: K. Ohkawa, *op. cit.*, p. 248.

BIBLIOGRAPHY

The following list of publications is intended to indicate the chief printed sources which have been used in the writing of this book and to provide guidance to those who wish to pursue further study of the topics discussed in it. Publications in the Japanese language are marked thus: (J). Pamphlets prepared for the Institute of Pacific Relations are indicated by the letters (IPR). Publications concerned with the period since 1945 are listed separately at the end of the bibliography.

I

GENERAL

(MAINLY STATISTICAL SOURCES)

(J) Bank of Japan, *Statistics of Factory and Mining Labour* (Monthly).

(J) Department of Commerce and Industry, *Factory Statistics* (Annual).

(J) Department of Commerce and Industry, *Statistics of Commerce and Industry* (Annual).

(J) Department of Commerce and Industry, Mines Bureau, *General Conditions of Mining Industry in Japan* (Annual).

(J) Department of Commerce and Industry, *References for Steel Works* (Annual).

Department of Agriculture and Forestry, *Statistical Abstract of the Ministry of Agriculture and Forestry* (Annual).

Department of Finance, *Financial and Economic Annual of Japan*.

F. V. FIELD (Ed.), *Economic Handbook of the Pacific Area*, 1934.

M. IKETANI, *The Japan Silk Year-Book*.

(J) Imperial Cabinet, Bureau of Statistics, *Reports of the Censuses of Population*, 1920, 1925, 1930, 1935.

Imperial Cabinet, Bureau of Statistics, *Population of Japan*, 1920, 1925.

Imperial Cabinet, Bureau of Statistics, *Resumé Statistique de l'Empire du Japon* (Annual).

(J) Imperial Cabinet, Bureau of Statistics, *Statistical Year-Book of the Empire of Japan*.

Japan Cotton Spinners' Association, *Cotton Statistics of Japan*, 1903-35.

(J) Japan Cotton Spinners' Association, *Bi-Annual Reports*.

The Japan Year Book.

The Japan-Manchukuo Year-Book.

K. KOHRI, *General Features of the Index Numbers of Japan*, 1932.

(J) Y. KOIDE, *Physical Volume of Raw Material Production in Japan*, 1936.

P

(J) Nagoya Imperial College of Commerce, *Japanese Economic Statistics*, 1936.

Oriental Economist, *The Foreign Trade of Japan: A Statistical Survey* 1935.

Asiatic Society of Japan, *Transactions*.
Kyoto University Economic Review (Quarterly).
Mitsubishi Economic Research Bureau, *Monthly Circular*.
Oriental Economist (Monthly).
Société d'Etudes d'Informations Economiques, *Japon: Bulletin d'Informations Economiques and Financières* (Quarterly).

II

THE TOKUGAWA PERIOD AND THE EARLY YEARS OF MEIJI

(CHAPTERS I AND II)

The Currency of Japan (A Reprint of Articles, Letters and Official Reports; published by the *Japan Gazette*), 1882.

T. FUKUDA, *Die gesellschaftliche und wirtschaftliche Entwicklung in Japan*, 1900.

W. E. GRIFFIS, *The Mikado's Empire* (2 vols.), 1903

E. HONJO, *A Social and Economic History of Japan*, 1935.

Y. HONYDEN, 'Der Durchbruch des Kapitalismus in Japan', in *Weltwirtschaftliches Archiv*, July 1937.

J. F. KUIPER, 'Some Notes on the Foreign Relations of Japan, 1798—1805', in *Trans. of Asiatic Society of Japan*, December 1924.

J. MURDOCH, *A History of Japan* (3 vols.), 1910.

E. H. NORMAN, *Japan's Emergence as a Modern State*, 1946.

S. OKUMA, *Fifty Years of New Japan* (2 vols.), 1909.

S. OKUMA, *A General View of Financial Policy during Thirteen Years, 1868-1880*, 1880

S. OKUMA, 'The Industrial Revolution in Japan', in the *North American Review*, November 1900.

M. PASKE-SMITH, *Western Barbarians in Japan and Formosa, 1603-1868*, 1930.

G. B. SANSOM, *Japan, A Short Cultural History*, 1931.

G. B. SANSOM, *The Western World and Japan*, 1950.

C. D. SHELDON, *The Rise of the Merchant Class in Tokugawa Japan, 1600-1868*, 1958.

N. SKENE SMITH, *Tokugawa Japan*, 1937.

N. SKENE SMITH, *An Introduction to Some Japanese Economic Writings of the Eighteenth Century*, 1935.

T. C. SMITH, *Political Change and Industrial Development in Japan: Government Enterprise, 1868-1880*, 1955.

T. C. SMITH, *The Agrarian Origins of Modern Japan*, 1959.

M. TAKAKI, *A History of Japanese Paper Currency*, 1903.

Y. TAKEKOSHI, *Economic Aspects of the History of the Civilization of Japan* (3 vols.), 1930.
M. TAKIZAWA, *The Penetration of a Money Economy in Japan*, 1927.
A. F. THOMAS AND S. KOYAMA, *Commercial History of Japan*, 1936.
T. TSUCHIYA, *The Development of Economic Life in Japan*, 1936.
T. TSUCHIYA, *An Economic History of Japan*.
United States *Consular Reports*, Vol. XIX.

III

MONEY, BANKING AND PUBLIC FINANCE

(CHAPTERS III, VI AND IX)

G. C. ALLEN, 'The Recent Currency and Exchange Policy of Japan', in *Economic Journal*, March 1925.
G. C. ALLEN, *Japan's Banking System* (*Japan Chronicle* Pamphlet), 1924.
A. ANDREADES, *Les Finances de l'Empire Japonais et leur Evolution*, 1932.
M. ARAKI, *The Financial System in Japan* (IPR), 1933.
Foreign Affairs Association of Japan, *A History of Japanese Finance*, 1938.
S. FURUYA, *Japan's Foreign Exchange and her Balance of Payments*, 1928.
J. INOUYE, *Problems of the Japanese Exchange, 1914-1926*, 1931.
Japanese Department of Finance, *A Brief Outline of the Financial System of Japan*, 1905.
Japan Economic Federation, *The Capital Market of Japan*, 1940.
T. JONES, 'The Recent Banking Crisis and Industrial Conditions in Japan', in *Economic Journal*, March 1928.
M. MATSUKATA, *Report on the Adoption of the Gold Standard in Japan*, 1899.
M. MATSUKATA, *Report on the Post-Bellum Financial Administration in Japan.*
Mitsui Gomei Kaisha, *The Mitsui Bank: A Brief History*, 1926.
G. ODATE, *Japan's Financial Relations with the United States*, 1919.
G. OGAWA, *Expenditure of the Russo-Japanese War*, 1923.
G. ONO, *War and Armament Expenditures of Japan*, 1922.
United States National Monetary Commission, *Reports*, Vol. XVIII, 1910.
United States Department of Commerce, *Japanese Banking*, 1931.
United States Department of Commerce, *The Currency System of Japan*, 1930.
United States Department of Commerce, *The Big Five in Japanese Banking*, 1929.

IV

INDUSTRIAL AND AGRICULTURAL DEVELOPMENT

(CHAPTERS IV, V, VII AND X)

G. C. ALLEN, *Japanese Industry: Its Recent Development and Present Condition* (IPR), 1939.

G. C. ALLEN, 'Recent Changes in the Organization of the Japanese Cotton Industry', in *Proceedings of the Manchester Statistical Society*, 1937.

I. ASAHI, *The Economic Strength of Japan*, 1939.

H. F. BAIN, *Ores and Industry in the Far East*, 1933.

D. H. BUCHANAN, 'The Rural Economy of Japan', in *Quarterly Journal of Economics*, 1923.

Department of Overseas Trade, *Report of British Economic Mission to the Far East*, 1930-31.

Department of Overseas Trade, *Report of the Cotton Mission to the Far East*, 1930-31.

Department of Overseas Trade, *Report on the Cotton Spinning and Weaving Industry in Japan*, 1925-26.

M. IKETANI, *The Japan Silk Year-Book*.

International Labour Office, *Industrial Labour in Japan*, 1933.

Japan Economic Federation, *The Heavy Industry of Manchukuo*, 1940.

K. KANAI, *The South Manchuria Railway Company's Part in the Economic Development of Manchukuo* (IPR), 1936.

K. KANAI, *Economic Development in Manchukuo* (IPR), 1936.

Katakura and Company (Works pamphlet), 1934.

S. KAWADA, 'The Japanese Agricultural Community and the Composition of its Population', in *Journal of the Osaka University of Commerce*, 1935.

U. KOBAYASHI, *The Basic Industries and Social History of Japan*, 1930.

Miyata Bicycle Company (Works pamphlet), no date.

(J) Nagoya Imperial College of Commerce, *The Present Status of the Woollen Industry in Japan*, 1935.

(J) Nagoya Imperial College of Commerce, *Business Analysis of Large-Scale Establishments in Our Woollen Industry*, 1936.

S. NASU, 'Ziele und Ausrichtung der japanischen Agrarpolitik in der Gegenwart', in *Weltwirtschaftliches Archiv*, July 1937.

S. NASU, *Land Utilization in Japan* (IPR), 1929.

Y. ONO, 'The Industrial Transition in Japan', in *Publications of American Economic Association*, Vol. 5, No. 1.

I. OTSUKA, 'The Survival of Small Undertakings in Japanese Industry', in *Kyoto University Economic Review*, December 1934.

A. S. PEARSE, *The Cotton Industry of China and Japan*, 1932

H. ROSOVSKY and K. OHKAWA, 'The Role of Agriculture in Modern Japanese Economic Development', in *Economic Development and Cultural Change*, October 1960.

SCHUMPETER, ALLEN, GORDON AND PENROSE, *The Industrialization of Japan and Manchukuo, 1930-40*, 1940.

United States Tariff Commission, *The Japanese Cotton Industry and Trade*, 1921.

T. UYEDA, *The Small Industries of Japan*, 1938.

S. UYEHARA, *The Industry and Trade in Japan*, 1926.

World Engineering Congress, Tokyo, *Industrial Japan*, 1929.

V

ECONOMIC ORGANIZATION AND POLICY

(CHAPTERS VIII, IX AND X)

G. C. ALLEN, 'The Concentration of Economic Control in Japan', in *Economic Journal*, June 1937.

(J) Department of Commerce and Industry, *General Conditions of Manufacturers' Guilds* (Kogyo Kumiai), 1936.

K. FUJITA, 'Cartels and their Conflicts in Japan', in the *Journal of the Osaka University of Commerce*, December 1935.

W. L. HOLLAND (Ed.), *Commodity Control in the Pacific Area*, 1935.

(J) E. HONJO, *A Study of Nishijin* (Nishijin Kenkyu), 1930.

(J) R. IWAI, *The Story of Mitsui and Mitsubishi* (Mitsui Mitsubishi Monogatari).

Japan Council, Institute of Pacific Relations, *The Control of Industry in Japan, 1933*.

Mitsubishi Goshi Kaisha, *An Outline of Mitsubishi Enterprise*, 1926 and 1935.

Mitsui Gomei Kaisha, *The House of Mitsui*, 1933.

(J) Nagoya Imperial College of Commerce, *Manufacturers' Guilds in Relation to Domestic Industry*, 1936.

M. ROYAMA, *The Control of the Electric Power Industry in Japan* (IPR), 1933.

(J) *Social Reform* (Shakai Seisaku Jiho), May 1934 and April 1935 (articles on structure of many small-scale trades).

Sumitomo Goshi Kaisha, *Sumitomo*, 1936.

(J) M. SUZUKI, *Essay on the Japanese Zaibatsu* (Nihon Zaibatsu Ron).

(J) H. WADA, 'How Big Capitalists Camouflage Themselves', in *Nippon Hyoron*, June 1936.

Y. YAGI, 'The Relation Between Japan Proper and Korea as seen from the Standpoint of the Rice Supply', in *Kyoto University Economic Review*, 1931.

N. YASUO, 'Manchukuo's New Economic Policy', in *Pacific Affairs*, September 1938.

VI

FOREIGN TRADE AND COMMERCIAL POLICY

(CHAPTERS V, VI, VIII AND X)

(J) Department of Commerce and Industry, *General Conditions of Export Guilds* (Yushutsu Kumiai), 1936.

Department of Finance, *The Import Tariff of Japan*

Department of Communications, *History of the Mercantile Marine in Japan*, 1883.

Y. HATTORI, *The Foreign Commerce of Japan Since the Restoration*, 1904.

Y. KINOSITA, *The Past and Present of Japanese Commerce*, 1902.

K. KOJIMA, 'Japanese Foreign Trade and Economic Growth', in *Annals of the Hitotsubashi Academy*, April 1958.

W. W. LOCKWOOD, *Trade and Trade Rivalry between the United States and Japan* (IPR), 1936.

Nippon Yusen Kaisha, *Golden Jubilee History*, 1935.

S. OGATA, 'The Control of Export Trade in Japan', in the *Journal of the Osaka University of Commerce*, No. 2, 1934.

S. OGATA, 'Probleme der Exportkontrolle in Japan', in *Weltwirtschaftliches Archiv*, May 1936.

Oriental Economist, *The Foreign Trade of Japan: A Statistical Survey* 1935.

K. TANIGUCHI, 'The Concentration and Dispersion of Japan's Foreign Trade', in *Kyoto University Economic Review*, Vol. II, No. 1, 1936.

Tokyo Association for Liberty of Trading, *A Brief Analysis of Japan's Foreign Trade*, 1935.

Tokyo Association for Liberty of Trading, *Trade Agreements Between Japan and Some Other Countries*, 1937.

Tokyo Association for Liberty of Trading, *Export Trade of Japan and Its Control System*, 1938.

United States Tariff Commission, *Recent Developments in the Foreign Trade of Japan*, 1936.

T. UYEDA, *The Recent Development of Japanese Foreign Trade* (IPR), 1936.

T. UYEDA, *Recent Changes in Japanese Tariffs* (IPR), 1933.

Yokohama and Tokyo Foreign Board of Trade, *Translation of Export Guild Law and List of Export Guilds*, 1934.

VII

MISCELLANEOUS

E. A. ACKERMAN, *Japan's Natural Resources and Their Relation to Japan's Economic Future*, 1953.

K. AKAMATSU AND Y. KOIDE, *Industrial and Labour Conditions in Japan*, 1934.

G. C. ALLEN and A. G. DONNITHORNE, *Western Enterprise in Far Eastern Economic Development: China and Japan*, 1954.

Bureau of Social Affairs, Home Office, *Social Work in Japan*, 1934.

Foreign Affairs Association of Japan, *Japan and World Resources*, 1937.

International Labour Office, *Industrial Labour in Japan*, 1933.

R. ISHII, *Population Pressure and Economic Life in Japan*, 1937.

(J) T. KAWANISHI, 'The Conditions of Living of the Japanese Farmers during the Agricultural Depression since 1930', in *Studies in Commerce and Economics* (St Paul's University, Tokyo), November 1934.

S. KOJIMA, *Natural Resources of Japan* (International Studies Conference), 1938

S. KUZNETS and others, *Economic Growth: Brazil, India, Japan*, 1955.

W. W. Lockwood, *The Economic Development of Japan*, 1954.
F. Maurette, *Social Aspects of Industrial Development in Japan* (ILO).
H. G. Moulton, *Japan: An Economic and Financial Appraisal*, 1931.
K. Ogata, *The Co-operative Movement in Japan*, 1923.
K. Ohkawa, *The Growth Rate of the Japanese Economy since 1878*, 1957.
J. E. Orchard, *Japan's Economic Position*, 1930.
E. F. Penrose, 'Japan in the World Economic Depression', in *Index*, September and October 1935.
E. F. Penrose, *Food Supply and Raw Materials in Japan*, 1929.
H. Rosovsky, *Capital Formation in Japan, 1868-1940*, 1961.
I. B. Taeuber, *The Population of Japan*, 1958.
S. Tsuru, *Essays on Japanese Economy*, 1958.
T. Uyeda, *The Growth of Population and Economic Changes in Japan, 1920-1935* (IPR), 1936.
T. Uyeda and T. Inokuchi, *The Cost of Living and Real Wages in Japan, 1914-1936* (IPR), 1936.

VIII

ECONOMIC RECOVERY AND EXPANSION, 1945-1960

(Supplementary Chapter)

(a) *Books and Articles*

G. C. Allen, *Japan's Economic Recovery*, 1958.
Asia Kyokai, *The Smaller Industry in Japan*, 1957.
Bank of Japan, *Money and Banking in Japan*, March 1961.
T. A. Bisson, *Zaibatsu Dissolution in Japan*, 1954.
J. B. Cohen, *Japan's Economy in War and Reconstruction*, 1949.
J. B. Cohen, *Japan's Post-War Economy*, 1958.
R. P. Dore, *Land Reform in Japan*, 1959.
Economic Planning Agency, *New Long-Range Economic Plan of Japan, 1961-1970*.
E. E. Ehrlich and F. M. Tamagna, 'Japan', in B. H. Beckhart (Ed.), *Banking Systems*, 1954.
S. Fujii, *Japan's Trade and Her Level of Living* (Science Council of Japan), 1955.
Holding Company Liquidation Commission, *Final Report on Zaibatsu Dissolution, 1961*.
S. Horie, *Banking System and Bank Liquidity in Japan* (International Credit Conference Rome) 1952.
S. B. Levine, *Industrial Relations in Post-War Japan*, 1958.
Ministry of Labour, *Japan Labour Code*, 1953.
Mitsubishi Economic Research Bureau, *Mitsui, Mitsubishi, Sumitomo*, 1955.
S. Okita, *Japan's Trade with Asia*, Reprinted from *Contemporary Japan*, 1954.

S. OKITA, *The Rehabilitation of Japan's Economy and Asia* (Ministry of Foreign Affairs), 1956.

K. OKOCHI, *Labour in Modern Japan* (IPR), 1958.

K. SEKI, *The Cotton Industry of Japan*, 1956.

S. SHIOMI, *Japan's Finance and Taxation, 1940-1956*, 1957.

E. B. REUBENS, 'Small Scale Industry in Japan', in *Quarterly Journal of Economics*, August 1947.

S. TSURU, 'Business Cycles in Post-War Japan', in International Economic Association, *The Business Cycle in the Post-War World*, 1955.

T. YAMANAKA, *Small Business in Japan*, 1960.

(b) *Periodicals*

Annals of Hitotsubashi Academy, continued from October 1960 as *Hitotsubashi Journal of Economics* (Quarterly).

Bank of Japan, *Economic Statistics of Japan* (Annual).

[1]Economic Planning Agency, *Economic Survey of Japan* (Annual); *Japan Economic Statistics* (Monthly).

Fuji Bank Bulletin (Quarterly).

Industrial Bank of Japan, *Survey of Japanese Finance and Industry* (Quarterly).

Kobe University, *Kobe Economic and Business Review* (Annual).

Ministry of Finance, *Quarterly Bulletin of Financial Statistics.*

Ministry of Labour, *Japan Labour Year Book.*

Ministry of International Trade and Industry, *Foreign Trade of Japan* (Annual).

Oriental Economist, *Japan Economic Year Book.*

Prime Minister's Office, *Japan Statistical Year Book.*

Sumitomo Bank Review (Quarterly).

Toyo Spinning Company, Institute of Economic Research, *Statistical Digest of Japanese Textile Industry* (Quarterly).

United Nations, *Economic Bulletin for Asia and the Far East* (Quarterly).

[1] This body has been known under different names during the last fifteen years, Economic Stabilisation Board (before 1953), Economic Counsel Board (1953-55), and Economic Planning Board (1955-57).

INDEX

Agricultural and Industrial Banks, 54, 108

Agricultural co-operative societies, 131, 153

Agricultural experimental stations, 32

Agriculture: after Second World War, 174-5; diversification of, 115, 175, 187; in Meiji era, 32, 62 *et seq.*; in Tokugawa era, 15-17, 28, 164; in World Depression, 104-5, 115-17, 139; number employed in, 15, 62, 114, 195; output of, 63, 113, 199-202; State intervention in, 63, 153; subsidies for, 128; technical advances in, 63, 115, 187

Aid, American, 172

Aikawa, 156

Armaments: expenditure on, 48-9, 136, 173, 189; manufacture of, 34, 57

Asano, 87, 134

Australia, trade with, 157, 158

Bakufu (military dictatorship), 14

Balance of payments, 32, 37, 59-60, 98, 100

Banking system, main features of, 50 *et seq.*, 106-10, 141-2, 222, 223

Bank of Chosen, 55

Bank of Japan: foundation of, 50-1, 53; note issue of, 50-1, 100, 138; operations of, 57-60, 99-100, 108-10, 137, 141, 183, 184

Bank of Taiwan, 55, 102

Bank of Tokyo, 183, 184

Banks: and industry, 54, 107, 184; and samurai, 44; after Second World War, 183-4; colonial, 55; commercial, 56-7, 106-7, 141; foreign, 35; national, 43-5, 51, 56; number of, 222, 223; savings, 141; 'special', 52 *et seq.*, 57, 59, 107-8, 127, 141, 183

Barley, 16, 63, 115

Benevolences (*goyokin*), 24, 39

Bicycle industry, 85, 123

Bi-metallic standard, 45

Breweries, 86

Building industry, 89

Camera industry, 176

Camphor monopoly, 48, 127

Canneries, floating, 117

Capital: import of, 54, 93, 108n; provision of industrial, 45, 53-4, 56 *et seq.*, 110, 112, 127, 134, 139, 163-4, 174

Cartels, 82, 152

Castle-towns, 17, 18, 37

Cement industry, 33, 87, 113

Chemical industry, 33, 113, 144, 145, 149, 176

China: influence of, 20, 21-2; trade with, 20, 64, 65, 72, 73, 80, 95, 111, 157, 177

Chosen Industrial Bank, 55

Clan governments, 14 *et seq.*, 22-3, 31

Coal: export of, 81, 93, 94; import of, 122; industry, 18, 80, 113, 122, 151, 177, 209

Colonial expansion, 55, 133

Colonies, trade with, 110-11, 116, 158-9, 170

Communications, 19, 35-6: *see also* Railways, Shipping

Co-operative societies, 130 *et seq.*, 153

Copper industry, 18, 36, 38, 80, 81, 93, 122

Cotton industry: after Second World War, 176; capacity of, 72-3, 118-19, 147-8, 206; in Meiji era, 33, 65, 71-4; in Tokugawa era, 18, 33; output of, 113, 119, 204, 205; structure of, 73-4, 119-20, 146, 148-9; technical advances in, 120, 139, 147-8

Cotton goods: exports of, 72, 93, 94, 105, 111, 119, 157, 205; imports of, 71, 94-5

Cotton, raw: cultivation of, 16, 64-5; imports of, 65, 73, 94, 96, 204

Dai Ichi (First) Bank, 55, 107

Daimyo, 14, 25, 33

Dan, Baron, 155

Debasement of coinage, 24, 39

Deflation, 51-2, 100, 102-5, 189-90

GEORGE ALLEN & UNWIN LTD
London: 40 Museum Street, W.C.1

Auckland: 24 Wyndham Street
Bombay: 15 Graham Road, Ballard Estate, Bombay 1
Buenos Aires: Escritorio 454-459, Florida 165
Calcutta: 17 Chittaranjan Avenue, Calcutta 13
Cape Town: 109 Long Street
Hong Kong: F1/12 Mirador Mansions, Kowloon
Ibadan: P.O. Box 62
Karachi: Karachi Chambers, McLeod Road
Madras: Mohan Mansions, 38c Mount Road, Madras 6
Mexico: Villalongin 32-10, Piso, Mexico 5, D.F.
Nairobi: P.O. Box 12446
New Delhi: 13-14 Asaf Ali Road, New Delhi 1
São Paulo: Avenida 9 de Julho 1138-Ap. 51
Singapore: 36c Prinsep Street, Singapore 7
Sydney, N.S.W.: Bradbury House, 55 York Street
Toronto: 91 Wellington Street West